About the author

John Madeley has been a writer and broadcaster specializing in Third World development and environmental issues for almost thirty years. From 1983 to 1998 he was editor of the renowned magazine *International Agricultural Development*. A contributor to leading British papers, including the *Observer*, the *Guardian* and the *Financial Times*, he has also written for many NGOs, including Christian Aid, CAFOD, the Catholic Institute for International Relations, the Panos Institute, and the Swedish-based Forum Syd. He is the author of the following books on development questions:

When Aid is No Help: How Projects Fail and How They Could Succeed
Trade and the Poor: The Impact of International Trade on Developing Countries
Land is Life: Land Reform and Sustainable Agriculture (co-editor)
Big Business, Poor Peoples: The Impact of Transnational Corporations on the World's Poor (Zed Books)
Hungry for Trade: How the Poor Pay for Free Trade (Zed Books)
Food for All: The Need for a New Agriculture (Zed Books)

Critical praise for John Madeley's recent books

Big Business, Poor Peoples (1999)

'Readable and persuasive.... A timely and cogent examination of transnational corporations, the engines that drive globalization.' *New Internationalist*

'An excellent book.' *African Farming*

'A readable account of the increasing power of big businesses.' *Christian Aid News*

'A sober and factual survey of a world economy dominated by big transnational corporations.' *Socialist Review*

'A grim account of exploitation and neglect.' *Church Times*

'A useful introductory critique of corporate involvement in developing countries ... [which] leaves readers knowing they have a lot of work ahead.' *Multinational Monitor*

'John Madeley produces the evidence which show that TNCs are not working to benefit developing countries.... A very easy, but disturbing, read.' *International Agricultural Development*

'Readers will be spurred to use their voices as consumers, investors and voters to resist the monopoly power of the new "global apartheid", a system which sucks the labour out of people and discards the skins.' Canon Christopher Hall, coordinator for One World in the Door

'Brings much useful information together [and] asks many fundamental questions.' *African Book Centre Book Review*

Hungry for Trade (2000)

'John Madeley's demolition job on the structure of international trade and finance, and the work of WTO, is convincing. This book needs to be widely read.' *Church Times*

Food for All (2002)

'Absorbing reading for anyone concerned about the risks of hi-tech farming methods.' *Appropriate Technology*

To Tods
Best wishes
Jos Rolly

A PEOPLE'S WORLD

Alternatives to economic globalization

John Madeley

ZED BOOKS
London & New York

A People's World was first published in 2003 by
Zed Books Ltd, 7 Cynthia Street, London N1 9JF, UK,
and Room 400, 175 Fifth Avenue, New York, NY 10010, USA

www.zedbooks.demon.co.uk

Designed and typeset in Monotype Bembo by Illuminati, Grosmont
Cover designed by Andrew Corbett
Printed and bound in the EU by Cox & Wyman Ltd, Reading

Distributed in the USA exclusively by Palgrave, a division of
St Martin's Press, LLC, 175 Fifth Avenue, New York, NY 10010

A catalogue record for this book is available from the British Library
Library of Congress Cataloging-in-Publication Data available

ISBN 1 84277 222 8 (Hb)
ISBN 1 84277 223 6 (Pb)

Contents

List of contributors   viii

Acknowledgements   x

PART I   Globalization understood – and the alternatives

1 What is there to worry about?   3

The globalizers · The globalized · The alternatives · The approaches

2 Globalization: what does it really mean?   15

The new colonialism · Undemocratic nature

3 Globalization: what's wrong with it?   27

Diversity disappears · It has not worked… · Corporate domination · The vulnerable suffer · Not a level playing field · Deregulation · Destructive competition · Susie Emmett on Poland · Peter Custers on disparate exchange

4 Alternatives to globalization: viewpoints from the South   62

Peggy Antrobus · Walden Bello · Manabe Bose · Kathy-Ann Brown · Jayanti Durai · Pedro Equina · Gustavo Esteva · Ha-Joon Chang · Martin Khor · Jane Ocaya-Irama · Bir Singh

Mahato · Nelcia Marshall-Robinson · Jennifer Mourin · Mohau
Pheko · Danilo Ramos · Devinder Sharma · Vandana Shiva ·
Victoria Tauli-Corpuz · Ruchi Tripathi · Nico Verhagen · Simeon
Waithima · Nugroho Wienarto · Mariama Williams

5 Alternatives to globalization: viewpoints from
the North   77

John Bunzl · Barry Coates · Fiona Dove · Susie Emmett · Peter
Fleming · Pippa Gallop · George Gelber · Ronnie Hall · Ted van
Hees · Hazel Henderson · John Hilary · François Houtart · Chris
Keene · David Korten · Maura Leen · Caroline Lucas · Aksel
Naerstad · Helena Norberg-Hodge · Ann Pettifor · Andrew Simms
· Carol Wills · Peter With

PART II   **Axis of change: what we must do**

6 Values on the move   109

7 Tackling corporate domination   112

Corporate colonization of the United Nations · Strategic options ·
Codes of conduct · Regulation · What's standing in the way? ·
Customer revolt is working · Changing behaviour · Shareholder
pressure · Cargill: the power of size

8 Tackling trade domination   136

The World Trade Organization · Corporate influence on the
WTO · The human rights challenge · Doha 2001 · What needs
to change? · GATS · Reform – or replace? · The MAI · A bad
master · Cancún 2003 · How subsidies distort

9 Tackling debt   158

The origins · The shackle keepers · HIPC's failure · Jubilee ·
The human cost · A short-lived flurry · The case of Malawi ·
Debt takes more · Debt relief works · Total cancellation ·
The World Bank's sister

10 Alternative strategies   177

Strategies for greater self-reliance · Food sovereignty · Agrarian
reform · Local money · Raising money globally: the Tobin tax ·

The Tabu currency in Papua New Guinea · Alternative trade: the future lies with the infant · Fairtrade mark · Fairtrade standards · Other products · The alternative to the flying food scandal · Local fight-back in Bolivia

11 Conclusion: the urgency of alternatives   202
Democracy · Sustainable development · Hope

ANNEX   Sources on alternative ideas and
campaigning social movements   212

Notes   218

Index   227

List of contributors

Peggy Antrobus, Development Alternatives with Women for a
    New Era (DAWN)
Walden Bello, Focus on Global South, Philippines
Manabe Bose, South Asian Peasant Coalition, India
Kathy-Ann Brown, Legal Advisor, Caribbean Regional
    Negotiating Machinery
John Bunzl, founder of the International Simultaneous Policy
    Organization
Ha-Joon Chang, University of Cambridge economist
Barry Coates, World Development Movement, UK
Peter Custers, Bangladesh People's Solidarity Centre, Brussels
Fiona Dove, Transnational Institute, Amsterdam
Jayanti Durai, Consumers International
Susie Emmett, environmental broadcaster
Pedro Equina, National Indigenous and Peasant Coordination,
    Guatemala,
Gustavo Esteva, Mexican social activist
Peter Fleming, policy analyst and author
Pippa Gallop, Corporate Watch, UK
George Gelber, CAFOD, UK
Ronnie Hall, Friends of the Earth, UK
Ted van Hees, European Network on Debt and Development,
    Netherlands.
Hazel Henderson, author

John Hilary, Save the Children, UK
François Houtart: Roman Catholic priest
Chris Keene, Anti-Globalization Network, UK
Martin Khor, Third World Network
David Korten, author
Maura Leen, Trocaire, Ireland
Caroline Lucas, Green Party Member of the European
    Parliament
Bir Singh Mahato, Member of Parliament, India
Nelcia Marshall-Robinson, Caribbean Association for Feminist
    Research and Action
Jennifer Mourin, Pesticide Action Network, Asia and the Pacific
Aksel Naerstad, Development Fund of Norway
Helena Norberg-Hodge, International Society for Ecology and
    Culture.
Jane Ocaya-Irama, ActionAid, Uganda
Mohau Pheko, Africa Gender and Trade Network, South Africa
Ann Pettifor, New Economics Foundation, UK
Danilo Ramos, Peasant Movement of the Philippines
Devinder Sharma, policy analyst, India
Vandana Shiva, Indian scientist and ecologist
Andrew Simms, New Economics Foundation, UK
Victoria Tauli-Corpuz, Tebtebba Foundation, Philippines
Ruchi Tripathi, ActionAid
Nico Verhagen, Via Campesina
Simeon K. Waithima, Agri-Health Initiative, Nairobi
Nugroho Wienarto, Farmers Initiatives for Ecological
    Livelihoods and Democracy, Indonesia
Mariama Williams, International Gender and Trade Network
Carol Wills, International Federation for Alternative Trade
Peter With, Dan Church Aid

*Contributors worked for the organization listed at the time of their
contribution.*

Acknowledgements

My heartfelt thanks to the contributors, all of them busy people, for responding so promptly to my requests. This book is dedicated to them and to the millions of lesser-known people around the world who are exposing the truth about corporate-driven globalization and implementing alternatives. My thanks also to Andrew Simms, of the New Economics Foundation, for reading the first draft and for his helpful comments, to Alison for her meticulous proof-reading, and not least to Robert for his guidance and unfailing enthusiasm. Any mistakes are entirely mine.

PART I

Globalization understood
– and the alternatives

I

What is there to worry about?

We must define our intent more carefully. Globalization means whatever you want it to.

George Monbiot

Globalization is like communism. It's an economic theory elevated into a life system

Czech pastor

The anti-globalization, questioning globalization, movement has become the largest movement of our time. But what exactly is globalization, and what are the protests about? And what are the protesters for? Henry Kissinger defined globalization in one word – 'Americanization'. John Kenneth Galbraith dismissed it as 'not a serious concept. We have invented it to disseminate our politics of economic entry into other countries'. Novelist Arundhati Roy asks if it's not 'a process of barbaric dispossession which has few parallels in history'.[1]

There are longer definitions – 'an aggressive programme for the imposition of Western norms of national economic management, economic deregulation and market opening, and facilitating take-overs of indigenous industries and agriculture by multinational companies', for example.[2]

The former chief executive officer of a transnational corporation defined globalization as 'the freedom for my group to invest where it pleases, in order to produce what it wants, by getting supplies and selling wherever it wants, supporting as few constraints as possible regarding workers' rights and social conventions.'[3]

Yet the debate on globalization suffers from a lack of clarity. In 2001 I reviewed a book containing the views of a number of people on globalization. The differing views were interesting and informative but, with only one exception, no one defined the beast. The result was confusion. 'It has to be asked whether people are talking about the same thing' was the perceptive comment in an overview chapter.[4]

The debate over globalization will not get far if people are unclear what it is, unless we begin by defining what we're talking about. I therefore decided to ask about 70 people from South and North, all of them with a special and in many cases unique experience or expert view of globalization, people who represent farmers and are involved in campaigns, and people who have otherwise given a great deal of thought to the alternatives:

- What is your definition of globalization?
- What's wrong with it, in your view, with an example?
- What are the alternatives?

The response was excellent: 46 people – coincidentally 23 from both the South and the North – gave their views, and these make up the first part of the book.[5] Some of the contributors are renowned thinkers and writers on the subject; 6 of them are members of the International Forum on Globalization (IFG), a grouping of academics and activists from South and North who have been working together since the mid-1990s to develop alternatives to globalization; many are with agencies that work alongside the poor and see the effects of globalization.

I began by asking for definition, because definition is important. If we can define globalization we have a better chance of tackling it. But if the definition remains ambiguous, we cannot be sure what we are dealing with. There's a Chinese proverb:

'Those who don't know the village they have come from will never find the village they are looking for.'

While people's definitions of globalization vary, there is an overwhelming consensus that by globalization people mean economic globalization, or neoliberal globalization, or more specifically corporate-driven globalization. It is the integration of people and countries into a single global economic system where the corporations have huge power, and represents a transfer of wealth from the public to the private sector.

Economic globalization should not therefore be confused with internationalism, or with the information and communication technologies that are bringing people closer together. Neither, as Helena Norberg-Hodge and others point out, should it be confused with cultural exchange or international collaboration and solidarity. The aim of the book is to contribute to building a coherent understanding of economic globalization and, most important of all, to the alternatives.

Western governments seek to whitewash globalization, even to the extent of confusing it with internationalism. 'Globalization means the growing interdependence and interconnectedness of the modern world', says a UK government White Paper.[6]

One thing is clear: contrary to what leaders of Western governments may say, globalization is failing the world's poor. 'The argument that globalization is working for the poor does not deserve to be taken seriously', says Kevin Watkins of Oxfam; 'between 1988 and 1998 the incidence of poverty fell by the derisory rate of 0.2 per cent a year. Already obscene global inequalities are widening'.[7]

Coming across from many of the contributors to this book is the aggressive nature of globalization. It is little wonder that corporate-driven globalization has generated such huge popular resistance and led to a worldwide movement not seen since the days of the anti-apartheid movement. 'There's considerable justification for being critical of the present arrangements [in the global economy]. Anti-globalization is a movement ... [with] some very serious forces and movements involved.'[8]

Globalization is an impersonal word; it is better to break it down into more human terms and to speak of the globalizers and the globalized.[9]

The globalizers

The economic globalizers are the powerful transnational corporations (TNCs) in league with Western country governments. The TNC dream is the world as a single market, without economic barriers, without anything standing in the way of them amassing profits for their shareholders. The overriding concern of this book's contributors is the way that TNCs are effectively running the global economic system.

Economic globalization is inspired and driven by corporate power. But, in one sense, the globalizers have long been with us. Nineteenth-century colonialism was partly corporate-driven. The first colonizer of Zambia was not so much the British government but the British South African Company, headed by Cecil Rhodes. Today there are even more powerful companies continuing and stepping up the process of exploiting countries and peoples.

Today's TNCs could have written the script themselves. 'The men who run the global corporations are the first in history with the organization, technology, money and ideology to make a credible try at managing the world as an integrated economic unit.' These words are in a 1974 book, *The Global Reach*, by Richard J. Barnet and Ronald E. Mueller. Allied to this is the political power they have to push governments firmly along the economic globalization track, to prevent any backsliding to developing the world the corporations want.

Recent estimates 'suggest there are about 65,000 TNCs today with about 850,000 foreign affiliates ... their sales of almost US$19 trillion were more than twice as high as world exports in 2001'.[10] The figure of 65,000 represents a tenfold increase since the 1970s.

Through economic globalization, the large TNCs especially are trying to carve up the world in their favour. Unelected, with no pretensions to democracy, they are powerful enough to persuade governments to pass laws, even to write the regulations of international bodies, such as the World Trade Organization (WTO), which further the corporate agenda.

The TNCs have a two-part strategy: they push free trade but also call for protectionism when it suits them. As Martin Khor points out, economic globalization is not just trade liberalization; it has not come about only as a result of free trade. Rather, it is a powerful mix of liberalization and corporate protectionism. TNCs enjoy the freedom of a single global market while being protected in those areas where it suits them. They may like open borders but they also want the system to protect their interests. The WTO's Trade-Related Intellectual Property Rights Agreement (TRIPs), for example, was the brainchild of thirteen major US-based corporations and protects TNCs through patent rights.

The power of these twenty-first-century globalizers over governments is seen in the WTO's General Agreement on Trade in Services (GATS). This is shaping up to allow corporations to sue governments that stand in the way of their expansion.

The TNC globalizers are active in every economic sector. In agriculture, the most basic of all industries, their power is huge and expanding. The corporations are attempting to control every part of the food chain, from seeds to retailing. A small number of corporations hold nearly 70 per cent of the patents on staple crops that are vital for the poor – rice, maize, wheat, soybean, potato and sorghum.[11] Fast-food chains such as McDonald's have expanded to virtually every part of the globe (but see Chapter 7). The danger is that local retail outlets are driven out of business, that countries lose their very heritage. Distinctive traditions could be swamped by a bland Americanism.

A number of contributors from the South see economic globalization as the new colonialism, with the big corporations the colonialists, supported by their governments. 'Our countries

are being colonized again' says Jennifer Mourin, for example. The
globalizers have become the new colonialists.

Economic globalization is a single ideology, a mirror image of
global communism. The rulers are not the politburos but the
corporations. Aided and abetted by governments, the corporate
globalizers use the system to their advantage to divide and rule
the world between them. A huge struggle is needed to combat
their privilege. Whereas the twentieth century was dominated by
a struggle against totalitarian systems of state power, the twenty-
first will be marked by a struggle 'to curtail excessive corporate
power'.[12]

The globalized

The globalized are the poor, the vulnerable and the disadvantaged,
overwhelmingly, although not exclusively, living in the Southern
hemisphere. Of central concern to many of the contributors is
the effect of economic globalization on the globalized poor. The
1999 *Human Development Report* from the United Nations
Development Programme says that economic globalization has
neglected the needs of people that markets cannot meet. This
process is 'concentrating power and marginalizing the poor'.[13]

The evidence of the last decade is that poverty is worsening,
that the poor are getting poorer, not just in relative terms but in
absolute terms, and that inequality is increasing. 'A new face of
apartheid seems to be spreading across the globe as millions of
people live in wretched conditions side-by-side with those who
enjoy unprecedented prosperity', says a UNICEF study.[14]

Among the globalized are the people who exist on less than a
dollar a day, over a fifth of the world's population. They include
the many millions of children who are malnourished, the 120
million who don't go to school, the millions of primary-school-
age children who work instead of going to school. 'The incidence
of extreme poverty is increasing in the least developed countries',
says an UNCTAD report.[15] But it is not only in the forty-nine

countries designated by the United Nations 'least developed' where poverty has worsened. During the last twenty years, African economies have been shrinking (at a rate of about 0.8 per cent per year, compared to a rise of 1.6 per cent a year before), while Latin America has been virtually stagnant.

In Africa, between 1960 and 1980, before trade liberalization, income per person grew by a third; since 1980, it has fallen by almost a fifth. In Latin America, between 1960 and 1980, income per person grew by 75 per cent: since 1980 it has grown by less than 6 per cent. Only in parts of Asia – notably China, India, South Korea, Taiwan, Indonesia and India to some extent – has there been any significant reduction in poverty, and those countries have made extensive use of trade restrictions when it suited them.

As developing countries have lowered their barriers to trade in the globalization process, so cheap food imports have flooded in, leading to millions of small farmers being dispossessed of their land. The globalized are being steamrollered by the globalizers.

At the United Nations Millennium Summit in June 2000, world leaders made a commitment to halve the proportion of people living on less than a dollar a day by 2015. They were talking about the globalized. But the policies do not match the words. Western governments especially continue to push the economic globalization which maintains the globalized in poverty.

The alternatives

It has been said that the only certain things in life are taxes and death. But there's something else. When politicians tell us 'there is no alternative' to this or that, one thing is certain – there is an alternative. So when Tony Blair says that globalization is 'irreversible and irresistible' and Bill Clinton describes it as 'not a policy choice, but a fact',[16] we can be sure that globalization is reversible and that it is quite obviously a policy choice. Otherwise humanity has lost control to an impersonal force. Do we have a say, or is there 'a momentum that is driving us unmindfully towards a landscape of consumer-robots and social instability, with a chance for self-determination probably diminished'?[17] Contributors to this book believe that we do have a say and that there are numerous alternatives.

In February 1998 I attended a conference in Geneva that looked unusual, even intriguing. It was billed as the 'First Conference of People's Global Action Against Free Trade and the World Trade Organization'. Unusual, in that in a Western city the conference was organized not by Northern-based NGOs, but by NGOs from across Africa, Asia and Latin America. A Spanish-based organization Play Fair Europe! helped with coordination.

The aim of the meeting was to allow people's movements from all continents to coordinate worldwide resistance against globalization, and to share and develop alternatives. As I watched proceedings in a rather battered old hall, I scarcely realized that what I was seeing was the start of something new – the birth of a new movement, a turning point in the headlong rush to corporate-driven globalization.

From the 300 participants from over fifty countries, the problems and their alternatives came tumbling out. Participants included people from Movimento Sem Terra in Brazil; the Karnataka State Farmers' Association of India; the Movement for the Survival of the Ogoni People, Nigeria; the Peasant Movement of the Philippines; the Central Sandinista de Trabajadores, Nicaragua; and the Indigenous Women's Network in Asia. The depth of feeling was considerable. 'Globalization is destroying millions of livelihoods', said Sarath Fernando of the Movement for National Land and Agricultural Reform in Sri Lanka; 'the alternative is for us to fight back for our survival'. 'We want to tell the governments that they are destroying humanity with these policies', said Alejandro Demichelis, of the Confederation of Education Workers in Argentina.

The problems may have been numerous, but the alternatives far outpaced them. People spoke of how they were developing their local economies, local monies, alternative trade, regional groupings.[18] The conference ended by launching the Peoples' Global Alliance and with a manifesto calling for direct democratic action against globalization and TNCs, saying this should be combined with the constructive building of alternative and sustainable lifestyles. The participants then marched on the headquarters of the WTO to protest about the damage they believe its policies are causing. It was the first international protest against WTO policies, and was followed three months later, in May 1998, by a much larger protest at a WTO Ministerial Meeting.

The movement was also growing in North America and Europe, and in November 1999 was seen in force on the streets and meeting halls of the US western seaport Seattle, at the next WTO Ministerial Meeting. While some people were protesting, some lobbying policymakers and some running workshops on the alternatives, all were united in a common belief that the system is wrong and that there is a better way. People the world over watched the street riots in Seattle on their television screens, but what they didn't see was the numerous meetings – so numerous it was not possible to attend them all – about the alternatives to the WTO's vision of the world. These alternatives have continued to develop.

In January 2001, 10,000 people went to Pôrto Alegre in Brazil for the first ever World Social Forum to discuss the alternatives. Twelve months later, 40,000 attended the second event. In January 2003, 100,000 attended the third forum, a tenfold increase in two years. Farmers from East Africa, fisherfolk from India, trade unionists from Thailand, indigenous people from Central America were among those who went to share their experiences, to learn, to plan campaigns, to be involved in solutions. 'Better we say what we are for rather than what we are against', Lori Wallach of Public Citizen told a workshop at the meeting. And the people who came did say what they are for: that they are opposed to corporate-driven globalization, but, of far more importance, they are in favour of the participatory democracy that opens the doors to alternatives.

The now annual World Social Forum has become an important milestone in the quest for alternatives, almost a clearing house for the multitude of burgeoning ideas on globalization.

Running through Part I of this book is a call for new visions, new dreams of what might be, new institutions, where necessary... 'It won't do to replace a neoliberal ethic among the IMF and World Bank with a more social-democratic one', says economist Walden Bello. 'We need new institutions that express the principles of what we should be calling deglobalization.' The battle is between a bland, monolithic, corporate-dominated and fundamentally anti-democratic global system that damages the lives of the poor, and a diverse, pluralistic and infinitely more democratic system where people have a real say in the things which affect their lives.

The approaches

The North's mainstream NGOs had mostly stayed away from the Geneva meeting in February 1998, possibly deterred by pre-conference publicity which said that a hallmark of the global alliance would be a confrontational attitude – fundamental opposition to the existing world trading system. Many of the Southern NGOs in Geneva did not think lobbying could have a major impact on changing policy. This highlights two approaches to alternatives to corporate globalization. The first is nonviolent direct action to build a better system, an option in which people are directly involved. In the South this may take the form of actively developing the local economy; in the North it may be people buying alternatively traded products and not buying products of certain corporations. In this approach, people are taking action themselves.

The second approach is more passive, and is the one largely favoured by most Northern NGOs. This is to persuade others to change – to persuade governments to change their policies, on trade, debt, corporate regulation, to persuade corporations. Lobbying is at the centre of most Northern NGO campaigns – even though there is little evidence of success. Trying to influence government from the inside has a role to play but it also has dangers. It can mean that NGOs are reluctant to criticize from the outside.

This difference is apparent in these pages: people from the South are often a great deal more critical of globalization than people from the North. Many from the South want to see globalization replaced; some from the North talk about making it work for the poor. 'For those of us living in the developing world, globalization is a dirty word. In the North it is a positive word', says Martin Khor.[19] The depth of hostility in the South to corporate-driven globalization is perhaps not fully understood by Northern NGOs, some of whom may take a passive role because of a wish to try to influence decisions from 'inside', or even by accepting funds from government. Too much criticism of government could mean a withdrawal of funds.

The make-up of NGOs in North and South is different. The North's mainstream NGOs generally consist of supporters – often generous and committed supporters – of the poor rather than the poor themselves, as is the case with many South-based NGOs. Unlike most NGOs in the North, Southern-based NGOs, like for example Movimento Sem Terra of Brazil, are more likely to consist of people whose livelihoods are critically affected by economic globalization.

This raises important questions: are development NGOs in the North, which exist to help the poor in the South, representing the interests of the poor? In some cases the answer is 'yes', but some Northern-based NGOs give the impression of not understanding how deeply people in the South feel about and are experiencing corporate-driven globalization. The views expressed in these pages suggest that at least some Northern-based NGOs need to rethink their policies.

Part II of the book looks at the alternatives and at how they can become mainstream reality, at what changes are needed to allow them to become practice on a wider scale. Combating the power of the transnational corporations is essential if change is to happen, in addition to changes in the 'power agencies': the WTO, the World Bank and the IMF. Resolution of the debt crisis that hinders freedom of manoeuvre of states is again essential.

'Globalization ... is of concern to ordinary people. Yet their voices are not being heard', says a former chief economist at the World Bank.[20] Some of those voices are heard in this book. They are voices for change. Changing the world is of course 'very difficult', as Gustavo Esteva reminds us, but people can create a new world, economically feasible, socially just and ecologically sensible. We are at a formative and exciting stage in the development of a new movement.

2

Globalization:
what does it really mean?

Victoria Tauli-Corpuz, a member of the International Forum on Globalization (IFG), defines globalization as

> the process wherein former imperialist countries are ensuring their continued economic, cultural and political domination of the world through the creation of international laws on trade, finance and investment liberalization. These international standards, laws, policies and programmes are made at the WTO, the World Bank, the IMF and through regional multilateral financing institutions like the Asian Development Bank, etc. Regional trading agreements like Mercosur, Free Trade in the Americas are also used to further the goals of globalization. The main goal of globalization is to ensure the continuing access of OECD (industrialized) countries to the markets of the developing or underdeveloped countries and for these countries to still remain as suppliers of primary resources and consumers of surplus industrial and agricultural commodities from the north.

This is fairly representative of the way that most contributors see globalization – in economic terms. Some stress the difference between economic globalization and the type of globalization that could be better described as internationalism. **Aksel Naerstad** of the Development Fund of Norway says:

It is necessary to be specific or to define what we mean when we talk about globalization. What I fight against is the corporate globalization and the economic globalization where all countries and people are forced into the 'same size fits all' where the reality is that it's designed for and decided by the few rich.

Green Party Member of the European Parliament (MEP) **Caroline Lucas**, co-author of *Time to Replace Globalization*,[1] says

It's important to make a distinction between globalization and economic globalization – which is what anti-globalizers are about. We need to distinguish economic globalization from the other things that people put in the same pot as globalization – such as the exchange of information, culture, technology and so on – which I'm in favour of, and which is internationalism. Economic globalization is the process whereby national economies are bound ever more tightly into one single global economy.

This point is made by several people. 'Economic globalization should not be confused with cultural exchange or international collaboration and solidarity', says **Helena Norberg-Hodge** of the International Society for Ecology and Culture. She defines globalization as a series of so-called 'free' trade treaties whereby

governments deregulate (i.e. remove restrictions on) inter-national capital flows and trade. The process depends on a continuous expansion of global transport and communi-cations infrastructures and favours large multinational cor-porations and speculative investors. At the same time that international trade is deregulated, a tightening of regulations at the local and the national level is destroying millions of small producers and local and national businesses worldwide.

Fiona Dove of the Transnational Institute defines globalization as

a process of greater global interconnectedness characterized by better means of transnational communications, increased transnational mobility of people, cultural hybridization, deregulated international trade and investment and thus the consolidation of global as opposed to international markets.

'Globalization is the integration of world markets, of world culture as well; it's the fact that we are no longer a mix of local communities, we are one global community', says **Jayanti Durai** of Consumers International. Broadcaster **Susie Emmett** believes that

At best, globalization is the positive essence of cultural exchange and trade (that) invigorates people and economies. At worst – and many believe the worst is yet to come – globalization is the relentless plunder of labour and natural resources whereby the powerful pay least and profit most.

Maura Leen of Trocaire points out that the word 'globalization'

is so all-embracing it can mask more than it reveals. For me globalization deals with the economic, social, political and cultural integration that is happening among nation-states. In the economic sphere it refers to the increasing integration of certain economies through trade, investment and other international financial flows.

John Hilary of Save the Children, UK, says:

The economic process is the central and most important aspect of globalization, and brings with it consequences such as the globalization of culture. It should be noted that globalization commonly refers not only to the phenomenon in general, but also to the process in its current form i.e. not just the incorporation of national and local economies into global markets, but the manner in which they are being incorporated today.

Walden Bello of the Philippines-based Focus on Global South defines economic globalization as the greater integration of the different economies into one integrated global economy, which means that the buffers that separate the different national economies are eliminated. This is done mainly through trade and financial liberalization and by giving freedom to capital to relocate different segments of its production in different countries.

'Globalization involves the increasing interdependence of national economies, financial markets, trade, corporations, production, distribution and consumer marketing', says **Hazel Henderson** in *Beyond Globalization*.

This globalization is driven by two mainsprings. The first is technology which has accelerated innovation ... and the global expansion of e-commerce and the Internet. The second is the fifteen-year wave of deregulation, privatization, liberalization of capital flows, opening of national economies, extension of global trade, and the export-led growth policies that followed the collapse of the Bretton Woods fixed current exchange regime in the early 1970s.

Cambridge University economist **Ha-Joon Chang** gives two definitions.

The first, more straightforward, definition refers to an increase in the importance of cross-border economic activities – flow of goods, flow of capital bank lending and flow of people in international migration (as the share of labour force). This kind of globalization has been going on at least for the last couple of centuries, although there were various setbacks and reversal of trends in particular periods. The second definition refers to not only the increase in the importance of cross-border activities but also to the spread of a single set of liberal rules that govern international economic activities, and indeed domestic activities as far as they have a bearing on the former.

'Globalization is old wine in new bottles', believes **Gustavo Esteva** of Mexico.

The old western ideal of One World took an economic shape in the last 300 years. It became a world project under the aegis of capital. After World War II, the US used its hegemonic power to shape it in their own image and interests. On January 20, 1949 it declared the cold war and launched the emblem for the American Era: development. At the end of the cold war, after four failed development decades, its emblematic substitute was introduced: global-ization. This is the emblem for an economic and cultural project, attempting to transform every man and woman on earth into homo economicus, the possessive individual born in the West. It has a political dimension: representative democracy. It has an ethical pretext: human rights.

The link with the past is stressed by debt-cancellation campaigner **Ann Pettifor**:

Globalization, in my view, is just a new word for an old, hopelessly utopian, economic model. A model in which impersonal, unaccountable financial markets, not democrati-cally elected governments, are deemed the most efficient and effective institutions for the management, allocation and distribution of human, financial and environmental resources. This model prevailed at the end of the nineteenth century, and again between the wars. It's a politically and socially unsustainable model that prioritizes market forces over democracy; money rights over human rights; and profits over environmental sustainability. It will therefore – inevitably – run up against social, political and environmental buffers as it did in 1914 and again in 1929. And, as happened in 1914 and 1944, the globalization 'genie' will, once again, have to be forced back into the bottle, with the reintroduction of capital controls. The only question outstanding is this: what level of human degradation, social and political disintegration and environmental damage will we have to endure – before the neo-liberal, market utopians are once again disproved?

And also by alternative trade specialist **Carol Wills**:

globalization is a process which is bringing the peoples of the world together, creating new bonds and connections, but also new poverty and marginalization. Although the word wasn't even coined until the 1990s, the process has been going on since isolated groups of human beings started to meet and influence each other thousands of years ago. The special aspect of globalization today is the acceleration of the process owing to better and faster communications and travel, the establishment of the World Trade Organization and its development of global trade rules and so-called 'free trade', plus the speed at which money can be moved around the world.

The new colonialism

Concern that economic globalization is the new colonialism is raised by a number of people. 'Globalization is unrestricted corporatization', says policy analyst **Devinder Sharma**;

globalization is the process that forces democratic governments to become subservient to financial power of the multinationals, promote the growth of the corporates, remove all hurdles in their relentless march towards exploitation of the poor, hungry and the available natural resources with impunity. Globalization is aimed at linking the elite and powerful, the bold and the rich, in each and every country. The rich and powerful must join hands to govern the world, use elected governments to make it easier and smooth for them to operate, and force the majority world to remain dependent on their alms and charity.

'I define globalization for what it is and not what it pretends to be', says **Vandana Shiva**, scientist, ecologist and agriculturalist.

Globalization is the corporate integration of the world, it's not the ecological integration of the planet and it's not the solidarity-based integration of world communities. It is a totally corporate driven affair; it has happened before in history, it came earlier as colonialism.

'An alliance of corporations, governments and the WTO', says **Nugroho Wienarto** of Indonesia, of globalization. According to WDM director **Barry Coates**, it is

> a process of economic integration undertaken by multi-national companies and facilitated by the policies of governments and international institutions, primarily the World Bank, International Monetary Fund and World Trade Organization. In its current extreme form, corporate-led globalization results from the removal of regulations on governments. Globalization is not the same as internationalization, which can be defined as the sharing of cultures, foods, music, experiences and mutual support across national, cultural and ethnic boundaries.

'Globalization means the global power of capital', says Roman Catholic priest **François Houtart**. 'The world economy has been dominated by the hegemony of the capitalist system, which has succeeded in building its two main bases for globalization: electronics and communication.'

Mariama Williams of the International Gender and Trade Network says

> Globalization is a process; it's not new, what we are in is a different phase of a process that has been ongoing. You can go as far back as you like, even to the Romans. But modern globalization started with colonial conquest and the integration of North America and Europe with Africa, Asia and Latin America. Globalization today is the integration of global financial markets in the world economy, and that process is driven by particular mechanisms; it has distinct characteristics and features such as technological change and speed of communications.

'Globalization is a system of dominance. Our countries are being colonized – again', says **Jennifer Mourin** of Pesticide Action Network. Says **Peggy Antrobus** of Development Alternatives with Women for a New Era (DAWN):

Globalization has economic, political, cultural and social dimensions. However, these dimensions are linked, with the emphasis on the economic. In economic terms, globalization is the promotion by Western industrialized governments and corporations of capitalism, the integration of global markets so as to expand their outreach to the rest of the world with a view to the enhancement of their profits and the extension of their influence. It is a process that wins the support of other governments in the expectation of market access for their products, and an opportunity to improve the standard of living of their people.

Mohau Pheko, of the Africa Gender and Trade Network, believes that

Globalization is the restructuring of the world economy, world politics, and the global arrangements in terms of how decisions are made, and centralizing all of that into the hands of very few people – mainly corporations and wealthy investors.

Economic globalization means 'increasing international commerce and investment at ever lower tariffs', says **George Gelber** of the aid agency CAFOD. 'There are very powerful forces that need and demand globalization – the transnational corporations which require global markets for their products because they cannot recoup their huge research and development costs without access to global markets.'

Pippa Gallop of Corporate Watch defines globalization as

a set of policies aimed at making it easier for corporations to operate anywhere they wish, however they wish, and harder for governments and citizens to regulate them, resulting in an increase in corporate power and corresponding erosion of the power of national governments and ordinary people.

'Corporate globalization, far from being a nebulous and apparently irreversible global phenomenon, is a very specific economic theory promoted quite deliberately by governments, who could decide not to do so', says **Ronnie Hall**:

> It is also a theory which when put into practice, tends to benefit rich people, rich companies and rich countries at the expense of poor people and countries, smaller businesses and the environment. It is a theory that is both unfair and unsustainable, meaning that people both now and in the future stand to lose out, especially when it comes to access to natural resources'.

Undemocratic nature

The undemocratic nature of globalization is highlighted by **Ted van Hees**. He defines it as the

> development of capitalist economic system on a global scale, led by private profit maximization through the establishment of free operating global markets on capital flows, goods and labour, at risk of undermining human and the globe's sustainable needs and rights and the responsible role of states. This is accompanied and steered by an increasingly uniform global system of conditionality and global rules, which are set and enforced by the world's rich countries and their governing and ruling powers (G7 governments and transnational corporations and banks) through undemocratically deciding and mainstreaming institutions which increasingly manage to integrate their global agendas – IMF, World Bank, WTO and increasingly UN agencies.

The theme is also raised by **Chris Keene** of Anti-Globalization Network in the UK.

> Globalization means the breaking down of economic barriers between nation-states, and as such could mean the end of democracy, as in a globalized economy power will inevitably pass from nations to global corporations, and there is as yet no global democracy.

'People experience globalization a bit like they experience God in their own way, believers or not', says **Andrew Simms** of the New Economics Foundation.

It can mean everything from, you're sacked, to, you're very, very rich. Sometimes it can mean both. More often it means the opposite, you've got a job but you're very, very poor. All these meanings stem from what globalization has become ... the attempt by big finance and big corporations to transcend geographic limits and democratic decision-making. And, to operate with minimum regard to social obligations and environmental realities, all in the narrow pursuit of the single bottom line.

The uniformity that economic globalization brings is raised by **Ruchi Tripathi** of ActionAid. 'The head of a major food company has said that globalization is when everyone lives in the same house, wears the same kind of clothes and eats the same food. That's globalization and that's scary.'
Jane Ocaya-Irama, of ActionAid, Uganda, turns the definition question around.

A hundred years ago, fifty years ago, we weren't talking about globalization because countries who are now developed were in the process of getting developed. And now that these countries have reached certain levels, all of a sudden they talk about globalization. But for many developing countries that have not reached those levels, globalization is a misnomer in many ways because we still depend a lot on our own production – our resource-poor farmers for example. I do not believe however that Uganda would benefit from more globalization.

The military angle is mentioned by **Peter Custers** of the Bangladesh People's Solidarity Centre in Brussels. He uses the term 'disparate exchange' to explain globalization.

While the term has hardly played a role in the critique of globalization so far, it brings out well how the system of free trade frequently harms the interests of countries of the South. The term 'disparate exchange' pinpoints the interconnection between the exports of arms from Northern countries on the one hand, and the imports of Southern raw materials, agricultural products, and industrial components on the other hand.

The terrorism aspect is raised by **Peter With** of Dan Church Aid. 'Globalization is a broad process including a lot of aspects – values like human rights, economics like liberalization, and now we have the globalization of terrorism.'

The divisive nature of economic globalization is summed up by **Pedro Equina** of Guatemala. He defines globalization simply as something that 'makes the rich richer and the poor poorer'. Indian MP **Bir Singh Mahato** says that globalization 'means competition between the even and the uneven, between the rich and the poor. Rich countries benefit, poor countries don't.'

Author **David Korten** reminds us that the the term 'globalization' was 'popularized by neoliberals and corporate lobbyists who were using a call for 'free' trade as a lever to deregulate markets and eliminate constraints on the consolidation of power of global corporations and financial markets'.

While most contributors have stressed the role of trade barrier slashing in economic globalization, **Martin Khor** of Third World Network adds another vital ingredient: protectionism of the powerful, by the powerful.

Globalization, the way it is being carried out, means opening the markets of developing countries in three areas – investment, finance and trade. Even though globalization is about liberalization, it is selective, it applies to developing countries, while at the same time we see protectionism, increasing protectionism, in the strong and rich countries – they protect, for example, their agricultural and textile sectors, and they make use of intellectual property rights regimes to protect their big companies from competition so that they can charge higher prices for their products and also prevent new entrants into the market. This is to preserve technological dominance and is a highly protectionist device.

It is not correct to equate globalization with liberalization anymore. Globalization is a system of world rules that enable the rich and powerful to impose liberalization on others when it suits them, and to have protectionism when it suits them. So eventually globalization is the globalization of policy in areas that in the past countries could devise for themselves.

Economic, corporate-led globalization is therefore a combination of liberalization and protectionism.

The 'destructive' nature of competition is stressed by **John Bunzl**, founder of the International Simultaneous Policy Organization. He describes globalization as

the latest phase in the natural evolution of human societies; a phase where the economic facet is characterized by fierce and global competition which, having outgrown the democratic governance structures of the nation-state, is now a truly destructive vicious circle which renders governments impotent and thus threatens all planetary life; a phase where, if we are to survive and to evolve as a species, destructive competition must give way to fruitful cooperation.

Perhaps the last word should go to **Danilo Ramos**, as his comments link up with the next section:

However you define it, globalization for peasant farmers in the Philippines means hunger and poverty. It is the reason why we are suffering. Globalization, to us, is imperialist domination. It strengthens control of monopoly capitalists over our resources, and makes use of cheap and docile labour in a increasingly borderless global economy.

3

Globalization:
what's wrong with it?

The damaging nature of corporate-led globalization is stressed by a large number of contributors. Says **Andrew Simms** of the New Economic Foundation;

> The problems with globalization are many; there are basic theoretical flaws to the belief that the free movement of trade and finance can produce the best of all possible worlds. There is also ample evidence of unsupportable social and environmental costs. Here is a flavour of some of them.

Historical flaws

Globalization is an old process that first needs to reckon with its violent past before its future can be properly planned. It continually harnesses new technologies, policies and political opportunities to pursue its ends, often regardless of consequences. In *Late Victorian Holocausts: El Niño Famines and the Making of the Third World*,[1] author Mike Davis argues that nineteenth-century economic globalization left India, China and Brazil tragically exposed to 'natural' disasters. According to Davis, the 'forcible incorporation of smallholder production into commodity and financial circuits controlled from overseas' fundamentally undermined food security, and left millions of people exposed to famine during El Niño cycles. Nineteenth-century globalization therefore represents 'a baseline for understanding the origins of modern global inequality ... how tropical humanity lost so much economic ground to western Europeans after 1850.'

Institutional flaws

We have a global marketplace but none of the institutional mechanisms to prevent the abuse of power and the exploitation of the weak by the strong. At the global level there is none of the regulation taken for granted at the national level. National rules, even when they are imperfect, still try to control the power of finance and corporations and are largely answerable to democratic processes. There are laws to protect consumers, prevent unfair business practices and break up monopolies. Management of the global economy, however, is like a horse with only two legs. The only groups and institutions with any power and leverage are economic, like the IMF and the World Trade Organization. Add the self-appointed annual Group of Eight (G8) nations meeting and the democratic colour of these arrangements is especially insipid. Institutions charged with protecting the environment and preventing poverty and social instability come a poor second best. Underfunded and powerless, they work behind mostly voluntary agreements.

Environmental flaws

Globalization is based on the promise of limitless economic growth. But already many limits have been exceeded. To fulfil the promise of US lifestyles for all would need another two planets' worth of natural resources that we do not have. We have become too big for our ecological boots. Already, to support the profligate lifestyles enjoyed by the minority rich, the earth's biosphere needs at least one year and three months to regenerate the amount lost to human consumption in a year. The result? Environmental decline. Disproportionate use by the rich of the atmosphere's limited ability to absorb pollution also means that wealthy countries and individuals are running up enormous carbon debts. Unlike poor country debt, which is rigorously policed, there is no mechanism to call in the ecological debts of the rich.

Cultural flaws

As global Anglo-Saxon brands of fast food, footwear and
musical fashion exploit their unfair multinational leverage,
culture suffers as diversity is lost. Cultural diversity is important for personal identity and well-being, but it also matters
because local cultural production is an important part of the
economy too. While the big brands suck out wealth from
local economies, repatriating most of their profits to head
office and on to shareholders, local producers both encourage
an enhanced sense of place and the creation and retention of
wealth where it matters, in the community. One pound spent
in a supermarket on globally branded goods is worth only
about half of the same spent in a local shop selling local
produce.

Economic flaws

Trade and financial deregulation have left the global economy
a more volatile place. The people most affected also tend to
be the people with the fewest ways of coping when things
go wrong. This is a problem because all the leading industrialized nations have signed up to a series of Millennium
Development Goals that identify ending global poverty and
protecting the environment as overarching goals for the international community. The advocates of orthodox globalization
have a case to answer. The Asian crashes of 1997-98 left millions in long-term unemployment, and the long-term decline
in primary commodity prices excluding oil – the value of a
basket of the main commodities is about half the value today
that it was in 1980 – leaves millions in the least developed
countries in poverty, and still dependent on a failed export-
led development model. Globalization also invites in a new
era of beggar-thy-neighbour competition among already very
poor nations. In a display of staggering double standards,
policymakers have pulled up the protectionist ladders that all
wealthy countries used during periods of their own economic development. Even the policies that worked for the
newly industrialized East Asian countries are now considered
economically incorrect for today's struggling nations.

Political flaws

Many of the problems in the global economy can be traced to the democratic deficit at the heart of globalization. Speaking about the International Monetary Fund, Nobel prizewinner and former World Bank chief economist Joseph Stiglitz commented that, 'In theory, the Fund supports democratic institutions in the nations it assists. In practice, it undermines the democratic process by imposing policies.' Competition for footloose capital further undermines democracy as governments gear policies not to meet the needs of their population, but to attract fair-weather investment. This also proves to be a classic catch-22. To attract investors, countries have to offer the lowest tax and regulatory environment. In doing so, they lose the ability to reap any benefits from the investment they have attracted.

'What's wrong with it?', asks policy analyst **Devinder Sharma**,

I wish I could tell you what is right with it. Globalization has become a major factor in widening the gap between rich and poor countries, and also within each country into the two distinct classes. The world did not realize the implications that lie hidden in a complex and intricate web called globalization. The die was cast even without our realization as to how it will reduce our existence, hit our economic sovereignty and make us re-emerge on the global scene with a begging bowl.

In 1960, before globalization became the buzz word, the richest fifth of the world's population were 30 times better off than the poorest fifth. By 1997, that figure had increased to 74. Between 1970 and 1995, the number of multinational companies jumped from 7,000 to 40,000. Five corporations have a combined income greater than the total income of the poorest 46 countries.

Globalization has helped corporates wield more power, it has helped the rich get richer while the rest of the world remains caught in an unending recession – the consequence of globalization.

Globalization aims at bringing new reforms in food and agriculture. It aims at pushing out millions of subsistence farmers from their meagre land holdings. It aims at destroying the inherent capability of poor and developing nations to produce food from within the country. It aims at taking away food security and letting the market dictate who should eat what, if at all. The world is being very conveniently divided into parts: the OECD countries as the food providers and the rest of the world as food receiver.

The WTO's Agreement on Agriculture, coupled with TRIPs, sanitary and phytosanitary measures, and foreign direct investment, are all aimed at limiting the role of developing countries in food production. With the developing world forced to remove trade barriers and QRs (quantitative restrictions), and with the OECD multiplying agricultural subsidies, the game is very clear. The developing countries should refrain from producing food and thereby playing havoc with natural systems. Instead, these countries should import cheaper and high-quality food from the West.

The sunrise biotechnology industry, which is completely in the hands of a few developed countries, makes this process of food dominance crystal clear. The developing world is forced to accept the unhealthy GM food and crops, making it possible for a handful of multinationals to control the entire food chain. Such a move will leave behind tremendous negative consequences for the developing societies, the impact of which will become clear as globalization gallops ahead'.

Gustavo Esteva, a distinguished Mexican social activist, says that

globalization is devastating cultures and environments all over the world. Capital has perhaps more appetite than ever. But it does not have enough stomach to digest all the people it pretends to control. While putting people out of its payroll, it closes the doors of the globalized market to millions of small producers and enterprises. More and more people become thus disposable human beings. And those falling under the control of capital are being uprooted from their cultures and places and reduced to a modern form of slavery. In the consumer society, they become prisoners of addiction or prisoners of envy.

The project brings violence to unprecedented levels and shapes, fostering and deepening authoritarianism. No economic figure about destitution, no sociological or anthropological description of miseries, no image of damaged environments, can render due account of the violence now generating a radical despair in millions of people. It is hardly conceivable. The feeling that your own life and the lives of the people dear to you do not count. They don't have any importance. It is something that appears in every aspect of daily life until it becomes total, un-appealable, like in totalitarianism … When you see your own people reduced to rubble because of resisting. When you see your own people assassinated. They are so many that there is no innocence left. This radical despair may generate rebellion, but it also produces global terrorism: a way of transcending and getting a feeling of triumph 'over passivity and bitterness, over the sense of absurdity that emanates from certain deepness of despair' (John Berger). Most people now suffering such deepness of despair do not become rebels or terrorists. They are doomed to carry on with it and even to transmit it to their children. Cynicism becomes an extreme form of violence. The obscene concentration of wealth is presented as the secret of prosperity for everyone. A structure of domination, increasingly closed and rigid, is advertised as democracy. Universal human rights, based on legal systems imposed by the few on the many, are predicated as a new universal ethic. They operate as the Trojan horse of decolonization, disseminating individualism among peoples and cultures whose own sources of morality cannot be reduced to the moral regime of homo economicus.

The renowned Indian scientist and ecologist **Vandana Shiva** says that globalization dismantles through brute power, through the coercive rule-making and rules of the World Trade Organization and other instruments, precisely those elements of our lives that are our best securities – ecological and cultural security and national sovereignty. And that is leading to a culture of an absolute epidemic of fear and insecurity, which is the breeding ground for terrorism and fundamentalism of all shades.

According to **Helena Norberg-Hodge**, who has spent much of her time working with the villagers of Ladakh,

globalization is a recipe for economic, environmental and cultural disaster. Local and national economies everywhere are being exploited by the activities of heavily subsidized investors and transnational corporations. Far from bringing prosperity, globalization is in fact triggering an international 'race to the bottom' – threatening to impoverish people and degrade environments in every corner of the world. The entire global financial system – based on banking, borrowing and debt – gives a massive and unfair advantage to TNCs over small and medium-sized enterprises. With the lessening of restrictions at the global level, TNCs are free to locate wherever they find the best 'investment climate' – meaning the lowest wages and the weakest employment and environmental controls. This has accelerated environmental degradation, raised unemployment, increased the number of sweatshops, destroyed small sustainable farming practices, reduced self-sufficiency and aggravated cultural and ethnic tensions worldwide.

Nowhere is the impact of globalization more evident than in the supply of food. The average meal now travels thousands of miles before it reaches the family plate. In French supermarkets, the garlic comes from Chile, while in the UK apples grown in New Zealand cost less than those grown half a mile away. This is not the 'free' market at work, but the result of huge government subsidies aimed at promoting global trade. Big business now has almost complete control over agricultural production and distribution. Meanwhile, small and medium-sized farms are squeezed out – even though they provide more jobs, have a higher total output and take better care of the land.

In our fast-paced Western world, the effects of globalization seem to have come upon us gradually, as an inevitable part of 'progress'. But there is nothing inevitable about economic development. Over more than twenty-five years, I have seen globalization descend like an avalanche on the people of Ladakh, or Little Tibet, a previously isolated region of northern India that was thrown open to development in 1975. When I first arrived over twenty-five years ago, the vast majority of Ladakhis were self-supporting farmers, living in scattered settlements in the high desert. Though natural resources were scarce and hard to obtain, the Ladakhis had a remarkably high standard of living – with beautiful art, architecture and jewellery. Life moved at a gentle pace, and people enjoyed a degree of leisure unknown to most of us in the West. Most Ladakhis only really worked for four months of the year, and poverty, pollution and unemployment were alien concepts.

Today, however, Leh, the capital of Ladakh, is littered with plastic waste and choked with diesel fumes, as lorries bring in shipments from India of packaged, processed foods, chemical fertilizers and pesticides, imported seeds and numerous plastic-wrapped consumer products. Because subsidized food is now imported from the outside, local farmers, who had previously grown a variety of crops and kept a few animals for themselves, are encouraged to grow cash crops, using non-native, ill-adapted plant varieties and toxic agrochemicals. They are not informed of the risks and consequences.

Media and tourism promote the idea that a Western consumer lifestyle is infinitely more desirable, powerful and glamorous than their own. Western-style education further perpetrates the image. The pressure on the young to conform to this model is overwhelming. These economic and psychological pressures are forcing people into urban areas, where they must compete for scarce jobs. Family and community ties are broken. All of these factors are not only aggravating but, in many cases, creating ethnic friction. What I have witnessed in Ladakh is not a unique phenomenon – one can see the very same impacts of globalization on cultures around the world.

Danilo Ramos, of the Peasant Movement of the Philippines, says that globalization

enhances free trade in the agricultural sector and that for us is destructive and disastrous. Before the WTO, the Philippines was a country with surplus food, we had an agricultural trade surplus; we have now become a country that is dependent on other countries, with a huge agricultural trade deficit.

'Accelerating globalization and ensuing deregulation and privatization of finance, markets, electronic commerce have often become destructive flows, disordering local societies, cultures and ecosystems across the planet', according to author **Hazel Henderson**.

The anti-democratic nature of globalization is again stressed by several contributors. 'An economic model that gives huge powers to impersonal, unaccountable markets, and financial markets in particular, has deep flaws', says **Ann Pettifor**, who worked tire-lessly in the 1990s for the Jubilee 2000 debt cancellation campaign.

First, globalization represents a conscious transfer of power to financial markets which have come to dominate the economy. As a result the interests of creditors, investors, speculators and gamblers have become paramount. Economic policies (such as the IMF's 'structural adjustment policies') are designed to protect the value of creditors' assets and to transfer assets from borrowers to lenders. Deflationary policies take precedence, which leads to falls in prices and wages often accompanied by increases in the price of money or interest rates. These policies lead to great concentrations of wealth, and to con-comitant impoverishment. Human suffering becomes unbear-able. Intolerable suffering leads in turn, and inevitably, to resistance, often violent and anarchic.

Second, the transfer of power from democratic institutions to markets hollows out democratic political systems. This disempowers voters, and leads to disillusionment. If governments shrug their shoulders and disavow responsibility for impoverishment and environmental degradation, voters will look elsewhere – to authoritarian, militaristic leaders, who will, they believe, stand up to international financial markets. This is what happened in Germany during the 'globalization' of the 1930s.

According to **Pippa Gallop** of Corporate Watch,

Globalization takes decisions yet further away from the people who are affected by them and conflates what is good for business. It takes the idea of the market through to its logical conclusion: that goods flow to those who can pay, which means those who need them least. It demands that everything is allowed to be owned and traded, although this means that people are losing their right to grow their own food and make their own medicines. It can only lead to a widening of the gap between rich and poor as companies control patents, genetic resources, and education, and demand payment for using them from those who cannot afford it.

'When you look at the centralization of politics, of decision-making, it leaves entire populations out of decisions about what happens to them, both at the local and the national level', says **Mohau Pheko** of the South Africa-based Africa Gender and Trade Network,

in particular, it leaves them totally out of decision-making at the international level, with no information, with nobody to account for what happens. At the economic level it is even more vicious. Seemingly, decisions are made by just a few people. Something is wrong with that. Again it takes decisions away from local people – decisions about their economic future, their development.

'Globalization imposes a "one size fits all" kind of straitjacket of all countries', says MEP **Caroline Lucas**;

> it takes away key elements of national decision making ability, it transfers democracy away from national governments, where people have been elected to carry out certain tasks, and puts it into an undemocratic, unaccountable, untransparent institution like the World Trade Organization. To give an example. On process and production methods, countries are not allowed to distinguish between products on the basis of the way they have been produced. So as far as the WTO is concerned, a football made with child labour is the same as a football not made with child labour. A genetically modified tomato is the same as a non-GM tomato. So that means that a country cannot make those key distinctions which it will want to make in order to shift its economy and production patterns onto a more sustainable path.

Lucas gives a further example:

> European Union member states, the European Commission, the European Parliament, had agreed there should be a ban on the sale of cosmetics that have been tested on animals. There was a date when that was due to come into force. And then suddenly that was completely backtracked by the Commission, who said that we're afraid that it might be seen as a barrier to trade by the WTO, and so we are not going to have this ban. So there you had a policy supported by over 90 per cent of citizens of the European Union being overturned, because of fear of a challenge. And that is a gross violation of democracy.

Diversity disappears

'The problem first of all is that globalization makes countries part of one monolithic global economy which stresses uniformity', says **Walden Bello**, one of the developing world's leading thinkers on globalization;

second, it means that diversity disappears, and diversity is one of the strengths of developing country economies because they are particularly suited to cultures and ways of life of different people. Third, the integration of economies means that when crisis hits everybody goes down. Once crisis hits the centre, the global economy, everybody begins to go down. What we have with globalization is a dinosaur type of arrangement of global economic centralism, and, as we know, this is always extremely dysfunctional. The current global recession is showing the dangers of this interlocking of economies.

The disappearance of diversity is also stressed by **Jennifer Mourin** of Pesticide Action Network:

From the point of view of peasant farmers and fisherfolk, globalization is essentially an erosion of our culture, our food diversity, our way of life. Our televisions reflect only one kind of face; music only one kind of music. It doesn't reflect us. Food is no longer as diverse; it doesn't reflect our culture, our wonderfully diverse, delicious culture. Diversity has been our soul, our life, our survival. Take that diversity away – and it's a recipe for disaster. Our food is disappearing, land is being taken away from people, women especially are suffering. We are struggling to maintain our identities, our essence. Globalization, and the way it is being pushed, is promoting monoculture – one kind of culture only. And that for us is untenable.

'Professor Byran Hehir, former dean of the Harvard School of Divinity, captured the challenge of globalization when he noted that globalization has logic but lacks an ethic', says **Maura Leen** of Trocaire in Ireland;

he pointed out that the failure to provide a structure of regulation to underpin globalization means that power runs free. Therefore the process of globalization requires regulation and should be subject to international law. Yet at present there is no international body charged with regulating TNCs – for example, the UN Centre for TNCs closed down around twenty years ago. UN Secretary General Kofi Annan has pointed out that world leaders have underestimated the fragility of the process of globalization, and that the spread of markets has outpaced the ability of societies and political systems to adjust to them, let alone to guide their course. Many have argued that what is needed is a new or much reformed global architecture to manage global affairs.

Victoria Tauli-Corpuz, one of Asia's foremost activists on globalization, says that globalization is wrong because

it does not allow the southern countries to develop their economies in a self-determined manner. During colonization their economies were distorted to fit within the framework designed by the colonizers. Thus even after political independence many of the economies of former colonies are still within the mould of being debt-dependent, mainly agricultural and geared towards exporting cheap raw materials. They have not industrialized to a level where they can process the raw materials into finished products. This huge disadvantage has not been addressed significantly. The key principle of the WTO agreement, which is creating a level playing field for all countries, glosses over these disparities. The special and differential treatment principle, which Southern countries fought hard for, is virtually ignored in day-to-day operations of the WTO.

It is wrong because the attempts of Southern countries to correct these historical injustices are not given much chance in bodies like the WTO, WB, IMF because the powerful countries can easily threaten and blackmail the politicians of these countries. It is wrong because it privileges the global capitalist market economy and transnational corporations and it destroys small livelihoods, small farms, non-market-oriented economies, which is what the majority of the world's people are depending on for survival. It imposes capitalist rules, values and norms as international standards which each country has to adhere to. For instance the TRIPs Agreement is a law which may be appropriate for the highly industrialized countries, but it is not appropriate for most of the countries and peoples of the South and even for the North. The indigenous peoples in North America, Australia, New Zealand and other developed countries also are against the way indigenous knowledge, sacred sites and artefacts, human genetic materials, etc. are pirated, commodified and privatized by corporations and governments. The commodification and privatization of genetic materials of living things through patents is legally and morally indefensible.

It has not worked...

Economist **Ha-Joon Chang** says that the globalization process has created

increased inequality, unemployment and poverty, because it has become easier to transfer economic activities across the globe. So financial speculation has created unprecedented amount of windfall income for the top earners, workers in advanced countries lose their jobs as the automobile factories move to lower-wage countries, developing country workers who used to work in protected industries lose their jobs as imports flow in, and so on. Many proponents of globalization ignore these problems, but even those who acknowledge them argue that globalization ultimately benefits everyone, as it accelerates growth and creates more wealth, which will eventually trickle down to everyone. This trickle-down argument has a point ... greater wealth creates at least the possibility that everyone can be made better off.

The ultimate problem with the current form of neoliberal globalization, he points out, is that it has failed *even in its own terms* — that is, growth.

- Roughly speaking, between the bad old days of 1960 and 1980, when globalization was much less progressed than today, the world economy was growing at just over 3 per cent per year in per capita terms, but during the last twenty years – the period of accelerating globalization – it has grown at only about 2 per cent.

- Growth slowdown has been especially marked in developing countries. They were growing at about 3 per cent between 1960 and 1980, but they grew at only about 1.5 per cent during 1980 and 2000. This means that they are falling behind the developed countries, whose growth also slowed down from 3.2 per cent, but only to about 2.2 per cent.

- Also note that even this 1.5 per cent average would fall to about 1 per cent or below if we excluded China and India, which have grown much faster during the latter period than in the fomer without pursuing the liberal strategy.

- During the last twenty years, African economies have been shrinking (at a rate of about 0.8 per cent per year versus a 1.6 per cent growth rate before), while Latin America has been basically stagnant (growing at 0.3 per cent versus 2.8 per cent before).

- Things are even worse in the former socialist countries, where after the fall of communism and their embrace of global capitalism, most of these countries have experienced a dramatic fall in living standards.

- In several countries, per capita income is still less than half what it was before the fall of Communism – the fastest collapse in living standards in modern human history.

So globalization has *not* delivered accelerated economic growth, in whose name we were told to accept a lot of unpleasant things, such as increased income inequality. In many cases, such as Africa and former socialist countries, the result was a retrogression, while in others such as Latin America it was an end to economic growth (from 2.8 per cent to 0.3 per cent). The only exceptions are countries like China and India, but note that these are countries that have not, as yet, fully embraced the global standards and have pursued largely independent nationalistic strategies.

Corporate domination

Corporate domination of the globalization process is an especially
strong theme that emerges. 'What's wrong with globalization is
that particular companies and cultures dominate; it's corporate
globalization', says **Ruchi Tripathi**, ActionAid's food trade policy
officer. **Barry Coates**, director of the UK-based World Development Movement, points to

> three main failings of the current policies of corporate-led
> globalization that are being aggressively pushed on the rich
> world and poor world alike. The first is the imbalance in the
> rules so that they discriminate against the poor, most starkly
> evident in the hypocrisy of trade policy and the WTO, in
> which the rich pressure the poor nations to open up their
> economies while refusing to do so themselves. The imbalance
> in rules governing the global economy reflects the deeper
> dominance of rich and powerful nations in their exercise of
> economic, political and military power. International agree-
> ments have become another tool for domination of the
> strong over the weak.
>
> The second is the failure of economics. The simplistic
> theories underlying the assumptions of comparative advantage
> is one of deregulation and unfettered free markets. This leads
> to policies that remove more and more restrictions on
> companies on the basis that such freedoms will result in
> benefits for all. However, this ignores the real world in which
> there are pervasive market failures (commercialization of
> knowledge and information, abuse of market power, etc.);
> huge social and environmental costs that are loaded onto the
> public by companies; increasing inequality and the concentra-
> tion of wealth into the hands of a few corporations and
> individuals; lack of attention to important aspects of life that
> should not be defined as commodities (health, education,
> right to water, knowledge and the ecological functions
> necessary for life).
>
> Third, a narrow version of neoliberal economics is being
> pursued above all other aims. Economic agreements are being

allowed to take precedence over local initiatives, national aims and international treaties on the environment, human rights and development.

Fiona Dove of the Transnational Institute in Amsterdam points out that

the globalization process, particularly on the economic front – but with major impacts on the cultural, social and political fronts – is informed by the ideology of neoliberalism and driven largely by transnational corporations in their own self-interest, with the help of their sponsors in government, and increasingly backed by military might. The neoliberal insistence on privatization and deregulation with a view to opening global markets has resulted in a myriad of problems with regard to what were public goods and services, access to such by the poorer sections of society, unreliability in transport systems, etc. In essence, what is wrong is that this process prioritizes the interests of powerful private corporations (profit) over the interests of the public, ordinary citizens. A revolution of sorts has taken place over the past couple of decades. This has subjected citizens to corporations, hollowed out any basic conception of meaningful democracy, resulted in vast gaps in wealth and quality of life, getting worse with privatizations of public goods and services (including the media), and now the military dimension to all of this is becoming ever more obvious.

'Globalization, as being advanced by corporate interests, is consolidating global governance power in global financial markets. Corporations deny any accountability for the social and environmental consequences of their action', says author **David Korten**; 'the result is growing inequality, the erosion of ethical cultures, social breakdown, and environmental destruction to the point of endangering the survival of the species.'

Peggy Antrobus, founding member of the network of Third World women DAWN, says that globalization operates in the interest of multinational corporations with little concern for the well-being of people, including people in the countries in which the corporations are based. It fails to acknowledge the structural imbalances between countries (political) and economies, and by using the terminology of 'free trade' pretends that there can actually be free trade between countries of unequal power and resources. This dishonesty is particularly unfair to small island developing states, which cannot compete with larger countries that benefit from economies of scale and wider options.

It capitalizes on imbalance in wealth and political power to promote policies and practices that are in the interest of the rich and powerful and results in an increasing gap between those who are in a position to benefit from the integration of economies and those who are not, in all countries. It facilitates injustices of all kinds – socio-economic, political and cultural. It uses the rhetoric of 'free trade' to uphold unfair practices that make trade between powerful and powerless countries anything but free; it speaks of a 'rules-based' trading system while leaving unregulated the largest corporations and financial flows of the wealthy; it claims to reduce poverty while exacerbating the impoverish-ment of increasing numbers of people; it claims to create a 'level playing field' while denying the major structural imbal-ances – political, economic and technological – between countries.

According to **Chris Keene** of Anti-Globalization Network UK,

globalization leads to a race to the bottom as transnational corporations seek the most favourable conditions for produc-tion, which means the lowest taxes, lowest wages, laxest environmental pollution controls, and weakest health and safety laws. An example would be the thousands of US and Canadian firms relocating to Mexico after the passage of NAFTA.

Aksel Naerstad, of the Development Fund of Norway, puts some figures on it:

Corporate globalization leads to a concentration of political and economic power in a few hands. A total of 143 countries in the world have a smaller gross national product than the annual turnover of the company Philip Morris. The assets of the 225 riches people in the world are the same size as the annual income of the 2.5 billion poorest people in the world. Corporate globalization creates a widening gap between the rich and the poor, pushing millions of people into poverty, and creates a small super-rich and super-powerful elite. A few people within a few companies and states decide the living conditions and destiny for billions of people. This monopolizing of power is in total contradiction with democracy. With corporate globalization it is impossible to create a democratic world where the people decide how the society should develop, and have the power to decide crucial issues in their own lives.

Nature, society and human life are diverse, and this diversity is crucial and a major source of life itself, for sustainable development in both nature and society, for happiness, challenge and creativity in human life. Economic and corporate-driven globalization is destroying this diversity, both in nature and in society. The exploitation of nature and industrialized agriculture, involving monocropping, the use of few varieties, patents on life, and genetically modified organisms (GMOs), is destroying the diversity in nature. Before the 'green revolution' in the 1960s more than 3,000 varieties of rice were cultivated in the Philippines. Now 8 varieties dominate totally, and just 200 varieties are cultivated. In the state of West Bengal more than 100,000 varieties of rice were known before 1965, but just 250 are grown today. Each day about 150 species of plants and animals become extinct, most of them because of human activity.

Corporate globalization is forcing one economic model, and also in many ways one culture, on very different societies. The power and the policy of the transnational corporations, the rules of the World Trade Organization, the policies of the World Bank and the International Monetary Fund, destroy local and national economies, and the possibility of using different models in different societies. Corporate globalization is based on and is pushing the neoliberal economic model, where a key element is reliance on market forces to develop economies and societies. Privatization of state enterprises and of public services, like health, education, water and energy supply, is part of this. The hunt for maximum profits will decide what sectors and services will be developed, not the needs of people and societies.

What is wrong with today's 'type of globalization, is the fact that profit is the main goal and not the needs of mankind', says Roman Catholic priest **François Houtart**.

A clear example is the action of transnational corporations, integrating the production and distributions processes with the idea of maximization of profit. Hence, the search for 'comparative advantages' in terms of labour, ecological norms, tax exemptions, etc. Production is aimed at profitable markets. Entire sections of the world population are excluded from it, because of lack of solvability. Social differences are increasing and sustainability is more and more difficult to maintain.

Ronnie Hall, of Friends of the Earth, also attacks the comparative advantage theory, saying that

neoliberalism promotes economic efficiency over and above any other social or environmental good. Its proponents argue that countries should specialize and trade in those products that they produce most efficiently (the theory of comparative advantage). The lowering of trade barriers also compels companies to compete on world markets, forcing them to cut costs and use their resources more efficiently. Everyone benefits as prices tumble, demand goes up and the wealth generated trickles down. It's an extraordinarily neat sounding theory and is no doubt particularly appealing to governments looking for triple whammy policies that appear to benefit the economy, big business and consumers all in one hit. Sadly, it's a theory that doesn't work in practice.

First, and perhaps most importantly, the 'everyone wins' theory of comparative advantage is way past its sell-by date. With the advent of new technology and the gradual erosion of investment barriers, capital can increasingly move around the world at the touch of a button. With governments also promoting private, liberalized investment flows instead of overseas aid, some countries – in particular, those with unstable economies, high operating costs or poor infrastructure – are finding it increasingly difficult to retain or attract investment. Absolute advantage is coming into play, which may go some way to explaining why inequality between countries is increasing rather than decreasing.

Second, the current economic model is based on increasing and unsustainable rates of resource use. There is no invisible hand guiding the market towards sustainability. These resources need to be husbanded and sustainable economies need to be managed. Other fundamental failings include measuring our economies inaccurately, failing to take proper account of key social activities that take place in the informal sector, and generally focusing on economic efficiency rather than social and environmental well-being.

Governments argue that there are no alternatives, but this is not true. In fact, there are almost unlimited alternatives. It is the one-size-fits-all approach of neoliberalism that is itself a problem. Yet this creates something of a dilemma for those seeking a way forward – how can we, as an international community, jointly develop a diverse array of sustainable economies? Friends of the Earth believes that the answer lies in changing the way we direct and manage our economies – so that countries and communities can determine their own economic agenda – and at the same time agreeing international 'ground rules' on equity and sustainability.

The vulnerable suffer

The effect on the poor and vulnerable is seen as a vital issue. 'Trade liberalization, a central aspect of globalization, is having severe economic consequences for the poor in developing countries', believes **Peter With** of Dan Church Aid; 'it's affecting our agriculture, our country's main economic sector'. 'Peasants are losing their access to the means of production. People are dying for lack of food', says **Manabe Bose**, of the South Asian Peasant Coalition in India, about globalization.

Globalization 'is essentially and too often at the expense of human values, needs and rights and the planet's scarce resources and survival. The IMF/WB (IFIs in general), G7 etc. have declared Poverty Reduction Strategies the major vehicle of a country's own development planning targeting poverty, but give precedence to "higher interests" such as opening up developing countries markets for their own economies' trading interests', says debt specialist **Ted van Hees**.

Nugroho Wienarto, of Farmers Initiatives for Ecological Livelihoods and Democracy in Indonesia, takes the view that what's wrong with globalization is that 'the powerful make use of global organizations to protect their interests. Small farmers, even in the North, suffer from this process.' According to **Pedro Equina**, of the National Indigenous and Peasant Coordination in Guatemala, globalization 'practically makes peasant agriculture and indigenous culture disappear. It is a global project of more profit for the few which destroys rural communities' power.'

'Globalization is seemingly irreversible but cries out for management that can make it "work for the poor", a phrase often on the lips of politicians who are advocates of globalization but cannot deny its malign impact on some of the poorest people in the world', says **George Gelber** of CAFOD.

Financial globalization brought ruin to East Asia in 1997, has bankrupted Argentina and is now destabilizing Brazil because the financial markets have more clout than Brazilian voters who dare to favour the mildly left-wing Workers' Party. The panic reactions of bond holders and financial institutions and the absence of exchange controls upset entire economies. In Indonesia alone the 1997 financial crisis pushed 20 million people below the poverty line and in Korea average income fell by over 20 per cent between 1997 and 1998.

Economic globalization creates winners and losers. Unfortunately the lock-in of Word Trade Organization agreements means that it is more and more difficult for governments to take action to protect or cushion the losers, through higher tariffs or subsidies. And the rich nations, particularly the European Union and the United States, have yet to correct the astounding distortions in international trade that they awarded themselves in the course of the Uruguay Round: they gave themselves the right to protect both their agriculture and textile industries, precisely the industries in which developing nations could make the most gains.

Cultural globalization has meant the creation of more and more global brands – Coca-Cola and McDonald's would be the most banal and most notorious – but local cultures are surprisingly resilient and adapt bland globalized brands to their own realities; make their own films, something that it is now easier and cheaper to do than ever before; and set up their own networks of exchange and protest. Whereas financial and economic globalization can be profiled in hard facts and figures, assessment of cultural globalization – even to the point of questioning whether there is such a phenomenon as cultural globalization – is much more subjective.

Nico Verhagen of Via Campesina stresses agriculture and food.

These are being undermined by the increasing emphasis on neoliberal economic policies promoted by leading political and economic powers such as the United States and the European Union, and realized through global institutions such as the World Trade Organization, International Monetary Fund and the World Bank. Instead of securing food for the people of the world, these institutions have presided over a system that has prioritized export-oriented production, increased global hunger and malnutrition, and alienated millions of people from productive assets and resources such as land, water, seeds, technology and know-how.

Not a level playing field

Globalization 'assumes that there is equality, that there's parity, which is not the case', says **Jane Ocaya-Irama** of ActionAid, Uganda; 'there's no parity in development. Maybe certain elements of globalization could be good, but globalization in the broad sense, in the sense of transnational corporations going into small countries, using their advantages to the disadvantage of the countries, is not good.'

Nelcia Marshall-Robinson, of the Caribbean Association for Feminist Research and Action, supports this view:

The current system and the policies and rules that apply within it are not honoured by all countries. All countries are not on a level playing field. Globalization affects countries disproportionately. For us in Caribbean, small-island developing states, it seems to be forgotten that we are very vulnerable, in terms of our size, our environment, our proneness to natural disasters, and in terms of what we are able to produce and trade. And it is women who are bearing the brunt.

Allied to this is the 'need to accumulate'. According to **Mariama Williams**, of the International Gender and Trade Network,

globalization has always been driven by the need to accumulate – goods, profit etc. During the slave trade that profit came from slave labour. Now it comes from exploiting cheap labour, primarily women's labour. The South is told to specialize in commodities where they have a comparative advantage and those goods are being produced by cheap women's labour in almost all areas.

Winners and losers there certainly have been, but among the 'losers', points out **Carol Wills** of the International Federation for Alternative Trade, are

the millions of traditional artisans, small farmers, and fisherfolk have lost their livelihoods as a result of their markets being flooded with cheap factory-made substitutes for what has traditionally been made by hand in the village (e.g. plastic buckets and sandals in place of metal buckets and leather sandals, power-loom produced polyester sarees in place of hand-woven cotton), or because they cannot afford the fertilizers required by the new high-yield strains of rice or because the price of coffee on the world market has sunk to a thirty-year low which does not meet the cost of production, or because the fishing fleets of rich countries are going further and further from home and closer and closer to the shore in their pursuit of a catch. Many of these newly dispossessed people have headed for the cities, where they believe there to be new opportunities. They have heard about this on the radio or even seen it on television because now that electricity has arrived (perhaps not in their own village but in a nearby town) they have seen that people in the cities enjoy a better standard of living than they do in the village. What they usually find is that life is just as hard in the city.

If they are lucky enough to find a job in a factory, the wage may be very low indeed. The global economy is placing all of us in a system which works continuously to provide more for less. One way it does this is by moving capital around the world to take advantage of low-cost labour and lack of regulation. (Even if there are good labour laws in a country, that country may well lack the means to enforce them.) If these new arrivals are thrown on their own devices, which is what happens to most of them, they have to use their own ingenuity and skills to the best of their ability (and they have lots of ingenuity, skills and ability), build their own house on a scrap of land and set up a tiny enterprise producing something, anything that can be sold. Unfortunately, the process of globalization has not developed sufficiently yet for most micro-entrepreneurs to be able to raise any capital to expand what they do.

'The process of globalization can be likened to treading water for fear of drowning. There is need for constant activity; mobilization of capital, human and natural resources towards one end – the profit motive; continual trade liberalization negotiations in all spheres', says legal advisor **Kathy-Ann Brown**;

> taken in the context of a multilateral trading system epitomizing the singular ideology of the post-Soviet era, globalization frequently evokes frustration. Frustration at being told of the great gains to be reaped from liberalization – in absolute figures – whilst failing to realize any gains at the domestic level, the result of our inherent capacity constraints; frustration at the notion that technical assistance is a panacea – the means to achieve sustainable development in a liberalized global economy. But market access is not market entry and for certain small and vulnerable developing countries enhanced and secured market access measures provide the only viable basis for exports. The frustration of being on the periphery; the frustration of not being an integral part of a world that 'matters' to international business investors, namely that 95 per cent of world trade which determines the pace and scope of globalization.

Simeon Waithima of the Nairobi-based Agri-Health Initiative suggests:

> Globalization's impact affects everyone. Decisions made in New York, in London, affect us all. Globalization is a top-down development tool and it has come at too fast a pace. We need to insert an ethical and moral dimension into globalization. Globalization is a tool of capitalism and this works under the elements of sub-politics. It is no good for developing countries because of inequalities. Corporations are not responsible to their own governments and are working without checks. If conditions are made safe for everyone, then globalization would work.

Deregulation

Deregulation is also highlighted. 'Today's globalization is driven forward by the liberalization of trade and investment regimes', says **John Hilary** of Save the Children UK;

> as well as exposing some of the world's most vulnerable communities to market forces which threaten their very existence, this liberalization in turn entails the removal of regulations which are termed unnecessary barriers to trade but which are often key means of achieving national policy objectives. This double agenda of liberalization and deregulation threatens to undermine development and pro-poor policies across the world, subordinating social and environmental well-being to the primacy of free trade.
>
> Nowhere has this been shown more clearly than in the international trade rules policed by the World Trade Organization (WTO). Through its disputes settlement mechanism, the WTO has repeatedly ruled that environmental and public-health concerns must take second place behind the demands of free trade. One of the strongest precedents for these rulings – cited approvingly by later WTO disputes panels – comes from 1990, in a judgement by the WTO's predecessor, GATT (General Agreement on Tariffs and Trade), on Thailand's long-standing ban on tobacco imports.
>
> The US government brought a complaint on behalf of its powerful tobacco lobby against Thailand's import ban, which was one of a range of measures that country had adopted on public-health grounds to tackle the problem of smoking. The Thai government argued in defence of the ban, pointing out that GATT free-trade rules still allow countries to take measures necessary to protect public health. It argued that the import ban was indeed a necessary measure, since allowing imported cigarettes into the country would lead to an increase in cigarette advertising and therefore greater pressure on people, especially young people, to smoke.
>
> The World Health Organization contributed evidence from Latin America and from other Asian countries to show

that opening up restricted tobacco markets in this way did indeed lead to an increase in smoking. According to WHO, public-health programmes alerting people to the harmful impact of smoking are unable to compete with the marketing budgets of the world's most powerful tobacco companies, and as a result cigarette consumption increases. In the Thai case, WHO noted that the presence of foreign brands and advertising would have a particularly harmful impact on young people and on women, who smoked local Thai cigarettes far less than adult men.

The GATT disputes panel agreed that smoking was a legitimate public-health issue. Yet in the final instance it ruled that the import ban should be removed, on the grounds that it represented an unnecessary barrier to free trade. While there was no doubt that the measure was effective in minimizing the public-health impact of smoking, the GATT panel ruled that the Thai government must allow the import of US tobacco into the country and look for other ways to deal with the public-health consequences of smoking.

As the WTO continues to expand its free-trade agenda, so more and more areas of public life are brought into conflict with its liberalization rules. The General Agreement on Trade in Services (GATS) threatens a range of basic services such as health, education and water by aiming to give multinational companies greater rights to enter new markets. It also undermines the ability of both local communities and national governments to meet their own public policy objectives, as global rules take precedence over local needs.

According to **Jayanti Durai**;

what's wrong with globalization is that without a parallel global regulatory force, businesses are the only ones who are directly benefiting at the moment. Big business can travel and use globalization, the way that political and economic barriers have fallen, in a way that other people haven't managed to capitalize on. Without having a global regulatory force to keep an eye on business in the way that you would

have at the national level, businesses are running away with
profits that would be better distributed across the world's
people.

Peter Fleming, policy analyst and author, makes the vital
point that globalization is

> wholly dependent on cheap oil and gas (the hydrocarbons). It
> depends on them directly for fertilizer, cultivation, processing,
> chemicals and transport, and indirectly for a strong global
> economy with the high incomes that can afford to buy its
> output ... the end of the era of unlimited supplies of these
> finite resources can be seen.

Destructive competition

Although there are many problematic symptoms of corporate
globalization, says **John Bunzl**, founder of the International
Simultaneous Policy Organization,

> there's really only one underlying causal problem; the prob-
> lem of destructive competition. Destructive because although
> most businesspeople, economists and politicians instinctively
> take competition to be exclusively beneficial, it can, in fact,
> be either constructive or destructive. Competition is only
> constructive if it occurs within a framework of proper,
> democratic governance. Without it, it becomes a destructive
> 'free-for-all' with its own negative dynamic which in the
> long run will benefit no one. And increasingly that's the
> situation we have today under corporate globalization.
>   So how does this destructive competition manifest itself?
> Since policies which encourage ecological and social sustain-
> ability generally cost industry more, governments resist
> imposing them for fear of capital or corporations moving
> elsewhere and of the knock-on consequences of capital flight,
> inflation, unemployment and a loss of votes. Businesses, too,
> resist the implementation of environmentally responsible
> technology, not because it cannot be done but because

increased costs will reduce their competitiveness. Mergers and acquisitions and their attendant job losses also occur, not so much out of greed, but out of fear for companies to retain competitive advantage and relative safety from themselves becoming the targets of hostile takeovers.

And national governments often permit increasing corporate consolidation against the public interest for fear of their own corporations becoming uncompetitive with those of other countries. Governments also pay vast sums of taxpayers' money in corporate welfare to compete for inward investment, and of course the corporations happily play one government off against another. Net result? Corporations win – and society and the environment lose. Developing countries, too, must compete with one another to attract investment from foreign multinationals by submitting to IMF-imposed 'structural adjustment', allowing their raw materials to be plundered, their forests clear-cut and their indigenous peoples displaced.

The main barrier to solving the problems with globalization is destructive international competition and the fear it induces in national governments – a fear which prevents them from regulating in the social or environmental interest. The problem is therefore that democratic governance today remains essentially national whilst business and markets have already become truly global. Democratic governance urgently needs to catch up and to operate at the global level.

In today's global economy, as capital and corporations now move across national borders to wherever costs are lowest and profits highest, far from increasing regulation to eliminate the effects of destructive competition, nation-states, whether developed or developing, must instead progressively dismantle the little regulation they already have in order to stay 'internationally competitive'. This translates into a deteriorating environment, a rapidly expanding gulf between rich and poor, and a noticeable tendency of underprivileged sections of society to resort to far-right political parties. Not for nothing have we recently witnessed rioting in many northern English cities and the rise of far-right demagogues like Le Pen.

So today's free movement of capital and corporations removes from governments of any political leaning the freedom to pursue those restorative policies their predecessors of the 1960s and 1970s were able to benefit from. Instead, the power of today's markets means that governments have effectively become the puppets of a quasi-dictatorship of transnational capital which demands business-friendly policies regardless of the party in power.

Susie Emmett, an environmental broadcaster, contributes a vivid picture from Poland

On a spectacular hillside in the southern Polish mountains, Marian Wegrzyn looks sadly down over the small farm he inherited from his father. The cherry and apple trees are pruned to perfection, the fruit brushes are comfortably mulched for the season's growth ahead and the three dairy cows look out from the byre. 'I never thought I would see the day when Polish children did not eat Polish apples', says Marian. 'Most of what we produce is worthless now. We've virtually no income. Everyone's in the same situation. We have to barter with our neighbours for fuel, clothes, whatever we need.'

Family farmsteads in Poland survived rule by the Russians, the Germans and Communism but they seem unlikely to survive the invasion by European supermarket chains. In just two years, five French, British and German supermarket food retailers – Tesco, Géant, Real, Auchan and Carrefour – have opened stores in the principal towns throughout Poland. Small farmers like Marian Wegryzn and his wife have found that the local wholesale trade in fruits, vegetables, meat and dairy produce from their mountain farms has collapsed. Their produce is of outstanding quality and diversity but, like others in their farming community, they are ill-equipped to find faraway specialist niche markets for the wide range of goods they produce. The supermarkets have made no pledge to source locally and, it is alleged, divert surplus produce from stores in France and Britain into Polish outlets.

'If my father and his father before him were able to produce
good food for local people on this land, then I cannot understand why it is better for Poland to be importing apples from
France and South Africa', says Marian despairingly. 'If the
imported produce was better, then it would be easier to understand. But I have heard that these stores sell in Poland what
they cannot sell in other parts of Europe and they don't even
charge what the food has really cost to produce and send all this
way. They can afford to sell at a loss.'

Big food businesses rule supreme and use their global reach
to source the greatest quantity cheapest, fastest. In this carnivo-
rous capitalism that crosses continents, farm livelihoods – and
the whole fabric of rural society – are thrown aside. As long as
the power to influence food policy and farm gate prices remains
in the hands of a few global food businesses, the ruination of
rural livelihoods looks, depressingly, set to continue.

Peter Custers, of the Bangladesh People's Solidarity Centre in Brussels, writes of 'disparate exchange'

The term 'disparate exchange' pinpoints the interconnection
between the exports of arms from Northern countries on the
one hand, and the imports of Southern raw materials, agricultural products, and industrial components on the other hand.
The interconnection consists in the fact that the income in
foreign currency which countries of the South derive from their
commodity trade on the international market is directly or
indirectly used for the purchasing of weapons and weapons
systems. Since these commodities frequently represent the very
most important forms of natural wealth possessed by Southern
countries, and since the products which the given countries buy
in exchange for their own commodities – arms – constitute a
form of economic waste, it is justified to speak of 'disparate
exchange'. The use of this term, moreover, makes it possible to
place the current discussions on 'free' trade and 'globalization' in
a historic context, and to revive the critical debate, which in
the past was staged so successfully, on the structural inequality

existing in the world economy between the rich Western World and the 'Third World'.

Disparate exchange, further, is no accidental phenomenon, but has emerged in part as a conscious reaction of Northern states, in particular of the United States, against the efforts which oil-producing countries have made to raise the international price of crude oil. As is well known, this economic struggle was initiated in the 1960s, when oil-producing and oil-exporting countries, exasperated with the continuously falling world price of oil, got together to found the cartel OPEC. The 'price revolution' they engineered in 1973, which in many cases was accompanied by the nationalization of oil companies and oil production facilities, at the time was welcomed by many countries of the Third World as an exemplary initiative. It was seen as the way to end neo-colonial domination over, and the perennial poverty of, people in the South. The United States, however, at the time of the price revolution had already mapped out its counter-strategy, as was gradually to become evident. Nixon, Kissinger and other leaders of the world's number one rogue state, the USA, before 1973 had already started encouraging the main oil-producing countries – Saudi Arabia and Iran – to allocate their enhanced incomes from oil exports towards the purchasing of expensive weapons systems. These Middle Eastern countries were actively encouraged to place weapons orders with armament corporations based in the USA, Great Britain and other Northern states. Thanks to the USA's close ties with Saudi Arabia's royal dynasty, Northern armament corporations benefit both whenever the production of oil in Saudi Arabia is expanded, and when the country's income grows due to a rise in the world's price of oil.

It demands no special intelligence to realize what is the true outcome of the mechanism of disparate exchange. Enhanced incomes from the exports of oil, gas and other raw materials by Southern states can, of course, be reserved for implementation of social programmes, such as the construction of new public-health facilities and the extension of educational programmes. Yet when priority is given to the procurement of expensive weapons systems, this generally occurs at the expense of public-

welfare programmes. Besides, a whole series of Southern
countries which have embraced the mechanism of disparate
exchange have meanwhile fallen prey to internal armed conflicts
or international wars. A striking example is that of the grue-
some and prolonged war of the trenches which Iran and Iraq
fought in the decade of the 1980s. The basis of this international
war was indisputably the mechanism of disparate exchange, of
the international exchange of oil against arms. The war's result:
hundreds of thousands of people killed. Right now, the trading
mechanism exerts its most horrifying impact on countries of the
African continent. Here, disparate exchange, among others, is
the source of finance of the war in the Congo, which has been
termed a 'world war' in view of the large number of countries
involved and in view of the huge number of persons who have
been killed within a few years. The example of Angola exposes
how the mechanism of disparate exchange contributes to the
prolongation of civil wars. The notorious rebel movement
UNITA, through much of the 1990s, has financed its international purchases of arms via the trade in diamonds heralding
from Angolan mines. Yet the Angolan government too has relied
primarily on the export of raw materials – that is, on the
extraction of oil – for the waging of its war campaigns.

In the past, during the post-Second World War period, the
negative consequences of the unequal relationships existing
between rich and poor countries on the world market were
widely criticized. The main topic for debate at the time was
that of 'unequal exchange', which theme referred to the continuously deteriorating terms of trade between commodities
traded by Southern countries and commodities traded by
Northern states. The discussion regarding this mechanism has
since been pushed into the background in the era of globalization, and in particular since the founding of the WTO.

Southern countries continue to be affected by unequal
exchange. Thus, African countries which depend on the export
of one single or just a few products, are seriously affected
whenever a minor drop in the price of their export product(s)
occurs. Still, the mechanism of 'disparate exchange', which is a

spin-off of unequal exchange, as stated, has even more devastating consequences.

The worldwide movement against globalization 'from above' has hardly broached the subject of disparate exchange. In my view, the theme should be considered a key element in any discussion on globalization and militarism.

4

Alternatives to globalization: viewpoints from the South

Peggy Antrobus: 'Protect people's rights'

Recognize the link between trade and development. There is a need for:

- *A new social contract* that acknowledges the rights of people to be protected from the rapaciousness and greed of unrestrained capitalist exploitation.
- *An economic model* that protects the rights and well-being of the majority of people, and practises sustainable development.
- *A development model* that recognizes the link between economic production and social reproduction and safe and sustainable environmental practices.
- *A model of fair trade* that includes: (a) provision for indexation of the prices of raw materials and manufactured products so that the prices of the former can be equitably related to those of the latter; (b) provision for effective and meaningful special and differential treatment for countries whose economies are especially disadvantaged by globalization – e.g. small island developing states and the poorest countries; (c) provision for the protection of the rights of governments to act in the interests of their own populations, especially when their human rights are jeopardized by trade liberalization.

Walden Bello: 'More separation between economies'

The alternative is that we should have more separation between economies, that while we are all part of the global economy we should be able to maintain the basis for different countries to follow their different, diverse paths of development. We need to create a flexible mode whereby countries can relate to one another, so that if the global economy goes down, everybody does not go down. We want diversity and flexibility; we want trade, but trade that enhances the diversity of different economies rather than diminishes them.

The way this can be done is quite certainly by not following the doctrines of free trade. We need more domestically orientated development and real international cooperation rather than integration. Civil society groups in both South and North have a key role to play in persuading governments to change course.

Manabe Bose: 'Take agriculture out of the WTO'

Agriculture should be taken out of the WTO. Agrarian reform is needed; people who farm the land should have ownership of the land.

Kathy-Ann Brown: 'A democratic multilateral trading system'

Progressive liberalization at a humane pace, recognizing that 'one size does not fit all'. Recognition of the need for periodic breathing spaces from negotiations on progressive liberalization to permit implementation and 'recovery'. A democratic multilateral trading system without political leverage exercised against small and vulnerable developing countries by multinational corporate giants who fund the 'democratic' process. A 'review and repair' of the multilateral trading system; equitable reform.

Jayanti Durai: 'Raise people's awareness'

Assess what the companies are doing and how they are operating. It's really the multinationals who are benefiting, not all companies. Then put into place guidelines, rules and regulations that can monitor what's happening with the corporations across borders. It is a matter of regulating business. In the same way that you have the United Nations bringing together people and setting up rules between states, we need to have rules that regulate business.

The close ties between government and the corporations are a problem for regulation. European and US politics show that governments aren't willing to challenge companies. That is one of the reasons for the rise of civil society – and increasingly everybody has a common agenda: development, environmental, labour, etc. – where there used to be conflicts. There is this common interest, there is hope of civil society working through some of the UN agencies; there's a lot of scope for improved dialogue between civil society and business. The scary thing in this is that governments are being bypassed. Governments are seen as puppets, in a sense.

There have been a number of instances in which civil society has worked with UN agencies to encourage and strengthen ideas – the framework convention on tobacco control, for example, at the World Health Organization. By working through an institution it is possible to get government support.

Some believe that the way forward lies with the consumer, that it's all about purchasing power. There's certainly a whole unwakened side that we have not managed to capitalize on as yet, but I don't think that's enough. There are limitations: only those who can afford to buy have purchasing power and can make choices (between products). There's a lot more scope to raise people's awareness of where things are produced and how they are produced and what that means for our world, for poorer people.

Pedro Equina: 'Solidarity and hope for the poor'

The alternative is the sovereignty and food security of poor countries in defence of seeds, different products and peasant agriculture, which has survived thousands of years. The alternative is the globalization of solidarity and hope for the poor as a mechanism between institutions working in poor countries, so that the development process does not come to a stop, and to rescue indigenous communities' own culture.

Gustavo Esteva: 'Creating a whole new world'

Localization is the opposite of globalization. It is an emblem for the current struggle of people affirming themselves more than ever in their own physical and cultural spaces, open to wide coalitions of the discontented.

An epic is thus evolving at the grassroots. Ordinary men and women are learning from each other how to challenge the very nature and foundations of the 'Global Project'. They recover and regenerate their own definitions of the good life, marginalized by development and globalization. They re-embed food in agriculture and regenerate their capacity to produce their own food. They escape from education, to regenerate their own art of learning and thus avoid the oppressive class division between the educated and the uneducated or undereducated. They are escaping from the dependency of health systems; they regenerate their autonomous capacity to feel and stay well, supported in diverse medical traditions.

They reclaim their ability to settle and crave their own places in the shapeless space constructed by the market or the state, instead of becoming mere residents and commuters. They reclaim and regenerate their own traditions of exchange; 80 per cent of what they consume is produced by people like them. Instead of one abstract market, ruled by the corporations, they organize a million differentiated markets, where people knowing each other control their exchanges, for example through local moneys.

Free trade implies subordination to transnational corporations and international institutions. People distrust free trade and protectionism, and they distrust bureaucracies. Escaping from that false dilemma, they attempt to bring the control of trade and investment to the local level, where people themselves can define what they want or not. They use representative democracy as a political umbrella to create a new regime of radical

democracy, in which people can govern themselves. In their
local places they express their art of living and dying and refor-
mulate nations as political spaces for the harmonious coexistence
of their cultures. Instead of One World they look for a world in
which many worlds can be embraced. They know that to
change the world is very difficult, next to impossible. But they
can create a whole new world, economically feasible, socially
just and ecologically sensible.

Ha-Joon Chang: 'Control globalization or risk collapse'

The proponents of globalization argue that there is really not
much we can do, because the process is driven by unstoppable
progress in transportation and communications technologies,
which is beyond anyone's control. They in fact often go one
step further and argue that those who try to control globalization are the modern Luddites. I argue that this is not true. If
it is technology that is driving this process, why was the world
more globalized in the late nineteenth century, when we relied
on steam ships and wired telegraph, than, say, the 1960s or the
1970s, when we had all the transportation and communications
technologies that we have now, except for the Internet?

The simple answer is that this was because governments
were a lot more willing to control cross-border economic
activities in the 1960s or the 1970s than in, say, the 1880s or
the 1890s. In other words, technology only sets the outer
boundary of globalization and it is policy, or politics, that
determines exactly where the boundary lies. If this is the case,
the extent and the pattern of globalization today can be
changed in a way that promotes growth and reduces inequality
by changes in economic policies adopted by the powerful
developed countries.

Of course, all this is not to deny the benefits of having some
international rules. The problem, however, is that currently
there is a strong belief that these rules have to be of liberal
kinds and have to be adopted by more or less every country.

However, different countries need different rules of course;
we cannot have different rules for every country, but at least a

few different sets of rules are needed for countries at different stages of development (this is partially recognized in various international agreements, but the exceptions granted to poorer countries are regarded as strictly transitional ones that need to be phased out over the next five to ten years). Moreover, even within each category, the rules need to be very broadly defined so that countries have sufficient freedom to design policies that suit them the best.

At the same time, the governance of the organizations that administer these rules needs to be made more democratic and accountable. Governance reform is important, because all rules are general statements and have to be actively interpreted; therefore whoever governs this process critically affects the outcome of that interpretation. Capital flows need to be fairly strictly regulated for all countries, while developing countries should have a greater ability to use trade protection. International migration should be controlled in a way that allows the receiving countries to assimilate immigrants better, but the receiving countries should be encouraged to accept more unskilled workers than highly skilled workers.

Unless the current process of globalization is properly controlled, reduced growth, increased inequality and greater instability (which tends to reduce growth and increase inequality) may lead to a collapse in the whole process, as indeed happened following the Great Depression.

Martin Khor: 'Each country should be free'

The alternatives can be discussed on two planes: policies and processes. It is the processes which are the more important because globalization is made by human beings, powerful human beings, making use of rules and institutions to impose a certain order. The alternative is to have a different system of international governance which is more democratic and participatory, where the developing countries can have their representative voice, not only heard but their views reflected in the decision-making process. Also, local communities, civil society groups etc. should be able to participate.

We should democratize decision-making: for example, change the system of decision-making in the WTO into one that is transparent, democratic and open, as you see in many United Nations processes. In the IMF and the World Bank, the quota system has to be changed, and developing countries given the right, if they so desire, to purchase shares beyond their present quota. If we change the decision-making process within these powerful organizations, or if we transfer the power of these organizations back to the United Nations, then there would be a better chance of fairer global rules.

Many of the global rules that now prevail can be transferred back to the nation-state – for example, rules relating to intellectual property. We should not have mandatory rules imposed in all countries simply because they belong to the WTO – which they need to belong to if they want to trade. Intellectual property rules should belong to other organizations like the World Intellectual Property Organization, which should then sponsor treaties, as it has done in the past. Countries should be free to decide whether or not they want to join these treaties, or to form new agreements of their own. This applies also to macroeconomic policy. Countries should not be dictated to by the IMF or the World Bank. Each country should be free to make its own macroeconomic policies.

Jane Ocaya-Irama: 'Put the poor first'

The alternative is to put people at the centre of all our development – people's needs and priorities, poor peoples' rights. That would help a lot. Even within the framework of the WTO, if governments took the perspective of the poor, then we would have a different world.

Bir Singh Mahato: 'Agriculture out of the WTO'

The alternative is special consideration for poor countries. They should be allowed to make use of subsidies so as to compete with rich countries. Agriculture should be taken out of the WTO. Land reform is essential.

Nelcia Marshall-Robinson: 'Re-craft policies'

Trade in itself is not bad – but it has become an end in itself. The alternative is for policymakers to take another look at the policies they have drawn up, to review what has taken place and to listen to the advice of civil society, because every day we are experiencing the negative impacts. If policymakers make full use of the available expertise, they will be able to re-craft policies.

Jennifer Mourin: 'Resist and appreciate'

The alternative is for people to resist – and I can see it happening at grassroots level. They are resisting by producing for themselves, by getting away from transnational corporations, by saving their own seeds, by re-appreciating their culture, their songs, their clothes. It's basically revisiting ourselves and appreciating what we are, what we have.

Culture is not static; it is a moving, living thing, but it has to be reflective of the many peoples in the world. So the strategies for alternatives are also varied. In agriculture, people are looking at reclaiming food diversity, of seeds and crops, finding ways that are appropriate for farmers, fisherfolk and women, to produce food and live our lives with dignity.

Mohau Pheko: 'Regional cooperation is essential'

We need to go to the local level and begin to give people the opportunity to decide how they want development to proceed and begin, in very small and communal ways, to go back to economic systems from which people are able to benefit from the resources of their own countries.

Regional cooperation, particularly for Africa, is absolutely essential if we are to protect ourselves from financial globalization, liberalization, etc. If we can work together as a strong unit at the regional level, we can begin to confront together, as a bloc, the decisions that are coming down from the global level, and that marginalize and exclude us.

Emphasis on the local means that agriculture should be taken out of the WTO. I doubt if there's any other agreement that impinges more on food and food security. The Agreement on Agriculture, together with the TRIPs Agreement, creates food insecurity.

Danilo Ramos: 'Enhance food sovereignty'

Alternatives? To implement genuine land reform programmes and develop agriculture as the foundation of the economy. Take agriculture out of the WTO and enhance food sovereignty – which means farmers having control over land and resources, water, technology, not like today when the agrichemical transnational corporations control the seeds, pesticides, etc. That is very harmful for us as peasants.

Devinder Sharma: 'Let democratic governments function'

The only alternative to globalization is to say no to globalization. The only alternative to globalization is to let the democratic governments function independently and fearlessly. This can only be possible if the role of the deadly trio – World Bank/IMF/WTO – is minimized and gradually phased out.

The only alternative to globalization is to deepen democracy, is to let the people decide their own future. This will eventually happen, with or without our suggesting an alternative model. After all, how long can the globalized forces go on pushing the common man against the wall? There is a limit to human tolerance. Like Communism, the days of the globalization era are also numbered. It is a phase through which the world is being forced to pass. It is a phase which will go down in history much quicker than socialism. Simply because globalization is built on exploitation of the poor and marginalized.

Nations will have to take control over their own destinies; they will have to take back control from the globalized forces. The only alternative is when nations begin to follow Abraham

Lincoln's definition of democracy: 'Democracy is of the people, by the people and for the people.' Unfortunately, in a globalized era, the definition of democracy has become 'government of the industry, by the industry and for the industry'.

Vandana Shiva: 'Local food security systems needed'

The alternative is to put people's security first, not the profits of corporations. These securities are well known, people have struggled for them for centuries: the right to food; the right to medicine, health, water security; to livelihood security and definitely political security – knowing that you live within a political system where democracy influences the conditions in which you live.

Bringing this about will mean changing government policy from pursuit of a free-trade agenda to following a people's security agenda; that means influencing debates in the WTO. Activists in India are joining up with opposition parties to demand that India's elections be fought on issues such as who will write intellectual property rights laws, how will agriculture be governed – by the rules of the WTO or by our national policies over which we have influence. We need also to put alternatives in place that will create 'free spaces' – for example, the alternative to a monopoly on seeds through patents is to create community seed banks; the alternative to globalized trade is to have local food security systems, and this is something that people can do even before governments start to shift.

Victoria Tauli-Corpuz: 'Alternatives, viable and sustainable'

There are already existing alternatives which are proven to be viable and sustainable. These are found in indigenous peoples' communities, local economies shaped by activists who want to live in more sustainable ways, etc. Many indigenous peoples in the world have economic systems which are not very much integrated into the global market economy, and they are resisting moves which will destroy these. These diverse systems of production and consumption should be allowed to flourish and develop at their own pace instead of being destroyed to give way to capitalist production and consumption systems.

Existing global trading and financial systems should be reviewed and changed to become more democratic and transparent. As it is now, these are still very much dominated by the OECD countries. The spirit of the UN system of one country, one vote should be instituted in the trade and finance institutions. Decisions made in these global bodies should be subjected to review by national parliaments and the civil society in these countries. The global trade and financial systems, and the transnational corporations which are the key players in shaping globalization, should be regulated.

Internationally agreed standards for the protection of basic human rights, women's rights, indigenous peoples' rights, protection of the environment, etc., should be the main frameworks guiding the behaviour and operations of global institutions such as the WTO, the World Bank and the IMF and also of transnational corporations. Diverse cultures, world views, economic systems, political systems, etc., should not be allowed to be dominated and destroyed by capitalist and Western systems, laws, philosophies and values.

Ruchi Tripathi: 'A people-orientated approach'

What's needed is some sort of balance between local solutions, starting with people, based on a people-orientated approach, putting people at the centre while not losing the positive aspects of internationalism that help us to see other people and learn about their cultures. So it's a balance between maintaining your local identity and priorities and being a citizen of the wider international community.

With governments we need to ensure that the poorest and marginalized, those who are left out, have a voice in the decision-making process. This we see more and more, at least in India, where we have a right-to-information bill and citizens' action movements that are becoming stronger, so government has to take notice. At the international level more support is needed for these kinds of initiatives.

Nico Verhagen: 'Multilateral regulation is needed'

To complement the role of local and national governments, there is clear need for a new and alternative international framework for multilateral regulation on the sustainable production and trade of food and other agricultural goods. Within this framework the following principles, among others, must be respected:

- people's food sovereignty;
- the right of all countries to protect their domestic markets by regulating all imports that undermine their food sovereignty;
- trade rules that support and guarantee food sovereignty;
- priority given to domestic food production, sustainable farming practices and equitable access to all resources, and support for small farmers and producers to own, and have sufficient control over, means of food production;
- an effective ban on all forms of dumping in order to protect domestic food production; this would include supply management by exporting countries to avoid surpluses, and the right of importing countries to protect internal markets against imports at low prices;
- prohibition of biopiracy and patents on living matter – animals, plants, the human body and other life forms – and any of its components, including the development of sterile varieties through genetic engineering;
- respect for all human rights conventions and related multilateral agreements under independent international jurisdiction.

In order to guarantee the independence and food sovereignty of all of the world's peoples, it is essential that food be produced though diversified, farmer-based production systems. Food sovereignty is the right of peoples to define their own agriculture and food policies, to protect and regulate domestic agricultural production and trade in order to achieve sustainable development objectives, to determine the extent to which they want to be self-reliant, and to restrict the dumping of products in their markets. Food sovereignty does not negate trade but, rather, promotes the formulation of trade policies and practices that serve the rights of peoples to safe, healthy and ecologically sustainable production.

Governments must uphold the rights of all peoples to food sovereignty and security, and adopt policies that promote sustainable, family-farm-based production rather than industry-led, high-input and export-oriented production. This in turn demands that they put in place, among others, the following measures:

- adequate remunerative prices for all farmers;
- the right to protect domestic markets from imports at low prices;
- regulation of production on the internal market in order to avoid the creation of surpluses;
- abolition of all direct and indirect export supports;
- prohibition of all forms of patenting of life or any of its components, and the appropriation of knowledge associated with food and agriculture through intellectual property rights regimes;
- a ban on the production of, and trade in, genetically modified (GM) seeds, foods, animal feeds and related products.

Global trade must not be afforded primacy over local and national developmental, social, environmental and cultural goals. Priority should be given to affordable, safe, healthy and good-quality food, and to culturally appropriate subsistence production for domestic, sub-regional and regional markets. Current modes of trade liberalization, which allows market forces and powerful TNCs to determine what goods are produced and how, and the way food is traded and marketed, cannot fulfil these crucial goals.

Measures should be initiated to remove food and agriculture from the control of the WTO through the dismantling of the Agreement on Agriculture. Intellectual property policies should be revised to prohibit the patenting of living matter and any of their components, and to limit patent protections in order to protect public health and public safety. All negotiations on GATS should be halted. Genuine agrarian reform should be implemented to ensure the rights of peasants to crucial assets such as land, seed, water and other resources.

Discussions should be initiated on an alternative international framework on the sustainable production and trade of food and agricultural goods. This framework should include:

- A reformed and strengthened United Nations, active and committed to protecting the fundamental rights of all peoples, as the appropriate forum to develop and negotiate rules for sustainable production and fair trade.
- An independent dispute settlement mechanism, integrated within an international Court of Justice, especially to prevent dumping.
- A World Commission on Sustainable Agriculture and Food Sovereignty, established to undertake a comprehensive assessment of the impacts of trade liberalization on food sovereignty and security, and to develop proposals for change; these would include the agreements and rules within the WTO and other regional and international trade regimes, and the economic policies promoted by international financial institutions and multilateral development banks. Such a commission could be composed of and directed by representatives from various social and cultural groups, peoples' movements, professional fields, democratically elected representatives and appropriate multilateral institutions.
- An international, legally binding treaty that defines the rights of peasants and small producers to the assets, resources and legal protections they need to be able to exercise their right to produce. Such a treaty could be framed within the UN human rights framework, and linked to already existing relevant UN conventions.
- An international convention that replaces the current Agreement on Agriculture and relevant clauses from other WTO agreements and establishes within the international policy framework the concept of food sovereignty and the basic

human rights of all peoples to safe and healthy food, decent
and full rural employment, labour rights and protection, and
a healthy, rich and diverse natural environment, and incorpo-
rates trading rules on food and agricultural commodities.

Simeon Waithima: 'Development from the bottom up'

Alternatives? Monetary considerations alone are not enough.
Economic principles do not answer issues of food and health.
The point is to empower governments and people. Let's put
people rather than money first, and let's have development from
the bottom up, not from the top down.

Nugroho Wienarto: 'Farmer alliances needed'

Strengthen the small farmers, show them how they can make
alliances, at local and district levels. Farmers have to defend
their interests; no one else can help them if they are not strong
enough.

Mariama Williams: 'Refocus policies and objectives'

There needs to be a refocusing of policies and policy objectives
to put people at the centre – a refocusing that gives priority to
the basic things that are critical to human life, that are enabling
and supportive of democracy. There is a role for the private
sector and for profit making but this should not be the centre, it
should not drive the economic system. We need a process, a
system, that is geared towards helping people be the best they
can be and make the best contribution they can. If you have that
as your starting point, it frees you from the narrow box of
concentrating on market access, completion, efficiency, profit,
without thinking out the implications. Policymakers should ask
what the economy is for, what's the purpose of it, and consider
what they need to do to restructure economies. When you start
from that perspective you get a whole different set of
relationships.

5

Alternatives to globalization: viewpoints from the North

John Bunzl: 'Simultaneous policy can help'

The solution can only come from the provision of adequate, equitable and democratic global governance. Governments of nation-states need to cooperate with one another to implement policies which remove the destructive elements of competition. So an integrated management approach which ensures that all three engines of our Tristar – economic, social and environmental – are all adequately and equitably fuelled to produce prosperity for the common good is vital.

It's for that reason some call for the WTO to build social and environmental concerns into its trade rules. Now that may sound like a great and fair idea, but 'rules' necessarily mean a 'one size fits all' regime for all nation-states that are not equal and find themselves at dramatically different stages in their development. A rules-based system ignores fundamental differences in each nation's ability to compete on a level playing field. So rules alone are not enough.

What is also needed are methods of raising global taxes; of redistributing incomes across borders to the poorest; of providing debt-free technical and financial assistance to non-industrial and developing countries to help them out of poverty and to meet higher environmental and social standards, and so on. In other words, what is needed are all those traditional strategies which were once available to governments during the 1960s and 1970s to keep all three engines running but which are now denied them. We need not just rules, but *governance*. However, to give such powers to the WTO, or even to the UN, when neither institution has any form of direct, democratically elected parliament would be to court global dictatorship – benevolent or otherwise. That is where the Simultaneous Policy – 'SP' for short – can help.

The SP technology represents a practical means by which all of us can work together to escape the present vicious circle of destructive competition and transit to a framework of international cooperation which eliminates the downsides of globalization leaving us all with the benefits. It allows us democratically to develop a range of measures to re-regulate global capital markets and transnational corporations; then gradually to bring politicians around the world to adopt those measures in principle; and then, finally, to get them implemented by all, or virtually all, nations simultaneously. But the stipulation of 'implementation by all nations simultaneously' should not be understood as a precondition 'cast in stone'. By removing governments' and business's key objection to being first to 'go it alone', and thus eliminating their fear of becoming uncompetitive, SP instead represents a new and vital consensus-building strategy. It provides the critical basis upon which governments can readily say 'yes' instead of 'no' to policies like the Tobin Tax or any other policy whose unilateral implementation might threaten their international competitiveness.

How to achieve this quantum shift in international relations? Since the adoption of SP represents a citizen's commitment to vote for *any* political party or politician – within reason – who also adopts SP, mainstream party politicians will increasingly have the incentive to do so or risk being unseated at future elections. For the adherence by all parties to market and corporate demands has severely narrowed the differences between them, so the number of voters needed to swing an election one way or another is becoming relatively small – as the last US presidential election showed. And it is the adoption of SP by that 'critical number' of voters in each parliamentary constituency in each country which is the aim of the SP campaign.

So SP is not an 'alternative' as such, but more a tool or 'technology' through which alternatives can come to be implemented. The problem is not any lack of alternatives, it's the lack of a practical means of getting them implemented which takes existing structures of power relations into account. That is what SP hopes to provide.

Barry Coates: 'Alternatives to irreversible GATS'

There is no single alternative to the current form of economic globalization – there are *many* alternatives. The one-size-fits-all model is a useful tool of standardization for global business, but destroys diversity in all forms and undermines democracy. The type of policies appropriate to societies should reflect their social history, economic capabilities, political culture, ecology and geography. The diversity of choices available to societies should not be closed down, as is occurring rapidly through the policies of the World Bank and the International Monetary Fund, and the agreements of the World Trade Organization, particularly the General Agreement on Trade in Services (GATS).

Economic history has shown that societies increase the standard of living of their citizens through many different paths; most dangerously, none has ever succeeded in making a major step forward using the policies currently being dictated by the rich and powerful nations. Equitable forms of development in the past have relied on an active state role in enabling all of its citizens to participate in the economy (eg. land reform, universal access to affordable services), strong regulation of domestic business and foreign companies, support for local businesses and the flexibility for the society to embrace and adapt to new ideas.

The first priority in creating the political space for governments and groups of citizens to pursue alternatives must ensure that these principles are not being prohibited. Yet this is exactly the case in current and proposed international agreements. The fight for alternatives must therefore start with the fight against those international agreements, such as GATS, that would close down the most important development options.

Under GATS, foreign suppliers of services are given new freedoms and governments are regulated so that they are required to remove any 'unnecessary' barriers to foreign companies. The rights of citizens, for example, to benefit from universal access to essential services, are subordinated to rights for companies. Similarly, governments are restricted in their pursuit of policies in the public interest, for example to restrict access to fragile ecosystems. These rules are locked in through GATS, through provisions that are effectively irreversible. At a time when millions of people around the world are mobilizing to demand greater accountability in the provision of services, it is deeply undemocratic for an international agreement to prevent public movements from persuading governments to change their policies. GATS includes in its aims to lock in privatization and liberalization, thereby preventing governments from responding to calls for change, and to deny democratic rights over the services that constitute more than half of the global economy.

Alternatives to GATS should start from the principle that basic services, such as water, decent health care and education should be an entitlement for all; promote universal access to a wider range of services (such as electricity, communications, public transport) that are important to the poor; and uphold the rights of governments to regulate services in the public interest, including limiting access to respect ecological limits and protect public health.

The GATS case demonstrates that the pursuit of the narrow commercial interests of large companies has been allowed progressively to dominate local and national government policy and international rule-making. Instead, economic policies should be reoriented to serve goals other than maximizing national income. There should be a means to achieve higher aims such as the right to basic needs and capabilities; the promotion of sustainable development; the achievement of an equitable distribution of wealth; the elimination of poverty; the promotion of human rights; and to sustain the ecosystems upon which life depends.

The political space for the pursuit of real alternatives will not be achieved without fundamental democratization of governments and international institutions. This is required to ensure that governments reclaim their obligations to set boundaries on markets and the activities of corporations, and are held fully accountable for acting in the public interest. The rise of a social movement internationally provides an opportunity to engage and empower members of the public to demand change. This movement brings together diverse interests to join in a campaign for real alternatives, drawing energy from international solidarity movements (e.g. anti-apartheid, international justice), campaigns to reform international institutions radically (IMF, World Bank, WTO), and local sustainable development initiatives.

Fiona Dove: 'Reassert social forms of ownership'

Hopefully, a counter-revolution is now developing as people wake up to the consequences of rule by corporations: a reassertion of basic democratic principles, which puts people first and the economy in the service of society, alongside a deepening of democratic practice such that the deficiencies of representative democracy, which have allowed the silent revolution by corporations to take root, are addressed. Key here would be the reinstitution of public media as opposed to commercial media, which would require state support, and a commitment to critical, independent information dissemination. We need to subject corporations to society; there should be no confusion about the supremacy of the rights of people over the rights of corporations. This requires judicial and constitutional support and public vigilance.

Citizens should be regarded as users of public goods and services and not as 'consumers'; the public should be regarded as the citizenry not as the 'market'. We need to reassert social forms of ownership and/or control/regulation of what should be public goods and services to ensure equitable public access and provision. This does not necessarily mean the state per se but can include non-profit collectives, mutual associations, etc. – popular elected bodies of citizens to play regulating roles.

Susie Emmett: 'Undesirable globalization bites back'

We are only just waking up to the fact that unjust, unsustainable and undesirable globalization bites back at the societies that sanction it. The responsibility lies with all of us – as consumers, producers, business managers or shareholders.

Peter Fleming: 'Oil shock coming'

The case for developing local economies in agriculture, food and indeed all primary resources is overwhelming because of the fragility of environmental resources. Yet while the argument for localization of food production is now widely accepted in principle among environmental NGOs, this consensus has little substance. There is no agreement on what a local economy is, or what localization means. Questions arising include the following: What is the scale of a local economy? Is it a village, a county, a region, a nation, the EU? Is such a thing worth worrying about?

The failure of globalization does not in itself mean the success of localization. Other perspectives of the future will have their supporters. The local, democratic, participatory, innovative and ecological perspective is not inevitable. A concentrated, high-tech, elitist, non-democratic response can also be imagined and might be easy to fall for.

Here are some suggestions as to how the case for localization can be strengthened and conditions created for its adoption:

• *Food: new measures of productivity* At present, the productivity of agriculture is usually measured as productivity per hectare of cultivated land; alternatively it is measured in terms of productivity of labour or the return on capital. We should begin to measure productivity in terms of the product per hectare of total resources, including the 'footprint' – the land required to sustain agriculture's energy demand, its transport dependency, its waste disposal and carbon emissions. In terms of this comprehensive measure, labour-intensive local-scale organic agriculture is incomparably more productive than current mainstream methods.

- *Energy generation and conservation* A fully developed solar economy of the future can reasonably be expected to produce energy equivalent to some 35 per cent of current energy demand. The remaining 65 per cent of energy demand will be met by conservation in its various forms. The generation, conservation and storage of renewable energy all imply a substantial role for local landowners and farmers. Conservation will require a reduced dependency on transport and on the hydrocarbons; generation suggests a role for farming in solar, wind and biomass energy; storage suggests a role in using solar energy to produce hydrogen.

- *Towards a mature science of cultivation* Organic cultivation is generally regarded as an option that offers consumers the benefit of a wider range of choice. This is, however, a misrepresentation. 'Organic' describes the agricultural method that is in a process of evolving towards a stable closed-system cultivation. Organic methods are at risk of being compromised by, for example, the current demand for designer food of low nutritional value, high transport dependency, and with few characteristics of a closed system, but these compromises will become increasingly irrelevant and unnecessary in the future, when the strength of organic methods, whose essential principles are correct and scientifically sound, will be demonstrated. Those principles can only be fully expressed in terms of a localized food production system with mixed farming, capable of providing a broad range of food locally; the food production of the future will therefore inherit a well-developed scientific method.

One of the reasons why a clear vision of agricultural policy is so extremely difficult at present is that we are facing a total discontinuity of policy. Current policy is discussed almost entirely in terms of perpetual business as usual, but future environmental and economic conditions will preclude that. Totally different policies will be required: to enable localities to maximize their self-sufficiency in terms of food, water, energy and materials. This in turn means that a short- to medium-term policy should start to make preparations now for the conditions that will exist in the not too distant future.

If localization of food production and consumption were to become a reality, this would have a substantial effect on agriculture. It would imply mixed organic farming to sustain a diverse range of local food supply and to reduce local agriculture's dependency on imports of materials such as fertilizer. It would also imply significant differences in regional and local practice, with a flexibility and freedom from regulations that encourages local evolution and solutions. How strong are these connections between agriculture and localization, and how widely are they recognized?

The coming of the hydrocarbon depletion phase can be expected to lead to destabilized and interrupted oil supplies, a severe downturn in gas supplies, and high prices for imported oil and gas. When these shortages develop, it will be impossible to sustain an agricultural and food system based on routine long-distance transport; it will also be increasingly difficult to ensure affordable supplies of nitrogen fertilizer. The only sensible option open for the food industry under these circumstances will be that of local, organically grown food. The oil shock, combined with an intensifying world food deficit and climate change, will lead to calamitous economic decline with high unemployment. The only possible response to this is a fully developed localization extending deep into economics, society and culture.

Pippa Gallop: 'Gain control over our lives'

Gaining control over our own lives should be the first aim of any alternative to globalization, since we can then make our own decisions about how our lives should be. A radical decentralization of power is needed, so that communities have control over their resources and labour. The point is not to prescribe what the alternatives should be, but to enable people to create their own.

In order for people to have the freedom to decide their own futures, they must have free access to, and control over, certain basic resources, such as seed, medicines and education, which should be locally relevant rather than globally uniform. This should not even have to be cited as an alternative, since these rights have frequently been the norm throughout history, and have been threatened by global corporations only recently. In order to realize this, land also needs to be more equally distributed.

There needs to be a move away from putting a price on everything, and an emphasis on needs rather than buying power. As much as possible should be produced locally, to provide stable livelihoods and to decrease the huge damage being done to job security, to the environment and to food security by the massive transportation of goods around the globe. This need not imply a return to parochialism, merely the preservation of some aspects of identities and cultures. Indeed the effect of supposed globalization in some places has been to create defensive, exaggerated varieties of parochial behaviour, such as religious fundamentalism, racism and exacerbated oppression of women.

George Gelber: 'Transfer more resources to the South'

It is unlikely that globalization will be tamed by a paradigm shift to yet another global model and, indeed, it is difficult to discern what such an alternative paradigm might be. In any case, the problem is not globalization itself but poverty and inequality between people and between countries. Inequality between the richest and the poorest grew in the 1980s and 1990s and the numbers of the very poor – the bottom 20 per cent of the world's population living on less than a dollar a day – are not declining in line with the Millennium Development Goal of halving by 2015 the proportion of the world's population living in extreme poverty.

The questions are: Is globalization exacerbating poverty and inequality? Can globalization be part of the solution? What has to change? And have the necessary changes got anything to do with globalization anyway? The UN Financing for Development Conference, held in Monterrey, Mexico, in March 2002, set out a long list of changes, many of which could be summarized by saying that developing country governments have to get their act together. Part of getting their act together is creating a business-friendly climate, especially for foreign direct investment – more globalization, in other words, but it does not have to mean allowing foreign companies to operate without any regard for their impact on the environment and communities of the host nation, so this means better-regulated globalization. But the Monterrey Consensus also called for more development assistance, more debt relief, which have nothing to do with globalization, except perhaps picking up the pieces. And it also called for the removal of trade restrictions by developed countries – better and more complete globalization.

In addition, and this was not part of the Monterrey Consensus, developing countries should be able to protect their agricultural sectors against cheap and dumped imports from rich countries which heavily subsidize their own farmers – better and more regulated globalization. Nor should developing countries be forced to open their markets to any transnational corporation that wants to set up shop – again this would be better and more regulated globalization. In the wake of the Enron and WorldCom scandals, where coroprations have been able to run rings round the regulatory authorities in the United States, this demand seems merely prudent.

Financial globalization urgently requires management and regulation. The herd instinct of financial institutions, first seeking out unsustainable returns and then retreating en masse when these returns show signs of faltering, has brought misery to millions and is often connected only tenuously with the real economies of the countries concerned. Governments need the flexibility of exchange controls to limit both inward and outward flows and should be able to put in financial speed-bumps that will deter short-term speculative investment. Governments should be able to assess the impact of their measures rather than be forced into one-size-fits-all policies by the IMF and the World Bank; if the consequence of these measures is that foreign direct investment is discouraged, that is a cost that they should take into account. This would amount to a severe restriction on globalization. Whether it would work for the poor would depend on the skill and the intentions of the governments making use of this flexibility.

Ultimately all global policies need to be scrutinized in terms of their impact on development. Having willed the end – the Millennium Development Goals – the world community, and the rich nations which have such unequal weight within it, must will the means; this entails making globalization a more equal race and transferring far greater resources from North to South.

Ronnie Hall: 'Take a decentralized approach'

Governments argue that there are no alternatives but this is not true. There are almost unlimited alternatives. It is the one-size-fits-all approach of neoliberalism that is itself a problem. Yes, this creates something of a dilemma for those seeking a way forward. How can we, as an international community, jointly develop a diverse array of sustainable economies? The answer lies in changing the way we direct and manage our economies, so that countries and communities can determine their own economic agenda, and at the same time agreeing international 'ground rules' on equity and sustainability.

It is now clear that high levels of economic growth do not automatically generate social and environmental benefits, and simply attempting to maximize GDP is no longer sufficient. A credible and productive system of economics should have as its goal the satisfaction of people's needs through the equitable and sustainable use of the planet's limited resources. Poverty eradication, social and cultural sustainability, intergenerational equity and human dignity must be the key objectives. Production and consumption levels need to be managed, and special and differential treatment of impoverished countries and peoples should be an integral component, allowing increases in consumption for those impoverished.

Furthermore, sustainable economies should be based on the principles of economic diversity and subsidiarity, allowing people around the world to reclaim the right to exert control over their local and shared natural resources and select those economic mechanisms and strategies they believe best suit their economic, social, cultural and environmental needs at any one time.

This decentralized approach needs to be complemented by stronger international rules ensuring reduced use of and equitable access to natural resources, repayment of the ecological debt, implementation of the precautionary principle, and regulation of corporate activity. This is not to say that international trade and investment have no part to play in sustainable economies. They can play a part in sustainable societies, but ultimately this will always be dependent on their impact on levels and patterns of consumption and production, the effective internalization of social and environmental costs and the distribution of benefits to all. In short, it is important to distinguish between free-trade ideology – the free-trade myth – and the freedom to trade; they are not the same thing at all.

Ted van Hees: 'Another type of globalization'

Global interests essentially reflect power relations; there is no monolithic bloc or global conspiracy. We need another type of globalization, where people and their interests are put first and their views, as well as those of their governments and parliaments (or other elected or democratic bodies), are taken seriously. Potentially, the framework for achieving people-centred development and anti-poverty planning are there. Therefore IFIs and WTO have to step back and open the political space for the genuine empowerment of poor people themselves, and for people's views to be expressed and actions be taken by civil society organizations. Usually, empowerment is not granted by those who are in power, nationally or internationally, but is achieved by people who are aware of contradictions in power relations and who organize themselves to take responsibility for their people's future.

Hazel Henderson: 'Reshape the global economy'

A reshaping of the global economy is needed, to address the new threats and dilemmas and to conserve our planetary resources, which are beyond the jurisdiction of nations and international agreements. Corporations, banks, speculators, scientific, professional and academic organizations, e-commerce, mass media including the Internet – all roam and rely on this open, largely unregulated, global domain.

Second, new trade rules are needed. The World Trade Organization has sought to roll back social and environmental policies which are seen to distort trade. The opposite approach should be taken: promoting patterns of trade which are not subsidised by exploitation, pollution and less than full cost pricing. There is a need to reconcile international trade regulation in order to promote social and environmental standards. One step towards this, at national or international level, would be to place an obligation on all major companies selling products internationally, to report their compliance or noncompliance with accredited standards. This would be termed a social and environmental disclosure requirement.

Taming the global casino of unregulated financial trading is the most urgent task of national governments. After a decade of financial shocks and debacles the Washington consensus policy logjam is crumbling – one essential first step is the cancellation of the debt of most indebted countries. The notion of an international bankruptcy court is now supported by the UN.

John Hilary: 'Reorientate trade and investment rules'

The alternatives to globalization in its current form are many and various, but they depend on a fundamental reorientation of global trade and investment rules. In particular, the free-trade agenda and the interests of multinational companies must be subordinated to the needs of people and the environment. Only in this way will globalization be able to contribute to sustainable development, rather than (as at present) militating against it.

Foreign direct investment (FDI), via the establishment of production facilities in poorer countries, can be beneficial for local economies, especially where there is a shortage of capital locally. However, FDI needs to be linked into the domestic economy if these gains are to be maximized in terms of extra jobs and capacity building. As one example, the Nissan factory built in the UK town of Sunderland in the mid-1980s employs around 4,500 people directly, but suppliers and subcontractors to Nissan have provided another 20,000 local jobs.

The traditional means for developing countries to ensure that FDI contributes to local economic development and job creation is through performance requirements and access conditions on multinational companies. Governments have required multinationals investing in their country to employ local staff in key positions, to source inputs from local suppliers and to protect the national balance of payments by undertaking to export a certain proportion of their products. Many also place equity ceilings on FDI participation, and/or require multinationals to form joint ventures with local companies so that there is more opportunity for skills and technology transfer.

Yet the WTO's TRIMs Agreement (on Trade-Related Investment Measures) bans local content and trade balancing requirements, undermining developing countries' ability to use FDI for development purposes. Similarly, the WTO's General Agreement on Trade in Services (GATS) bans access conditions on FDI in services, progressively prohibiting countries from setting equity ceilings on FDI or from requiring multinationals to establish joint ventures with local partners.

The alternative approach would allow developing countries the space to make globalization work to their benefit. Instead of the race to the bottom, in which governments compete with one another to offer multinationals the most attractive investment environment by minimizing requirements on them, the alternative model would create a race to the top, where multinationals would be engaged on the basis of their ability to contribute to the development of the local economy. Some countries already adopt this approach to engaging FDI. India, for example, reserves the right to give preference to foreign service suppliers which offer the best terms for technology transfer.

Similarly with trade, a positive approach can bring developing countries and poorer producers genuine benefits, rather than the negative experiences of trade liberalization in many countries to date. In place of the level playing field of free trade, which pits the world's strongest companies and countries against the poorest communities in unequal competition, this approach acknowledges that the poorest producers are in need of special assistance if they are to benefit from globalization. The WTO actually concedes that the world's least developed countries (LDCs) require special and differential treatment, but there has been no mechanism for ensuring that the richer economies open their markets to exports from LDCs. So far only New Zealand has honoured the long-standing pledge to provide duty-free and quota-free access to all LDC exports; if other rich countries are made to follow suit, the benefits to LDCs such as Bangladesh, Malawi and Tanzania will be significant.

At the producer level, a similar preference for fairly traded produce would start a race to the top akin to that described above for the globalization of production. Instead of the ortho-dox free-market model, where the returns earned by the primary producer are kept low and the profits are reaped by those higher in the value chain, the fair-trade model guarantees producers a premium above the world market price, as well as stable returns and good working conditions. A reconfiguration of trade according to this positive model would address the chronic problem of plunging commodity prices and declining terms of trade for the poorest countries and communities.

Some developing countries can benefit from the export opportunities that the globalization of trade brings. However, all must be allowed the space to develop their own economies free from the fear of unequal competition from the world's most powerful companies. This flexibility for developing countries to open their own markets at their own pace is equally important across the agricultural, manufacturing, industrial and service sectors if they are not to be forced out by foreign competition. Only with sufficient space to protect their domestic industries will developing countries be able to take advantage of global-ization without suffering the negative impacts of exposure to global market forces.

Globalization could bring genuine benefits to developing countries and poorer communities if it were reoriented towards development needs. Yet there will always be countries which are unable to benefit from investment and trade opportunities, through reasons of their own poverty and underdevelopment.

The international community will continue to bear a responsibility for the development of the poorest, and globalization will only be made to work for these communities through a long-term commitment to development assistance and the meaningful transfer of resources to where they are needed most.

François Houtart: 'Three levels of alternatives'

The alternatives exist at three levels. The first is the level of utopia, not in the meaning of impossible goals, but in terms of what kind of society we want and, in particular, what type of agriculture, what type of transportation, what type of mass media, what type of education, health, social security, culture, etc. Such a utopia has to be constantly redefined and should be the result of a contribution of social groups across the universe and of various cultures. The second level is a middle-range level, because of the technical difficulties for their achievment or because of the resistance of the system. They can be found in many sectors of activities: economic, political, ecological, cultural. A good example can be the regionalisation of the economy, as a first step to creating another type of globalisation. The third level is the short range, which is characterised by measures of regulation – for example, the Tobin Tax, which will never change fundamentally the capitalist system, but which can alleviate the situation.

All those alternatives are situated within two different perspectives: a post-Keynesian one, thinking that the system can be humanized; and a post-capitalist one, thinking that it is necessary to transform radically the logic of the economic capitalist system, being aware that this is not something which can happen at once. For the moment, a convergence between those two main orientations seems to be fundamental and this is what is happening, for example, in the World Social Forum of Pôrto Alegre.

Chris Keene: 'Local production for local needs'

Localization: a rebuilding and protection of local economies worldwide. This will lead to local production for local needs, except where a commodity cannot reasonably be produced locally. Long-distance trade would be confined to goods which could not be easily produced locally. A corporation not producing goods locally would not be allowed to market its products. Finance would be kept local by reintroducing exchange controls. (Any systems engineer knows that systems should be designed with firewalls between the component parts to prevent instability in one part of the system spreading to other parts; yet this is exactly what globalization destroys, so it is not surprising that the world economy suffers from frequent crises.)

David Korten: 'Address real human needs'

The alternative is a planetary system of strong local and national economies with distributed, locally rooted ownership that function according to real market principles within a framework of democratically determined rules and that address real human needs.

Maura Leen: 'Ethical globalization needed'

The alternatives to the current problems evident in processes of globalization are not what some might label as anti-globalization per se. In fact development NGOs, which have raised many concerns about the inequality and polarization in the current phase of globalization, have also been some of the strongest proponents of multilateralism (e.g. strengthening the role of the UN, itself a key dimension of an equitable process of globalization), yet they have been labelled as anti-globalization. Globalization is about interdependence; so are human rights, which are now recognized by virtually all states as being universal, indivisible and interdependent. Hence the need for ethical globalization. It is increasingly clear that states, international agencies and TNCs cannot escape the surveillance of the wider global community. Hence the call for a globalization from below, involving global civil society in decision-making, as distinct from only approaching globalization and global policy agendas from above.

Ethical globalization requires effective global institutions and global accountabilities. Take the EU. Although it is the world's largest aid and trade bloc, the EU did not have a specific overall policy on development cooperation until the year 2000. So how could it, let alone its citizens, effectively monitor its actions to address issues of global development. Ireland knows more than most the impacts of economic globalization. The integration of Ireland within the world economy has been accompanied by major changes in the composition of national income, with agriculture now accounting for only 4 per cent of GDP, a figure that underestimates the political weight of the agriculture sector.

Ethical globalization requires good global governance, which in turn needs an active global citizenry. It requires global solidarity and alliance-building between civil society organizations. Irish NGOs are becoming more global in their outreach and are members of international alliances such as CIDSE and Caritas. All this is part of a wider recognition that international alliances are essential in seeking global solutions to poverty and injustice. Equally important is the emergence of civil society groups in developing countries calling on their governments and the international institutions of which they are part (e.g. the World Bank, the IMF and the WTO) to put in place policies that tackle rather than exacerbate poverty.

Good global governance will require new and reformed structures of global governance. A number of areas for reform are evident: for example, an end to the veto by permanent members at the UN Security Council; reform of the voting shares within the IFIs (at present Africa only accounts for 2 per cent of voting shares at the IFIs despite being the region where IFI policies and finance are most influential); the need to set up a fair and independent arbitration procedure for sovereign debt and structures to ensure adequate investment in global public goods.

In the wake of September 11, and the creation of a global coalition against terror, the UN Security Council and other bodies should promote adherence to international human rights standards law as the framework for states' actions. Otherwise the world will be a less secure place for all. While the international coalition against terrorism was put in place almost immediately, there is a lack of adequate commitment to tackle the terror manifested in hunger and acute poverty – themselves a form of violence against the poor.

Finally, in recognizing the importance of global citizenship, further investments should be made in public education on development issues for all sectors of society, as such education provides the public with information on life in developing countries, explores the causes of poverty and injustice, and fosters action to address these concerns. Significant progress in support of international development will only happen when societies in both developed and developing countries, and key political leaders and decision-takers therein, believe that structural change to tackle global inequalities is necessary.

At the World Social Forum the UN High Commissioner for Human Rights, Mary Robinson, spoke of the need to make globalization a vehicle for human development and equality, with poverty eradication the first priority, and pointed out that our task is to turn our vision of ethical globalization into a programme for action. In essence, as she recently stated, in our globalized world the human rights challenge remains one of implementation.

Caroline Lucas: 'Put democracy back into place'

The alternative is to put democracy back into place, at national and local levels, and to reinstate trade to what it used to be. Trade used to be about exchanging the different, the exotic; it was not about sending goods from one end of the world to the other for the sake of it, in the hope that someone, somewhere, is going to make a profit out of it – profit which never gets to the poorest people. Instead of globalization we need policies of re-localization, which means providing far more of our own goods from within our own borders. This is obviously a policy that is good for domestic industry, and it's good for both North and South. It's not a policy that can come about overnight by putting up tariff barriers in the North, but the cancellation of the debts of poorer countries would mean they do not need so much foreign exchange.

We have to help build up the economies of the South so that there is more potential for them to do more trade regionally rather than depend so much on markets in the North – which are fickle and which don't give them the benefits they deserve.

Aksel Naerstad: 'The future is within societies'

Margaret Thatcher pushed the TINA concept – 'there is no alternative' to the neoliberal model. She was wrong; but I also think those who are looking for the alternative are wrong. The world is diverse, and therefore I think that seeking for one alternative concept to the dominating economic and political model is wrong. Yet even if we are not seeking one single model, I think it's possible to find some common guidelines for what we who are in opposition to the present world order and corporate globalization are or should be working for:

- Respect for and promotion of the diversity in nature, culture and society.
- Fulfilment of the human rights of all people.
- Democratic and transparent societies and economies where people's elected assemblies make the main decisions and where people have real influence on the conditions of their daily lives.
- Respect for national and people's sovereignty.
- Real international solidarity and cooperation based on equality, respect for sovereignty and diversity, common and differentiated responsibility for poverty eradication and protection of the environment.
- Sustainable societies and sustainable development (real, not just a slogan) and the (real) adoption of the precautionary principle.
- Equality for all people in the use of natural resources (equal shares of CO_2 emissions, use of non-renewable resources, etc.)

- Small units and local economies as the basis for national and international economy.

Alternative models for societies and development to what we have today must be created in real life, through people's struggle and lives. There is also a need for theoretical work; however, new societies will not be constructed in studies, but in real life. The theoretical work and outlining of alternatives have to be done in close connection with the social movements and people's struggle.

New societies grow out of the old, and there is a lot to build on in the world of today. Smallholders all over the world are practising sustainable and organic farming. It is possible to feed a growing population with nutritious, healthy, safe and good food produced in a sustainable manner. Factories are producing necessary and valuable goods for people, without polluting and with good conditions for the workers. There is enough knowledge, human resources and capital to produce the necessary goods for a decent life for all people. There is a diverse and rich living culture all over the world. Democracy is practised in many people's organizations and societies, and there are thousands of ideas about how to deepen, strengthen and develop democracy. There are good examples of combining political planning and a market economy. A big part of people's daily life is based on friendship and cooperation. You are not thinking about money or what you get back when you help your neighbour, or when your colleague gives you good advice.

The future is within societies today. The main problem is that the multinational companies, the international institutions like the WTO, the IMF and the World Bank, the rich states and the people in power, don't allow the alternatives to live and grow – because they are a threat to their power. We who are against corporate globalization are always asked to say what our alternatives are. We must work hard on developing realistic and good alternatives, and on promoting the many alternatives we find in people's lives all over the world today. But sometimes the alternatives are very simple. The alternative to slavery is no slavery. The alternative to patents on life is no patents on life.

The alternative to conditions imposed by the IMF are no such conditions. The alternative to multinational monopolies is no monopolies.

I end my contribution with the slogan from the farmers' and smallholders' international organization Via Campesina: 'Globalize the struggle. Globalize hope!'

Helena Norberg-Hodge: 'People longing for community'

If globalization is the root of so many problems, localization – a shift away from the global and towards the local – is an obvious part of the solution.

Strengthening local economies would not mean encouraging every community to be self-reliant; it would mean simply shortening the distance between consumers and producers wherever possible and striking a healthier balance between trade and local production. Localization would not mean that everyone must 'go back to the land', but that the policies now causing rapid urbanization would be changed to ensure that a better balance between urban and rural could be maintained. Localization would not mean that people in cold climates would be denied oranges or avocados, but that their wheat, potatoes and milk – in short, their basic food needs – would not travel thousands of miles when they could all be produced within a fifty-mile radius. Rather than ending all trade, steps towards localization would aim at reducing unnecessary transportation while encouraging changes to strengthen and diversify economies at the community as well as the national level. The degree of diversification, the goods produced and the amount of trade would naturally vary from region to region.

Reversing our headlong rush towards globalization would have benefits on a number of levels. Rural economies in both North and South would be revitalized, helping to stem the tide of urbanization. Farmers would be growing primarily for local and regional rather than global markets, allowing them to choose varieties in tune with local conditions and local needs, thus reviving agricultural diversity. Most production processes would be far smaller in scale, and therefore less stressful to the environment. Transportation would be minimized, and so the greenhouse gas and pollution toll would decrease, as would the financial and ecological costs of energy extraction. People would no longer be forced to conform to the impossible ideals of a global consumer monoculture, thereby lessening the psychological pressures that often lead to ethnic conflict and violence.

Ending the blind pursuit of trade for the sake of trade would reduce the economic, and hence political, power of TNCs. It would eliminate the need to hand power to such supranational institutions such as the World Trade Organization, thereby helping to reverse the erosion of democracy.

For a shift towards the local to occur, steps will be needed on several levels. Already, many individuals and organizations are working from the grassroots to strengthen their communities and local economies. There are also initiatives to control corporate activity at the national level. For these efforts to succeed, civic society also needs to formulate and be involved in implementing a multilateral treaty to control and reduce the power of TNCs. A moratorium on further deregulation would be a good first step. A second step would be to replace the WTO with a WEO – a World Environment Organization. This may sound fanciful, but things are changing quickly in the global economy. Who would have thought that it would be necessary for governments to meet behind steel barricades in order to negotiate treaties that are supposedly increasing prosperity worldwide? Resistance to globalization is growing stronger by the day. The knowledge that it is destructive is like a genie that has got out of the bottle- and it can't be stuffed back in again!

In addition to these policy shifts we need countless small, diverse, local initiatives of the kind that are already emerging. Unlike actions to halt the global economic steamroller, these small-scale steps require a slow pace and a deep, intimate understanding of local contexts, and are best designed by local people themselves. If supported by policy changes, such initiatives will, over time, inevitably foster a return to cultural and biological diversity and long-term sustainability.

My organization, the International Society for Ecology and

Culture (ISEC), has been working in Ladakh for more than two decades to help the people there resist the pressures of globalization. Our numerous activities include information-sharing campaigns, cultural exchange programmes, renewable energy projects and helping to set up indigenous groups, such as the Women's Alliance of Ladakh (WAL). The WAL works to raise the status of farming women and maintain agricultural and cultural diversity. Thankfully, our efforts have had a significant positive effect in helping to rebuild self-sufficiency and self-respect in Ladakh. ISEC has also carried out work outside of Ladakh to inspire people around the world to be part of a shift towards localization. ISEC's Global to Local programmes address the wide range of globalization-related issues, focusing particularly on food and farming. ISEC promotes the localizing of food systems – a remarkably strategic way of solving a whole range of environmental, economic and social problems at once.

Around the world a wide range of efforts are emerging to reweave the social and economic fabric in ways that mesh with the needs of nature – both wild and human. Positive changes like these point to people's longing for community and for a deeper connection to the natural world. People are ready, even eager, for a fundamental shift in direction.

Ann Pettifor: 'The world must be turned upside down'

We need an alternative economic model, powered by values that uphold human rights, celebrate diversity and respect environmental limits. Above all, money rights must once again be put back in their box, and subordinated to human, animal and environmental rights.

Markets must once again be integrated into our social, political and cultural arrangements, not dominate them. And all economic policies must be constrained by the limits placed on the natural capital of our seas, soil and atmosphere. This will require new regulation. There will have to be controls over capital; regulation of trade, taxes on speculation, and a new framework of justice for negotiations between international creditors and sovereign debtors. We will have to bring back the ancient form of regulation known as Sunday – periodic correction to imbalance by setting aside one day a week for limiting consumption, and avoiding the exploitation of people and the land. And we will need a plan for the contraction and convergence of greenhouse gas emissions.

There must be an end to the dominance of creditors and bankers; and to the poor financing the rich. Rich countries must be structurally adjusted towards the sustainable use of natural resources. Ecological accounts must be settled, and debts paid by the rich to the poor, for the overuse of the earth's resources. The unpayable and uncollectable debts of the poorest countries and the poorest people must be written off. This requires a complete re-engineering of economic thinking. We need to abandon utopian economic models which idolize money and militarization, and which lead to debt creation and ultimately serfdom. The world must be turned upside down.

Andrew Simms: 'The new agenda'

Economic historian Robert Heilbroner points out that for most of the last millennium the 'notion that a general struggle for gain might actually bind together a community would have been held as little short of madness.' After Enron, WorldCom, Xerox, Andersen, Vivendi ad infinitum, we may think the same again for most of the next millennium.

We need to reattach the arm of business to the body of society and make the markets our servants not our masters. To do this there are countless detailed proposals to regulate and reform the way business is done, nationally and globally. There are informed calls for: a global currency transactions tax to pay for sustainable development and poverty reduction; a transparent insolvency procedure to end the torture of indebted countries; and an equitable global framework to tackle the greatest collective threat, global warming. This short space, however, is best devoted to the principles from which the necessary, myriad proposals for alternatives should flow.

If it is raining you put on a coat or take an umbrella. If the sun is blazing, it's sunglasses and sun cream. We organize our affairs to meet the challenges facing us. Three main trends threaten us today: economic instability, environmental instability and political instability. Planning a response to such trends means looking through the lens of risk reduction. The poorest and most marginalized people suffer when economies crash due to the inherent instability of liberalized markets, or when extreme weather events driven by climate change hit communities. The question to be asked of every new policy, and every new project, must now be: does it increase people's vulnerability, or does it strengthen their resilience?

This is the acid test of policy under globalization. It must be applied to everything, from decisions over privatization to building transport infrastructure, agricultural planning, the management of foreign debt, how to generate energy and manage disasters. To do this, the official guiding principles of national policy need to be supplanted. Governments currently aim to maximize competitiveness in order to maximize orthodox economic growth. This happens in the context of maximum integration in the global economy, up to the point that it contradicts national self-interest, as in the cases when the United States has sought to protect its steel industry and agriculture.

The new agenda embraces a different set of criteria for universal economic well-being. Echoing Gandhi, Keynes said that ideas, knowledge, art, hospitality and travel are things which should by their nature be international; goods, however, should be homespun whenever reasonable and convenient and, above all, finance should be primarily national.

It was another way of describing what today we would call subsidiarity or the proximity principle. That is the idea that economic transactions are better at the lowest appropriate level. It is a way of both creating and keeping wealth where it is needed and helping to live within our environmental budget. As anti-globalization protesters move from opposition to proposition, they are starting to promote localization as a considered alternative to globalization. New economic research supports them. Spending money on local food in a local retail outlet, rather than a globally connected supermarket, brings double the value back to the community. The supermarket acts like a vacuum cleaner sucking wealth away, while the local outlet is like an irrigation system. The success of a business or investment then comes to be judged by its local multiplier effect rather than by the profits extracted to pay distant shareholders.

The alternative to conventional globalization will also be built on open and democratic institutions. Conservative philosopher Karl Popper wrote that an open society needed democratic or free institutions. He believed that only genuinely democratic institutions could solve problems. From financial crises to the debt crisis, the World Bank and the IMF have proved appalling at solving problems. Popper also crystallized the inherent contradiction of the free markets championed by financial institutions, writing that 'the paradox of economic freedom, which makes possible the unrestrained exploitation of the poor by the rich, results in the almost complete loss of economic freedom by the poor'.

Seen like this the financial institutions become enemies of an open global society. At the same time that they aspire to be truly universal, they ferociously protect minority rule of the world economy. If you tried to buy votes in a national election there would be allegations of gerrymandering and court cases. At the international financial institutions buying votes has been considered a virtue ever since Harry Dexter White of the US Treasury department said at the founding of the World Bank and IMF: the more money you put in, the more votes you have. That is how the Group of Seven wealthy countries, who don't even use the services of the Bank and the Fund, ended up controlling nearly 50 per cent of the votes on their boards. It is global governments' modern-day equivalent of seventeenth-century rule by the aristocracy.

The challenges are many: to restore the primacy of democratic political processes over the rule of the market and closed, unrepresentative financial institutions; to reform and revitalize the United Nations system; and to build a culture of daily, civic democracy through the use of innovations like citizens' juries and people's forums.

Two hundred-plus years of economic development have seen

the global economy expand, and the gap between rich and poor widen. But the economy has expanded so much, based on the exploitation of natural resources, that we are living beyond our environmental budget. We now face bankruptcy of an irreversible nature. Disproportionate consumption by the rich has created an enormous ecological debt. To balance the environmental budget and tackle the gaps between rich and poor we need a plan that both reduces our environmental impact and redistributes our natural wealth. A model called 'contraction and convergence' is rapidly gaining support. It works by setting a global cap on greenhouse gas concentrations, with an appropriate emissions budget that is reduced over time in a carefully negotiated fashion.

Carol Wills: 'Develop fair trade, improve livelihoods'

Harness the good things about globalization (e.g. wide availability of Internet access and email facilities throughout the world) and organize to challenge the way it is progressing. Build a global movement of concerned citizens who actively (but peacefully) campaign for change.

Make contacts with university researchers and think-tanks who can provide the evidence that rampant globalization can cause great harm to ordinary people everywhere, and that a different kind of thinking can expand opportunities for all. For example, the rich North needs growing markets for its products in the South (where else can they go with declining populations at home?), but these markets won't exist if most people in the South sink into destitution. Greater equity for all is in all our interests.

Work out the real cost of cheap food which travels half-way across the world to reach our local supermarket and then our table. When you've done that you will find it isn't quite so cheap after all. What does it cost in terms of fossil fuels and environmental impact to bring New Zealand lamb and butter to England? What is the real cost of a fruit yoghurt in which the strawberries were picked in Spain and then travelled by lorry to

Poland to be combined with the yoghurt before being brought to the UK?

Support local production. Develop fair trade as a means to improve the livelihoods and well-being of marginalized producers and workers. Celebrate cultural diversity.

Peter With: 'Confront our politicians'

We must get more balance into trade liberalization; poor countries need the right to protect their markets more than they have now, and rich countries should open their markets – they talk about trade liberalization but are not practising it themselves. There should be more globalization of values like human rights, basic labour standards and environmental standards – this is growing but very slowly. And we need a global governance to take care of the broad agenda, not only of trade liberalization.

For global governance we need rules on trade agreements, the climate, etc. at the international level. There are a lot of nice plans of action around – arising out of the big conferences of the 1990s – but they are not binding. It's very difficult as long as the economic system is so unbalanced in favour of the rich countries. You cannot expect poor countries to agree to global rules on labour standards since their situation is so different to that of Western countries.

NGOs in the North have to confront our politicians and say that it's not acceptable that transnational corporations define the rules. We have had successes. Two years ago we feared that there would be more binding rules on trade-related intellectual property rights. Now, because of the campaign of Oxfam and others, and the South Africa case, this is not morally acceptable. The balance of power has shifted and this is due to campaigning. We need much more of this. We need a similar campaign in agriculture, exposing double standards, for example.

PART II

Axis of change: what we must do

6

Values on the move

Corporate-driven globalization cannot work for the world's poor. When there are no barriers to trade, a 'one size fits all' system, the poor swim in the same economic stream as the transnational corporations. Putting a tiddler into the same stream as a shark can have only one outcome – and it's not good for the tiddler. The poor cannot be expected to survive, let alone gain, in a system where they have no say, control, power or influence. There is no way that the stream can be organized to give the tiddler a chance. It would be naive to think that the poor can survive in such a system, that it could be turned round to benefit them. The shark has either to be removed from the river or muzzled so that it cannot cause any harm. Thus there is an urgent need for alternatives.

The alternatives in the first section of this book show the huge range of options that are available and, in some cases, being put into practice. These alternatives give firm grounds for hope.

The alternatives suggested are decentralized, democratic and pro-poor. For them to have a chance of being implemented there need to be substantial changes in the institutions that control the present system – the corporations, the World Trade Organization and international financial institutions (IFIs), especially the IMF and the World Bank. These bodies do not encourage debate on the alternatives because alternatives are seen as a threat to their power, a threat to a monolithic system ruled by the free play of international market forces. But unless alternatives are accepted and phased in, the global economy is heading for a crash where the poor will suffer most, the rich–poor divide will only worsen, and the world will become more unstable.

The corporate-driven globalization lobby has tried but failed to stigmatize alternatives. It has tried to characterize its opponents as 'protectionist', as people who would take the world back to the 1930s or to the days of state control. This shows, however, the double-mindedness and hypocrisy of the corporate case. The prevailing system has given TNCs corporate control, a control maintained by persuading governments to protect their interests when it suits them. The corporate criticism is also outdated – none of the contributors to these pages envisages a return to old-style protectionism. The alternative to corporate-driven globalization is not protectionism. Rather the 'alternative' is a wide range of alternatives, some of which envisage selective safeguards, especially for the poor, none of which envisages continuing protection measures for the rich. Far from being 'protectionist', most contributors want a scrapping of the vast bulk of the protectionist devices such as subsidies which the corporations now enjoy.

This part of the book looks in more detail at the alternatives and what needs to be done to enable them to become reality. It looks specifically at changes that are needed in three crucial areas: transnational corporations, international trade, and developing country debt. These are not the only areas where change is needed – they do not, for example, deal with effects of financial liberalization – but they are the major issues which contributors have highlighted.

Many contributors see *localization* as the alternative to corporate-driven globalization. An epic is 'evolving at the grassroots', says Gustavo Esteva, referring to localization. The epic is many-sided, as the following pages show. Localization is needed, but is not enough. It has to be accompanied by changes in the forces and institutions behind corporate-driven globalization – TNCs, the WTO, the World Bank and the IMF. A key question is how to curtail the power of these bodies and make them more democratically accountable. Contributors perhaps tend to overestimate what corporate regulation can do, and underestimate the power of the TNCs to resist it. Too much faith in governments to bring about regulation could be seriously misplaced. Governments and corporations are partners. Citizens, by contrast, are independent; 'regulation' by citizens, in for example what they choose to buy, has a key role to play.

The kind of economic system that develops in the twenty-first century will depend on values. It was a change in prevailing values that played a key role in the rise of capitalism in the nineteenth century, paving the way for the Industrial Revolution. Until this happened, social mobility was little known in the agrarian societies.

We now appear to be witnessing a change in prevailing values. Again there is mobility, but this time mobility of ideas and practice. More and more people are speaking out for a system that works for human beings not corporations, for a system where people are more important than profits. More are demanding a system where communities have a real say over the factors which affect them, in which human rights, genuine democracy, the rich diversity of people's cultures and environmental limits are valued. It is values such as these that will determine the kind of society that emerges this century.

People the world over are finding vehicles to put these values into practice, struggling against corporate power and institutional inertia. Some of the struggle is through non-governmental organizations and popular movements – like, for example, in Bolivia over water (see Chapter 10) – and some through political parties, like the successful Workers' Party (PT) in Brazil.

If the majority of people share values that place people before corporations, then another world is possible and will eventually emerge – a true alternative to corporate-driven globalization.

7

Tackling corporate domination

Alternatives to corporate-driven globalization urgently need to be implemented. TNCs have abused their size, reach and power to turn the international economy into an economy that benefits them and their shareholders at the expense of the poor. They have twisted the arms of national governments to get policies favourable to them, warded off regulation, and corrupted the role of the United Nations.

Alternatives are needed because a global economic system that functions as a single market can only be worked efficiently by those who know the market intimately and who want to make profits from it. Corporate-driven globalization is that system. TNCs have turned 'one world' into 'one market'.

The corporations may argue that the world needs them to produce goods efficiently – to feed people, for example. They claim that industrial agriculture is more efficient than traditional farming. Yet the evidence shows that industrial farming's so-called efficiencies are sustained only by substantial government subsidies, plus the heavy use of chemicals. If corporate power is to be reduced, then the subsidies that Western governments afford them must be reduced and WTO agreements changed (see Chapter 8).

Corporate influence over key bodies like the United Nations, national governments and international financial institutions is huge but often secretive and hidden.

Corporate colonization of the United Nations

The United Nations exists for all the peoples of the world, but its role is in danger of being corrupted by the corporations. At least since the mid-1970s TNCs have exercised enormous influence over the UN. From 1975 to 1992, negotiations on a code of conduct on TNCs took place in the UN; they were abandoned in 1992 because the corporations were powerful enough to prevent a successful outcome. They had persuaded the UN that a code was unnecessary.

The United Nations Centre on Transnational Corporations (UNCTC) – set up in 1974 to serve as the UN Secretariat's focal point on TNC matters – had tried to draw up a code to 'establish standards for the conduct of TNCs from all countries, to protect the interests of host countries, strengthen their negotiating capacity and ensure conformity of the operations of TNCs with national development objectives'; also to 'set standards for the treatment of TNCs by countries to protect the legitimate interests of investors … and create a climate for foreign direct investment which is beneficial to all parties in the investment relationship'.[1]

TNC influence was supreme, however. In 1978 a Swiss-based organization, Association pour un Développement Solidaire, published excerpts from internal files which showed the extent of that influence. The files show that TNCs succeeded in 'subversively infiltrating the UN and its agencies and neutralizing them as a potentially countervailing force, or even utilizing them for the corporations' own purposes'.[2]

Western countries urged in the negotiations that developing countries should encourage TNCs and protect their investments. Developing countries stressed the need for the companies to adhere to their development objectives – they wanted a code that would pinpoint the responsibilities of TNCs to their economies, peoples and environments. But this aspect of the code received far less attention than the issue of how governments of developing countries treated the companies.

When, in the late 1980s, a growing number of developing countries removed barriers to trade, and began to offer guarantees about the protection of TNC investments, so Western countries, influenced by their TNCs, lost interest in the code. In 1992, the negotiations were abandoned, and the UNCTC was downgraded and renamed 'The Transnational Corporations and Management Division'. The centre's inability to frame a TNC code of conduct underlined the deep influence of the corporations, both in the UN system and over governments – they effectively turned the UNCTC into a centre for TNCs rather than on TNCs.

Yet worse was to follow. At a meeting in July 2000, chaired by the UN secretary-general, Kofi Annan, and attended by senior executives from 50 major corporations, a 'Global Compact' was launched. The UN claims that the compact is 'a uniquely positioned instrument for promoting the aims of global corporate citizenship and social responsibility'.[3] But the compact is a corporate coup on a massive scale. It allows the participating TNCs to claim that they are partners with the UN in overcoming world problems. The compact is, however, a weapon in the corporate bid to convince publics of their responsibility. While the TNCs involved are not allowed to use the UN logo in their publicity, chief executives of compact TNCs have used pictures of themselves with the UN secretary-general in front of the UN flag.

The compact is based on nine principles of behaviour, but to be part of it a company does not have to uphold all nine. It only has to 'annually submit an example to uphold just one of the principles'.[4] Some of the companies in the compact are highly controversial – including Bayer, Shell, Nike, Du Pont and Rio Tinto.

German-based Bayer, a major producer of chemicals, pharmaceuticals and pesticides, has attracted NGO action in the form of the Coalition Against Bayer-dangers. The coalition alleges that Bayer uses the Global Compact as 'bluewash' – using the 'good image of the United Nations to present a corporate humanitarian image without a commitment to changing real-world behaviour … Bayer has cited its membership of the compact as a means of dealing with public criticism'.[5] Bayer was named as one of the ten worst corporations of 2001 by the magazine *Multinational Monitor*.[6] In October 2001, the food company Nestlé joined the compact, despite its long-standing record of poor compliance with the World Health Organization's International Code of Marketing of Breastmilk Substitutes (see below).[7]

In the 1990s TNCs successfully persuaded UN conferences to overlook their role. At both the 1992 UN Conference on Environment and Development – the so-called Earth Summit – and the 1995 World Summit for Social Development, TNCs were successful in keeping demands for their regulation off the agenda.[8]

They were less successful at the World Summit on Sustainable Development (WSSD) in Johannesburg in 2002. Growing public concerns and concerted NGO lobbying ensured that the TNCs were on the WSSD agenda. 'One of the few achievements of the WSSD', believes Martin Khor, 'will be a commitment to promote corporate responsibility and accountability through the full development and effective implementation of intergovernmental agreements and measures'.[9]

Urgent action is needed, said the plan agreed by ministers at the Johannesburg summit, 'to actively promote corporate responsibility and accountability … including through the full development and effective implementation of inter-governmental agreements and measures, international initiatives and public–private partnerships, and appropriate national regulations, and continuous improvement in corporate practices in all countries'.[10] This could help, if only in a limited way, to curb corporate power.

The United Nations could have a key role to play in the international regulation of the corporations, but has shown serious misjudgement and naivety over the Global Compact. It has associated its good name with corporations that show few signs of changing their practices. The compact puts the UN's very credibility at stake.[11]

Strategic options

There are a number of strategic options for tackling corporate power, believes the International Forum on Globalization, 'ranging from the more reformist ones to the more transformative ones'.[12] They are corporate responsibility, accountability, removal, the revoking of charters to operate, eliminating limited liability and corporate 'personhood', and dismantling. The options described below draw partly but not exclusively on the report.

Corporate responsibility The corporate responsibility strategy urges TNCs to act in a more socially responsible manner, often in relation to specific environmental, labour and human rights issues. This is a long-standing strategy but one that has had little success. Its rationale is that corporations want the public to see them as responsible. TNC statements often stress that the company is aware that it must act in a responsible way. But appealing to corporations to act more responsibly seems unlikely to lead to anything more than minor changes. Corporate actions often betray corporate words; there is little to suggest that TNCs are giving responsibility a higher priority.

This strategy has made use of shareholder action tactics. Such activity, on Shell for example, has attracted support from a large minority of shareholders and given publicity to the issues. Shareholder action may be a first stage of gaining changes eventually (see section below). The scandals over Enron, WorldCom, etc. in 2002, drew the attention of the public to the need for increased corporate responsibility. But this alone is not enough. The debate 'should shift its focus away from corporate responsibility towards corporate public accountability. It should move away from relying on corporate statements of intent towards creating legal and political institutions to monitor and sanction socially and environmentally harmful corporate practices', says Judith Richter.[13]

Corporate accountability The objective is to make corporations operate in a more publicly or democratically accountable manner in society at large. Often, these strategies are pursued through legislative initiatives that seek to ensure that United States-based corporations, for example, act in a more publicly accountable manner through their overseas operations, by establishing standards along with some enforcement mechanisms. The standards could include the payment of a living wage to workers; bans on mandatory overtime for workers under 18, respect for basic International Labour Organization (ILO) standards such as the right to unionize, and health and safety protections.

A corporate accountability convention has been proposed by Friends of the Earth. The envisaged convention would levy duties on TNCs to take account of social and environmental concerns, and enshrine in international law the right of people to seek redress from the corporations. This last point is of huge importance. If TNCs could be sued by people under international law, they would have to be a great deal more careful about their activities.[14]

Corporate removal   Activists have acted to expel unwanted TNCs from their communities or to stop them entering. In Tamil Nadu, India, for example, the entry of the US company DuPont was blocked after villages launched a concerted protest about a planned nylon manufacturing plant which they believed was hazardous. DU Pont had wanted to relocate the plant from the USA to India. In India, as a whole, communities have a sound record of campaigning for the removal of corporations that abuse workers, cultural integrity, or natural resources. Similar movements have succeeded in the Philippines.

Revoke charters   In some countries, notably the United States, citizens are reclaiming their right to participate in government decisions about whether or not specific corporations should be granted the authority to operate, or whether their charter should be revoked. In California, for example, a coalition of citizens' organizations petitioned the authorities to revoke the charter of the Union Oil Corporation, because of alleged environmental devastation, exploitation of workers and violations of human rights. Revoking charters begins to put teeth into the idea of accountability.

Eliminate limited liability and corporate 'personhood'   Limited liability laws restrict the liability of the shareholders who own a public company. When, for example, gases erupted from a chemical factory in Bhopal, India, owned by the Union Carbide corporation, to kill some 20,000 people and leave 150,000 survivors chronically ill, the shareholders were not held liable. Justice would suggest that investors are liable for damage to people and the environment. Corporations are not people and should not have rights, as they do in some countries, that are accorded to persons.

Corporate dismantling   Strategies are being developed to dismantle the corporation as it is presently constituted. One strategy is to limit size and mobility. A TNC could be limited to one economic sector, for example, either foodstuffs or pharmaceuticals, not both. In the case of foodstuffs, a corporation could be confined to only one part of the food chain. No patents on life forms, including plants, should be allowed. No enterprise might be allowed to own more than one television or radio station.

The paramount concern of a TNC, as now constituted, is to make the best possible profit, to perform for its largely absentee shareholders. Otherwise it will be considered to be under-performing and will be ripe for takeover. It is profit, not concern for community, people's welfare, the environment, or their wider impact on national and global society, that drives the corporations. Policies are needed to support changes that involve breaking up large-scale corporations into human-scale enterprises, owned by local stakeholders rather than absentee shareholders.

The IFG report does not specifically mention codes of conduct, or examine a way of controlling the corporations that has possibly the biggest potential – namely, citizen power, expressed in the marketplace.

Codes of conduct

Corporations dislike having a poor image, not least because it can lower the morale of their staff and affect recruitment. No one likes to admit working for a company that is under attack for its poor record. A worsening company image can also make investors less likely to buy its shares. Share prices and market value both therefore depend to some extent on image.

To improve their image, a number of TNCs, including manufacturers of toys and shoes, have drawn up codes of conduct. But they have done so without any system of independent monitoring, making them of limited value. Neither have codes been able to stop corporate abuses. The WHO's International Code of Marketing of Breastmilk Substitutes is an example. This was approved by governments at the World Health Assembly in May 1981. Its provisions call for 'no advertising of breastmilk substitutes, no free samples to mothers, no promotion of products through health care facilities, no company mothercraft nurses to advise mothers'. The idea behind the Code was that companies should change their policies and that countries would put its provisions into effect in either a legally binding or a voluntary way.

While the milk companies changed some of their advertising practices, they also changed the Code to suit their own interests. After the Code was adopted each company wrote its own version, 'none of which came near to the WHO basics'.[15] In 1994, an attempt was made to tighten up loopholes in the Code. The World Health Assembly then adopted unanimously a resolution to strengthen breastfeeding worldwide. This resolution removed any possible ambiguities that the companies claim existed in the 1981 Code. But little seems to have changed and violations continue to be alleged. 'Hundreds of violations of the Code from just 14 countries were brought to Nestlé's attention last year.'[16] Violations include the dumping of free supplies in Thailand, aggressive promotion in India, and advertising in a number of countries, all of which are contrary to the Code, according to

Baby Milk Action. Nestlé dismissed as 'invalid ... the vast majority of violations'.[17] (See also section on Nestlé below.)

TNCs are 'too important and too dominant a part of the
global economy for voluntary codes to be enough', says the
UNDP *Human Development Report 1999*.[18] Corporations need to
be regulated if their power is to be tackled.

Regulation

Although around two-thirds of world trade is between TNCs,
there is no international regulation of the corporations. There is a
widespread feeling that corporations should be more accountable
to society. '[The] corporations are already a dominant part of the
global economy – yet many of their actions go unrecorded and
unaccounted.... They need to be brought within a frame of
global governance, not just a patchwork of national laws, rules
and regulations.'[19]

While the need is for regulation, the opposite occurred in the
latter years of the twentieth century. Even national legislation was
seriously weakened. The 1980s and 1990s witnessed massive deregulation – the dismantling of legal and administrative controls
that the corporations claimed interfered with the free play of
market forces. Restrictions on their activities were lifted, with
governments boasting about deregulation. A brochure from the
UK government's Invest in Britain Bureau, for example, adver-
tises 'labour costs significantly below other European countries'
and assures potential investors that

> no new laws or regulations may be introduced without
> ascertaining and minimizing the costs to business.... The UK
> has the least onerous labour regulations in Europe, with few
> restrictions on working hours, overtime and holidays....
> There is no legal requirement to recognize a trade union.
> Many industries operate shift work, and 24-hour, seven-
> days-a-week production for both men and women.[20]

Weak laws have been passed; guarantees of no labour rights, etc., have been given by many countries so as not to deter foreign investment. The laws are inadequate to tackle corporate power and there is no sign of any international regulation or international body that could legislate.

It is against this background of deregulation that a number of development agencies are calling for binding regulation of TNCs. Corporations often plead that they can regulate themselves, that they can be trusted. But one of the central lessons of the collapse of Enron is that corporate self-regulation will not work; that when left to their own devices, at least some corporations will gravitate towards irresponsible behaviour. Enron took advantage of the deregulatory nature of globalization to push for domestic and international arrangements that suited the company's bottom line. Its activities were hugely controversial in a number of developing countries – including, for example, its involvement in the Dabhol power plant in India's Maharashtra state.

Industry self-regulation is not possible when it interferes with industry's maximization of profit, points out Judith Richter. The questions that should be raised over regulation include:

- In which areas are binding laws needed? In which areas are other arrangements sufficient?
- Who sets the rules and on what basis?
- Who implements the rules and how?
- How can society ensure that any regulatory arrangement effectively prevents – or at least minimizes – potential harm to people and the environment from industry activities?[21]

'A new global body is needed to oversee the regulation of multinational business, to ensure that its activities safeguard people's basic rights and contribute to the eradication of poverty globally', recommends Christian Aid. 'The regulation of transnational business is perhaps the most pressing problem of globalization … never in human history has a comparatively small number of private corporations wielded so much power … the power of the TNCs needs to be brought under democratic control.'[22]

The Global Regulatory Authority (GRA), proposed by Christian Aid, would not itself legislate; this would be the responsibility of national governments. The GRA would:

- draw up and establish a code of conduct for TNCs;
- monitor compliance with the code;
- have a citizens' support unit to help organizations bring cases in national courts;
- conduct investigations into breaches;
- have the power to make legally binding rulings against TNCs breaching the codes;
- set minimum standards for the disclosure of information on TNC activities;
- monitor market abuses, such as cartels and monopolies;
- monitor direct foreign investment and advise on whether it would contribute to sustainable development.[23]

Democratic governance is stressed by the International Forum on Globalization. Alternatives

> must include a plan of action for replacing corporate rule with effective forms of democratic governance; for most national civil society alliances, this will likely require a two-pronged programme of action:
>
> 1. Eliminate corporate welfare, special corporate rights, and the mechanisms by which corporations exert influence over public policy. Corporate dominance of the political process not only deprives people of a meaningful voice, it also excludes a voice for the local businesses that public policy should seek to favour. While corporate executives have every right to participate in the political process as citizens, corporations themselves have no rightful place in a democratic political process, except to the extent government officials or citizen groups may call on them for advisory input.
>
> Appropriate initiatives include measures to:

- eliminate all prevailing patterns of bribery and corruption;
- impose tight rules on big business lobbying operations;
- eliminate corporate welfare (e.g. subsidies), rights and special exemptions;
- establish the liability of corporate officers and shareholders for corporate wrongdoing.

2. Policies are needed to rebuild economies responsive to human needs. As corporations have appropriated public policy to their own ends, national policy has come to favour global corporate interests over the national and local interests of people and communities. This process must be reversed. The policy process must respond to people and their needs, and the priority of national policies must be to build national and local economic security for all. Necessary actions include limiting corporate mobility, strengthening local ownership and radically reforming systems of money and finance to end, or at least strictly limit, financial speculation, and restore the integrity of money.[24]

Another proposal is for governments to put some economic transactions, such as services or resource management issues, 'off-limits' to TNCs, and regulate for them to be handled only by non-corporate or non-market mechanisms. Water supply and health care would come into this category. In other words they would not be treated as a commodity, available only to those who could afford to buy, but rather as something to be provided to all citizens as a basic right.[25]

What's standing in the way?

Regulation of TNCs is needed but there are huge problems in bringing it about. The corporations claim that they too believe in regulation, 'appropriate regulation'.[26] However, when the corporations talk of 'appropriate' regulation what they really mean is 'toothless and useless' regulation. And TNCs are powerful enough to persuade governments of their case. Regulation would have to be done by government, but the TNCs have corrupted the political system to the extent that governments are in bed with corporations. Their close connection would mean that governments would be most reluctant to regulate, and, if they did, they would closely consult with the TNCs over the shape of that regulation. The corporations would resist it in the way they resisted an international code of conduct on TNCs. Some token steps they may agree to, but TNCs would do their utmost to ensure that regulation did not act as a brake on their activities.

The skill of powerful corporations in getting around what they do not like should not be underestimated. TNCs already manage very successfully to find a way around national legislation that does not fit in with their plans. If international legislation is proposed, they will fight hard to keep their privileged position and to prevent anything becoming law that they do not find 'appropriate'. They have the funds to pay the best lawyers to block regulation and to find loopholes in legislation.

Public pressure for international regulation would ultimately persuade governments to act, but this could take years to achieve and is it not enough. It is hardly surprising that TNCs have little fear of regulation. 'We don't fear regulation, what we fear is customer revolt', admits a Shell official.[27]

Customer revolt is working

Corporations are powerful but they are also vulnerable. They depend for their survival on the marketplace. They depend on people buying their goods and services. If people do not buy a corporation's wares, then it is finished. This is appreciated by a growing number of people who refuse to buy the products of certain TNCs and have mounted campaigns to protest against their activities. Citizen revolt over TNC products – often called a boycott, a refusal to buy – is capable of bringing about changes in corporate policy, quickly and effectively: a great deal more quickly than government regulation.

GM foods

The most astonishing change in corporate policy in recent years came in the late 1990s when shoppers in the UK refused to buy genetically modified foods. This led to a major change in the policies of the giant food retail corporations and fast-food chains. 'The movement against genetically engineered and modified foods has leapt from one policy victory to the next, first getting many GM foods removed from the shelves of British supermarkets, then getting labelling laws passed in Europe.'[28]

The change came about after fears over the safety of GM foods were raised, fears that were not calmed by government assurances. Britain's BSE crisis had occurred only a short time before GM foods became available, and the public remembered the worthless utterances from government ministers over the issue. Opposition to GM foods developed in the UK in 1996 when concerned customers would fill shopping trollies with processed food at their local supermarket, and 'take them to the checkout where they would ask questions about products containing GM ingredients'.[29] Public meetings and debates raised the profile of these foods and supermarkets began to take notice. The super-market chain Iceland was the first to take GM foods off its shelves, in early 1998, although it had begun to remove them in 1996. The ban encouraged thousands of extra shoppers into Iceland supermarkets, and the company's profits rose.[30]

As Iceland was not among the largest food retailers, there was no immediate response from rivals. But, in June 1998, an article, 'Seeds of Disaster', by the Prince of Wales in a national UK daily paper, confirmed the growing doubts of many people about GM foods. He pointed out that we do not know the long-term consequences of these foods and ended by saying: 'I personally have no wish to eat anything produced by genetic modification, nor do I knowingly offer this sort of produce to my family or guests.'[31]

The next fifteen months were to witness an about-turn in corporate policy. Within weeks of the Prince of Wales's article, a major biotech company, AgrEvo, backed down over plans 'to grow Britain's first genetically modified commercial crop'. The company said it would not go ahead because the market 'is not ready'.[32] This was borne out by public opinion and consumer surveys. A Monsanto advertising campaign in the UK, in 1998, to try to persuade the public about GM crops, was a disaster, as the company later admitted. The public did not accept its claims. In October 1998, a study commissioned by Friends of the Earth found that 58 per cent of a sample of two thousand supermarket shoppers wanted their stores to go GM-free. Marks & Spencer customers were the most opposed, with 65 per cent favouring a ban. Within six months, Marks & Spencer had pulled all GM products off its shelves. Sainsbury's came next, in July 1999,[33] followed by the other leading supermarkets.

The fast-food chains also acted in response to customer tastes. By March 1999, Pizza Express, Domino Pizza and Wimpy had banned products with GM ingredients.[34] McDonald's and Burger King also announced they would phase out GM ingredients.[35]

All these changes in policy were due to customer revolt. And the preference of consumers in Europe for organic foods led to further changes in supermarket behaviour. They had to stock more organic produce or risk losing business to competitors. Again there was increased demand for better labelling of food-stuffs. Shoppers wanted more information on the label and many favoured goods that are well labelled.

Results: the most successful customer revolt of recent times led to changes in company policy in months rather than years.

McDonald's

Probably the biggest worldwide customer protest against the policies of a corporation is the Anti-McDonald's campaign. This is a protest 'against the promotion of junk food, the unethical targeting of children, exploitation of workers, animal cruelty, damage to the environment and the global domination of corporations over our lives.'[36] The campaign is active in many countries including Argentina, Australia, Austria, Belgium, Brazil, Canada, Croatia, Finland, France, Germany, Greece, Ireland, Israel, Italy, Malta, Mexico, the Netherlands, New Zealand, the Philippines, Portugal, Romania, Russia, South Africa, Sweden, Switzerland, Taiwan, the UK and the USA. An annual Day of Action in support of McDonald's workers is held every October.

In Britain protests have included handing out leaflets outside McDonald's – over 3 million leaflets since 1990 – and campaigning against new stores, including for example a successful 552-day occupation of a proposed McDonald's site by residents of Hinchley Wood in southeast England. In 1990 McDonald's served libel writs on two British protesters, Helen Steel and Dave Morris. In what came to be know as the McLibel trial (lasting 314 days), the judge ruled that McDonald's marketing pretended 'a positive nutritional benefit which their food [high in fat and salt etc.] did not match'; that McDonald's 'exploit children' with their advertising strategy, are 'culpably responsible for animal cruelty, and pay low wages, helping to depress wages in the catering trade'. But the court ruled that the couple had libelled McDonald's on some points and ordered them to pay £40,000 damages, which they refused to pay. The trial generated a huge amount of bad publicity for the company.

In France there have been mass anti-McDonald's protests by farmers, including the dismantling of a store and a 30,000-strong demonstration. Farmer José Bové was jailed for dismantling a McDonald's restaurant, a case that attracted widespread publicity and led to increased questioning over their food. At the Sydney 2000 Olympics there were protests against McDonald's mass use of refrigeration chemicals linked to global warming. In the United States, People for the Ethical Treatment of Animals (PETA) launched a billboard poster campaign in 1999 attacking McDonald's as 'The US No. 1 Serial Killer' (in response, they said, to the McLibel verdict), with pictures of slaughtered chickens and cows. Eric Schlosser's *Fast Food Nation*, a seminal work on the fast-food industry, includes a devastating critique of McDonald's.[37]

'Over a million and a half people worldwide work for McDonald's', says McSpotlight (the Anti-McDonald's campaign website);

> they work in similar conditions, carefully created and controlled by management to maximize company profits. McDonald's have pioneered methods of exploitation which have been widely taken up by other companies and corporations ... McDonald's is an excellent symbol of a global economy dominated by institutions geared to profiteering. Resistance to McDonald's – whether communities opposing the siting of new stores, campaigners undermining their public image, or from store workers standing up to management power, shows that people everywhere can think for themselves and fight back.[38]

Results: the revolt is working. McDonald's sales and profits fell in 2002 and expansion is being cut back. Questions are even being raised about the company's very survival. 'There are so many chinks in the armour now, nothing short of reinventing the brand will save it over the long term', said an analyst about McDonald's.[39] This is astonishing for a corporation that once seemed invincible. Again it shows company vulnerability to customer choice. In November 2002 McDonald's announced that it was closing 175 restaurants in ten countries. 'The burger business ... may have had its 50 years of fame.'[40]

Esso

A boycott of ExxonMobil (Esso) operates in six countries – Canada, France, Germany, Luxembourg, the UK and the USA – coordinated by the 'Stop Esso' campaign. The campaign alleges that the company

> uses its wealth and power to stop any international action on climate change. Esso ran an advertising campaign in the US press condemning the Kyoto Protocol and lobbied [President] Bush to pull out. Esso also funds multimillion dollar propa-

ganda fronts to dismiss the case for action to protect the climate. It frequently exploits selective, outdated or incorrect scientific studies in order to back up its position. Using tactics perfected by tobacco companies, these campaigns confuse the public and policy makers about global warming and sap the political will to address it.[41]

As soon as George W. Bush became president of the USA in early 2001, he pulled the United States out of the Kyoto Protocol, the international agreement to address global warming – exactly the policy that Esso was promoting. As the USA, with 5 per cent of the world's population, is responsible for 25 per cent of the pollution that causes global warming, this was hugely damaging for the protocol. Two days before President Bush's inauguration, Esso published an op-ed in the US press outlining its recommendations for 'An Energy Policy for the New Administration', stating that 'the unrealistic and economically damaging Kyoto process needs to be rethought'. One advertisement declared that 'the Kyoto Protocol approach would be a serious mistake.'

Esso was a long-time supporter of the Global Climate Coalition (GCC), the industry front-group that took a lead role in undermining initiatives to solve global warming. BP left the coalition in 1997 when it admitted that climate change required action. Large-scale defection of companies such as Ford, Texaco and General Motors occurred in 1999 and 2000. Esso had to leave when the GCC decided that only trade associations would be suitable for membership. In 2002 the GCC 'deactivated', claiming it had served its purpose 'by contributing to a new national approach to global warming'. With the USA out of Kyoto, the coalition had no need to continue its fossil-fuel-funded lobbying. The Stop Esso campaign says that Esso continues to deny the 'reality of global warming ... refuses to invest one dollar of its US$15 billion-a-year profits in clean, renewable energy like wind and solar power ... and is sabotaging global action'.[42]

Results: the campaign shows the power of citizens in the marketplace. A million motorists in Britain alone are boycotting

Esso, and an investment bank has warned the company that being tarred with the label 'environmental enemy number one' is a risk to its business.[43]

Nestlé

The products of Nestlé, the market leader in 'infant formula', are boycotted by groups in twenty countries that form part of the International Baby Food Action Network (IBFAN). This is co-ordinated by the UK-based group, Baby Milk Action. In the UK, the boycott is supported by 'over 90 church, health and consumer groups, over 1,000 businesses, 80 student unions, 17 local authorities, 12 trade unions, 51 politician and political parties'.[44]

In 1984 the boycott was lifted after Nestlé said it would keep to the WHO Code (see above), even in the absence of national laws. Much of Nestlé's large-scale advertising of breastmilk substitutes stopped, but other marketing practices continued. In 1986 an investigation in the Philippines revealed that 37 per cent of babies were fed in hospital on free supplies from Nestlé. The provision of such supplies is in direct contravention of the Code. In Pakistan, Malaysia and Singapore there was also evidence of the milk companies breaking the WHO Code. The consumer boycott of Nestlé was reimposed and at the end of 2002 showed no signs of being lifted.

Results: probably little perceptible effect on profits, but Nestlé's alleged violations of the WHO Code are being highlighted.

Bayer

The Coalition Against Bayer-dangers alleges that German-based Bayer – a major producer of chemicals, pharmaceuticals, pesticides and plastics – has a long history of giving profits precedence over human rights and a sound environment. 'Bayer is best known for aspirin and for the antibiotic Cipro, but it has also provided many useless and dangerous medicines.... Beginning in 1997 Bayer paid three of its competitors a total of US$200 million to abandon efforts to bring cheaper generic versions of Cipro to the market.'[45]

Bayer was forced to withdraw one of its leading pharmaceutical products, the anti-cholesterol drug Baycol or Lipobay, which was linked to over a hundred deaths, claims the coalition, and was one of the pharmaceutical companies who took the South African government to court for allowing the production of cheap generic versions of HIV drugs.

In October 2001 Bayer bought the GM seed company Aventis CropScience and became the leading genetically modified crop company in Europe, with over half of the GM crop varieties up for approval for commercial use.

If the European moratorium on the commercial growing of GM crops is lifted, Bayer will be set to flood Europe's fields with GM oilseed rape and maize. In most European countries Bayer will be responsible for the majority of GM field trials over the next year. Bayer is the third biggest manufacturer of herbicides globally, and dominates the insecticides market. Bayer made public promises in 1995 to withdraw its most toxic pesticides, but has yet to do so, and still sells pesticides rated by the WHO as 'extremely' or 'highly' hazardous.[46]

Result: the company's policies are under close scrutiny.

Changing behaviour

People are the all-important link in corporate plans and can play a central role in upsetting the corporate applecart. When people in the millions stop buying, change their buying habits or demand labelling, the corporations have to respond or die. TNCs have shown that they only act when their customers act.

While all TNC products have customers – in retail shops, on farms and factories, and so on – it can be harder for people like farmers to stop buying corporate products, especially if the economic system has given those companies monopoly or patent powers. Four corporations, for example – DuPont, Syngenta, Monsanto and Mitsui – hold 70 per cent of the patents on six leading staple foods: rice, maize, wheat, soybean, potato and sorghum. In total, the companies between them have taken out over 600 patents on these crops.[47]

Of particular concern is that the food chain will fall into corporate hands, and that farmers will become subservient to the corporations, losing sovereignty over their food supplies. Neither does the patent system reward farming families for their labour and knowledge. The United Nations 1999 *Human Development Report* says that the patent system is leading to the 'silent theft of centuries of knowledge from developing countries'.[48]

There are also corporate-held patents on aloe vera, broccoli, kava (a popular Fijian drink), Indian black pepper, the hoodia cactus of the Southern African desert, the nuña bean of the Andean people, Zimbabwe's snake-bean tree, Borneo's Bintangor trees, the Andean plant maca, and many others.[49] Patents on crops have emerged as a threat to food security. Direct opportunities for consumer action here are limited.

Shareholder pressure

Some motorists stopped buying Shell petrol following the execution of Ken Saro-Wiwa in Ogoniland, Nigeria, in 1995. Saro-Wiwa, president of the Movement for the Survival of the Ogoni People (MOSOP), had urged Shell to halt 'the ecological war' it had waged over thirty-five years and to clean up the mess it had made. He was awarded the Right Livelihood Award in 1994, but was convicted the following year of inciting youths to murder four Ogoni politicians. Amnesty International adopted Saro-Wiwa as a prisoner of conscience, saying that the accusation against him was unfounded, that he had neither used nor advocated violence, and that his detention was solely because of his campaign against environmental damage and the inadequate compensation by oil companies operating in Ogoniland. Activists judged that Shell had caused some of the environmental damage in Ogoniland and

could have used its influence to stop Saro-Wiwa's death, which it
failed to do.

At the annual meeting of Shell in May 1997, 130 shareholders
tabled a resolution which attracted the support of institutional
shareholders in the form of managed pension funds. The resolution – initiated by a group called The Ecumenical Council for
Corporate Responsibility – asked Shell to 'establish an independent review and audit procedure' for its environmental and human
rights policies'.[50] This earned the support not only of NGOs such
as Amnesty International, the World Wide Fund for Nature,
Friends of the Earth, but also of a London-based organization,
Pensions and Investment Research Consultants. Although defeated,
the resolution was backed by eighteen pension funds with investment assets of over £25 billion. Shell agreed to consult environmental and human rights groups on sensitive projects, and has
since withdrawn from a number of projects – in Bangladesh and
Colombia, for example – on human rights grounds.

Shareholder pressure at and around company AGMs can be
effective even without a specific resolution. In April 2002, for
example, five NGOs – Berne Declaration, Foro Emaus, the Pesticide Action Network PAN Asia Pacific and PAN UK, and the
Swedish Society for Nature – attended the AGM of Syngenta, the
world's largest agrichemical company with around 20 per cent of
the global pesticides market. (Syngenta is a merger of the agro-
chemical and seeds interests of the Swiss company Novartis and
Swedish–British AstraZeneca.) They urged the company to phase
out the production and use of the herbicide (weedkiller) Paraquat.

Paraquat is one of Syngenta's most successful products and also
its most controversial, a potentially lethal substance that has caused
many injuries and deaths. Symptoms can include a burning of
the mouth and throat, abdominal pain, nausea, vomiting and
diarrhoea. Effects due to high acute exposure to Paraquat may
include excitability and lung congestion, which, in some cases,
can lead to convulsions, lack of coordination and death by
respiratory failure. Other toxic effects include kidney failure, lung

sores and liver injury. In the opinion of informed groups, such as PAN, Paraquat cannot be used safely in developing countries. Yet Syngenta sells the herbicide to over a hundred countries. While the NGOs' plea was rejected by the company, the issue attracted considerable attention and the case against Paraquat is now firmly in the public domain.[51]

Corporations are assisted by governments and protected by company law. But even if company law changed, size remains a key factor (see also Chapter 6). Cargill, for example, is a private company and also one of the world's largest.

Cargill: the power of size

Cargill describes itself as 'an international marketer, processor and distributor of agricultural, food, financial and industrial products and services with 97,000 employees in 59 countries. The company provides distinctive customer solutions in supply chain management, food applications, and health and nutrition.'

Cargill's size enables it to perform what are normally seen as the tasks of government or international bodies. There are clear dangers in private companies playing that role. 'While the Romans ... had to rely on highly visible, expensive and unreliable armies of occupation. Cargill ..., along with other major TNCs, has developed and used more subtle – and more reliable – mechanisms and structures of occupation and control. Building a global food system, and establishing their toll booths along every route that food travels allows the company ... to be a determinative part of everyone's food future.'

Cargill's activity in Zimbabwe shows something of the way it operates. Cargill arrived in Zimbabwe in the late 1980s ... its entry strategy was seed production and trade (maize, then sunflower), commodity trading infrastructure (it set up the Zimbabwean Agricultural Commodity

Exchange, ZIMACE), and cotton processing (by buying a chunk of the former state-owned Cotton Company of Zimbabwe's ginning capacity).

By 1996, Cargill had an established 'regional trading team' in Harare, and was producing maize trading intelligence and Food Early Warning System reports. The company kick-started a fast-growing Commodities Exchange, initially enabling the company to make 'huge margins' (10–15 per cent). An official said that as commodity trading becomes 'more sophisticated, there will be more position-based trading. There will be more swings as things get more open and freer.'

Cargill disliked the way that Zimbabwe's strategic grain reserve – equal to half the average annual feedgrain demand in Zimbabwe – was kept as physical stocks. Most of the storage that Cargill had been acquiring, slowly but surely, is around the commercial farming sector. In the summer of 1995, around the time of grain price liberalization, Harare ran out of maize for eight days. Malawi maize was trucked in. Clearly, Cargill's vision of food security goes directly against the grain of any efforts towards regional food security based on large local, district or national level physical stocks; especially so if the vision involves the government, farmers' organizations, or farmers and rural communities themselves in managing stocks.

In a country 'driven by people with cash', Cargill knows it has more than a head start in getting what it wants out of the very institutions that it believes are such an impediment to good business. 'My gut feeling is that this region is on the way up', said a Cargill official; 'the less politicians get involved the better'.

Sources: Cargill website: www.cargill.com; Brewster Kneen, 'Cargill: corporate food security' in *Hungry for Power*, London: UK Food Group, 1999; Alistair Smith, 'Cargill in Zimbabwe' in *Hungry for Power*.

8

Tackling trade domination

Trade should be non-exploitative; local needs should come first.

> Bangladeshi farmer Farhad Mazhar,
> from *Recipes against Hunger*

While the world's corporations have globalized, rules and regulations have not followed suit. Regulation of TNCs is difficult because of existing international trade arrangements and rules. These give trade policy a dominant role; they effectively elevate trade above development, putting the free movement of goods and services across borders over people. The supremacy of trade is seen by governments and free-market academics in the West as all-important. Anything that interferes with international trade – and anything that interferes with the traders, the transnationals – is generally opposed by established institutions.

International trade is but a means to achieve something else – a higher standard of living, a wider choice of goods and services. That at least is how it should be. Instead, trade has been turned into almost a god, dominating economic thinking and policy. Unless this dominance is challenged and changed, there is little hope for corporate regulation, little hope for changing the exploitative and coercive nature of trade.

Setting the rules of international trade is the Geneva-based World Trade Organization. Changes in WTO rules are vital if there is to be more justice in world trade.

The World Trade Organization

In an economic world dominated by trade, the WTO dominates trade rules. The WTO was the outcome of the Uruguay Round of trade talks, held from 1986 to 1993 under the auspices of the General Agreement on Tariffs and Trade (GATT). Like the GATT, the WTO is not a United Nations agency. At the insistence of the United States, the Uruguay Round talks included agriculture and services for the first time. With 147 member countries (in April 2003) the WTO enforces the 1993 Uruguay Round agreements: the Agreement on Agriculture (AoA), the General Agreement on Trade in Services (GATS), the agreements on Trade-Related Intellectual Property Rights (TRIPs) and Trade-Related Investment Measures (TRIMs). WTO rules are prolific, running into thousands of pages.

The WTO presents itself as a forum for members to negotiate over trade liberalization. In practice the organization is a trade liberalization juggernaut which has been ceded enormous power by its members and, on some issues, has assumed the role of global economic governance.[1]

The WTO furthers the cause of liberalization, to the chief benefit of those who stand to gain most from liberalization – in practice the TNCs. The organization's first director-general, Renato Ruggiero, said in 1998:

> We stand at the very beginning of a whole new phase of internationalism. We are living through a time of deep and rapid transition towards a very different world. [We have] an opportunity to reaffirm our political will to move towards a better system of global governance … shaping the institutions of an increasingly borderless economy. The great promise of the new global age demands nothing else.[2]

The vision is therefore one of a borderless world economy, of global governance, based on free trade.

The WTO is an organization 'that mediates trade disputes, seeks to reduce barriers between countries and embodies the agreements', WTO director-general Mike Moore told a meeting in Seattle in 1999 at the time of the WTO's third ministerial meeting. But the WTO is far more. Its free-trade philosophy has a powerful influence on other international negotiations. The OECD's proposed Multilateral Agreement on Investment (MAI) was based on the notion that free trade is paramount; the MAI was essentially a development of the Uruguay Round TRIMs agreement (see below). Negotiations between the European Union and African, Caribbean and Pacific countries for a new trade and aid package to succeed the Lomé Convention were heavily influenced by WTO philosophy. The EU insisted that a new agreement had to conform with WTO rules. This has become the standard thinking among Western governments.

The WTO is both a forum for trade liberalization and a judge on those who transgress, exercising considerable and direct power through its disputes settlement mechanism. This mechanism has been used mainly by the developed countries. While this may not be surprising, as developed countries account for most world trade, developing countries often lack both the funds and the legal and technical personnel to use the mechanism.

A panel of three people normally adjudicates on a dispute. The panellists are not necessarily lawyers but their judgements have to be obeyed on pain of sanctions, even if they contradict national laws. The panels invariably uphold the strict letter of free trade, with pronouncements tending to benefit TNCs.

Trade in bananas, for example, is a long-running dispute between the EU and Caribbean countries on the one hand, and the USA and Latin American countries on the other. A number of EU countries, chiefly Britain, wanted to maintain special arrangements for the small-scale, but higher cost, banana farmers of the Caribbean. These guaranteed access to the EU despite the influx of cheaper bananas from Latin America, where the fruit is grown on plantations by large US-based fruit companies, such as Chiquita and Dole. The WTO panel ruled for the USA and Latin America – and effectively for the fruit companies – and against special treatment for Caribbean growers. This led the prime minister of Dominica, Mr Edison James, to speak of the 'blind and insensitive application of WTO rules'.[3]

The WTO's Agreement on Agriculture (AoA) reaches deep into the agricultural sectors of developing countries. The AoA covers market access, export subsidies, and domestic support for agriculture. Non-trade concerns, including food security, are mentioned in the agreement's preamble. Developing countries can provide investment subsidies, input subsidies to low-income or resource-poor producers, and give support to encourage diversification from illegal narcotic crop cultivation so long as they do not exceed 1992 levels.

Under the AoA, two sets of rules have been enforced, says Rashid Kaukab of the South Centre;

> one for those who were responsible for distorting the market through tariff and non-tariff barriers and high domestic and export subsidies. They have been allowed to continue to do so with only minor adjustments. The second set of rules is for those, including developing countries, who were not indulging in such practices. Now they are legally prohibited to do so.[4]

In any fair system of trade rules, poorer countries might expect to receive special treatment. But a WTO arrangement on special treatment is practically worthless. In practice, it's Western countries that receive special treatment under WTO rules.

Corporate influence on the WTO

A key responsibility of the state is security for its citizens. The WTO effectively provides security for investors at the expense of citizens. 'What the WTO does is to provide mechanisms for accelerating and extending the transfer of people's sovereignty from nation states to global corporations.'[5] WTO agreements and the dispute settlement procedure ensure that free trade is given higher priority than citizens and the environment.

Transnational corporations are powerful enough to exert considerable influence on the WTO's agenda. Nearly 70 per cent of world trade is between TNCs. The role of 'foreign affiliates' in export market shares has increased dramatically for some countries. For China it rose from 17 per cent in 1991 to 50 per cent in 2001; in Mexico from 15 per cent in 1995 to 31 per cent in 2000; in Malaysia from 26 per cent in 1985 to 45 per cent in 1995.[6]

While it is corporations rather than countries that trade, the WTO is made up of countries. Its decisions are usually in line with corporate expectations. Government ministers and their officials conduct business at WTO meetings under the gaze of representatives from major corporations, who may even be part of the official delegation. The company people expect to be heard when they lobby for decisions which help their business. 'The role that TNCs can play in a nation's economy can make their host government a very accommodating and attentive audience; the corporations have much more access to WTO decision-makers than citizens groups and NGOs.'[7]

WTO rules are biased in favour of the corporations. Based mainly, although by no means exclusively, in Western countries, the corporations benefit primarily people in their base countries. The WTO principle of non-discrimination is enormously beneficial for the TNCs. The principle means that foreign companies have to be offered the same treatment as domestic companies; governments are not allowed to discriminate in favour of local enterprises. This takes precedence over national interests such as development needs, socio-economic impacts and environmental considerations, and even legislation. Governments are no longer expected to govern in the interests of their citizens: their prime task is the pursuit of free-market economic growth. The mania for trade liberalization ensures that society is organized in a way which promotes corporate profit.

TNCs can even be powerful enough to turn WTO member applications to their own advantage – urging that a developing country wanting to join should not be allowed membership unless it does more to liberalize its economy. A corporation that is barred from selling its products to an aspiring WTO member country may urge, for example, that it lifts the ban before it can join. Lobbying by TNCs has secured new international trade rules that are intended to create 'a world order moulded in the image of multinationals'.[8]

The requirements of countries under the WTO cannot be separated from obligations to other international bodies. While, under WTO rules, developing countries are allowed to protect their farmers by placing tariffs on agricultural imports, the structural adjustment programmes of the World Bank and the IMF may not permit them to do it (see Chapter 9).

The human rights challenge

The WTO is being challenged on human rights grounds. 'Anything, any institution, that negates people's right to food needs to be challenged', says the New York-based People's Decade for Human Rights Education (PDHRE). The WTO is in this category, it believes. 'The promotion and protection of human rights and fundamental freedoms is the first responsibility of governments', it says; 'the WTO has no immunity from human rights.'

PDHRE claims that the WTO must adhere to the UN's Universal Declaration of Human Rights.

> The WTO must mainstream human rights principles and goals throughout the organization and incorporate them in policy formulation, implementation and review. It must admit the primacy of international human rights law over its trade rules and agreements. It must counter fears that its trade sanction powers will lead to human rights protectionism by

ceding enforcement authority to fully empowered United Nations human rights bodies and machinery.

'The World Trade Organization stands at a crossroads', says PDHRE;

> it must choose whether international trade rules will actively promote a fairer, more sustainable world ... the WTO has so far refused to acknowledge its human rights obligations under international law or examine the human rights dimensions of international trade policy. Human rights are not for trading away.[9]

Doha 2001

The WTO's fourth ministerial meeting in Doha, Qatar, in November 2001, was seen by developing countries as an opportunity to change WTO rules and to influence the trade agenda.

Four months before the meeting, ministers from the thirty least developed member countries of the WTO declared that they were not prepared to take on negotiations for any new issues in the WTO. They insisted that their development concerns must first be addressed. The new issues they chiefly objected to were investment, competition, transparency in government procurement and trade facilitation. These were floated for inclusion in the rules of the WTO at its first ministerial meeting in 1996, becoming known as the Singapore issues.

The Singapore Ministerial Decision states that 'future negotiations, if any, regarding multilateral disciplines in these areas will take place only after an explicit consensus decision is taken among the WTO Members regarding such negotiations.' Tanzanian ambassador Ali Mchumo, on behalf of LDC countries, said before the Doha meeting:

> given the fact that the issues involved are complex, that divergent views exist and that the new issues are yet to be fully understood, especially regarding their implications on

LDCs' development, the Ministers were of the view that the study process should continue in the working groups and that time is not ripe for LDCs to undertake negotiations for multilateral regimes on these areas.[10]

The atrocities of 11 September 2001 injected a new dynamic into the preparations for the Doha meeting; the USA and the EU appeared to use the aftermath of the atrocities to push the need for a new trade round.

The free traders didn't take much time to mourn after September 11th. The US and EU are using this moment of distraction to ram through their trade agenda. It's obscene. The US is re-branding the trade talks as part of the war on terrorism – if you're not with us you're against us.[11]

Forty-one African ministers of trade meet in Abuja, Nigeria, on 18 September and issued the 'Abuja Declaration'. This says:

Most African countries remain to be convinced of the potential of the proposed new multilateral agreements to deliver tangible benefits to them; African countries are concerned over the added burden of obligations in the face of present implementation challenges facing them; with a similar concern over the dangers of overloading the agenda of the WTO; African countries note that so far there appears to be no consensus among members of the WTO to launch negotiations in these areas.

Seven countries – Kenya, Mozambique, Nigeria, Tanzania, Uganda, Zimbabwe and Zambia – asked the secretariat to carry out a study of the impact of trade liberalization before launching another trade round. The countries pointed out that many developing countries were subjected to what they termed an overambitious liberalization programme as a result of structural adjustment policies that did not offer much flexibility in their tariff-cutting exercises and that many businesses were shut down as uncontrolled imports flowed into the countries, resulting in widespread unemployment and the collapse of local industries. 'The reduction in customs tariffs has led to losses in government revenue leaving many countries with budget deficits and insufficient resources for development', they went on.[12] Their request was turned down by the secretariat.

As the arguments moved to Doha, developing country delegations in Geneva were unhappy about what they believed was the biased role of the WTO Secretariat, with negotiations being promoted on a much broader agenda than all its members were willing to accept. They were also concerned that the EU and USA were using their power to change country positions and break developing-country coalitions.

A few days before the Doha meeting started, the Indian trade minister Murasoli Maran threatened to leave the WTO because developing countries had no part in shaping the trade agenda. WTO procedures were again called into question. Procedures at the WTO in Geneva make life difficult for developing countries and put them at a disadvantage with regard to Western countries. There are a wide variety of meetings at the WTO – daily meetings, green rooms, informals, super informals, bilaterals, closed meetings, and so on. There are no written procedures or accounts of all the types of meetings. But it seems that the unspoken rule in the WTO is that if anyone is not present at a meeting, does not raise opposition in a meeting or speak up, then the absentee is in consensus with the outcome of the meeting.

Tight security meant that the Doha ministerial meeting was very different on the streets to the upheaval at the WTO's previous meeting in Seattle in 1999. But there were many similarities inside the conference hall. Working together well, developing countries were united in standing up for the kind of trade round they wanted. And once again they were subjected to considerable arm-twisting by Western countries to agree to launch a new round. This time the arm-twisting paid off.

A Jamaican delegate at the talks said 'we are being made to feel that we are holding up the rescue of the global economy if we don't agree to a new round here'. Two countries were threatened with the removal of access for their goods to rich country markets if they did not support a new round. A few months before the Doha meeting, Uganda was asked by the USA to remove its trade ambassador in Geneva on spurious grounds. The real reason was the ambassador's effectiveness in opposing US trade policy.

Towards the end of the meeting, Britain's prime minister Tony Blair telephoned India's prime minister, Behari Vajpayee, with a 'request'. India's trade minister Murasoli Maran had threatened to reject the ministers' final declaration in Doha because he thought it was biased against developing countries, many of whom were taking his lead. The UK secretary of state for trade and industry Patricia Hewitt phoned Blair to ask him to contact India's prime minister to persuade him to tell Mr Maran to back down and support the declaration. The global economy will suffer if these talks are not launched, making it difficult for us to maintain our aid to you, seems to have been Mr Blair's message. The tactic worked: Mr Maran was told by his prime minister to back down.[13]

Trade-related intellectual property rights (TRIPs) was one of the most hotly contested issues. Developing countries were concerned that intellectual property rights in the form of patents on drugs could impede access to lifesaving medicines. The declaration agreed by trade ministers in Doha says that the TRIPs agreement 'does not and should not prevent members from taking measures to protect public health'. Brazil, joined by India and a number of African countries, led the fight for this clarification of the TRIPs agreement, especially over compulsory licensing of drug patents.

On agriculture, the European Union agreed that negotiations be conducted 'with a view to phasing out all forms of export subsidies'. Phasing out is likely to take some time, making the potential gain for developing countries a long-term one. But for developing countries, the issue is nonetheless crucial. Tanzania industry and trade minister, Iddi Mohamed Simba, said: 'Rich countries will lose elections if they don't get agriculture right. We will lose lives.'[14] There was no mention in the agriculture text of an issue that could help food security and save lives – a 'Development Box' in the WTO to protect low-income farmers who grow staple food crops (see below).

On the Singapore issues the declaration says: 'we agree that negotiations will take place after the Fifth Session of the Ministerial Conference (in 2003) on the basis of a decision to be taken, by explicit consensus, at that session on modalities of negotiations.' The meeting's chairman, Mr Kamal, added in a statement that at the fifth ministerial meeting, any WTO member country could veto negotiations on the issues. Negotiations on them may therefore be delayed indefinitely.

Ministers finally concluded with a declaration – the so-called 'Doha development agenda' – that launches a 'work programme … to address the challenges facing the multilateral trading system': in other words a new round of talks to liberalize world trade. This will cover agriculture, services, textiles, tariffs on industrial goods, electronic commerce, WTO rules and limited aspects of the environment. But on agriculture, services and textiles, talks would have gone ahead anyway. They did not require the launch of a new 'agenda'.

The Doha 'development agenda' could be more accurately described as the 'Doha agenda'. Development is the missing element. World trade rules stay much the same despite the overwhelming evidence that trade liberalization is not reducing poverty. Developing countries had tried, without success, to change the rules. 'Before the meeting, developing countries had made more than 100 concrete proposals to make WTO rules fair to the poor. Very few of these were taken on board. This makes a mockery of the idea of a development round to help reduce poverty', said WDM director Barry Coates.[15]

'The ministers' declaration does not alleviate the imbalances in the WTO. Over half of the WTO's members said they had problems in implementing the current agreements. Doha was a lost opportunity to move towards a fairer multilateral trading system', said Jayanti Durai of Consumers International.[16] Neither was there any commitment to review the impact of the TRIPs agreement on agriculture, which allows companies to take out patents on food crops. For example, a patent has been taken out by a US company on basmati rice, although this has been grown by Asian farmers for centuries.

Probably the most serious gap in the agenda is that there is no mention of tackling the extensive corporate influence in world trade. The role of transnational corporations was not raised in Doha. No ideas were put forward as to how they might be regulated. 'It was like a conference on malaria that did not discuss the mosquito.'[17] But the corporations lie outside the WTO's remit.

Yet something else could have emerged from Doha. 'We are too beholden to trade', said an official of one developing country.[18] Trade has failed to deliver for most developing countries and has become too dominant in their development agenda. The growing realization of trade's failings was perhaps the most important outcome.

What needs to change?

The WTO has generated a huge amount of opposition in its short existence. 'The more power the WTO gets to itself, the more its rules are enforced, the more opposition it's going to generate to defeat it and to replace it with a renegotiated pull-up trade agreement, instead of what it is now, a pulled down trade agreement in terms of world standards', believes Ralph Nader.[19]

The overriding need is for developing countries to have special treatment in international trade, in WTO rules. Under the Uruguay Round agreement 'special and differential treatment' is supposed to be afforded to developing countries. As noted above, this has proved to be of little or no value. A section on anti-dumping says, for example, that 'special regard must be given by developed country members to the special situation of developing country members.' This has been overlooked by developed country members.

Developing countries want special and differential treatment to be an integral part of future negotiations in order to take fully into account their development and food security needs. 'The WTO should be given a much narrower trade-orientated remit. It should be confined to trade issues and trade issues only', believes Murasoli Maran, India's trade minister.[20] A review of special treatment was promised as part of the Doha agenda.

Several developing country governments and many NGOs are calling for a 'Development Box' in the WTO. They envisage that a number of measures, notably support for small farmers growing staple foods, could be placed 'in a box' and be exempt from WTO requirements. The box would allow governments to give more support to these farmers, helping them to increase output without conflicting with existing trade rules. At present they cannot offer such support if it conflicts with their obligations under the rules. A box would give them the flexibility to take measures to protect the rural poor.

The idea of special measures for the poor is however not new; it has been around since the Uruguay Round negotiations began in 1986. If countries are to be free to implement the measures that are proposed for the Development Box, agriculture needs be taken out of the WTO. A number of this book's contributors from the South have stressed the importance of this. The only argument for keeping it there is that the EU and the USA will be bound by its stipulations on reducing subsidies. But neither shows any sign of doing this. On the contrary, they find ways around their WTO commitments when it suits them, as witness the new farm bill which the USA plans to introduce and the decision of EU ministers in October 2002 to leave the Common Agricultural Policy little changed. Unless the USA and the EU act to cut subsidies, rather than making pious statements about how they will cut them one day, they can expect the movement for agriculture to be taken out of the WTO to grow. There would be advantages if agriculture was free of WTO constraints; countries would have the freedom to implement the measures they want to see in the Development Box.

There are possibilities for developing countries to export processed agricultural produce and selected manufactured goods such as textiles. But, as discussed above, under the WTO's Trade-Related Investment Measures (TRIMs) agreement, governments cannot give special help to lift their own companies off the ground. The TRIMs agreement needs amending to allow developing countries to give special treatment to local companies. No industrialized country has developed without the freedom to help local enterprise. Industrial countries can hardly deny developing countries that right.

The Trade-Related Intellectual Property Rights (TRIPs) agreement is also in urgent need of change. This agreement is proof that the WTO's business is free trade, unless the corporations say otherwise. For TRIPs is a protection racket that has nothing to do with free trade. The agreement was largely written by a consortium of corporations, including Bristol Myers, DuPont, Monsanto and Pfizer. It gives corporations the right to protect their patents in WTO member countries. But the consequences of this for small farmers in developing countries are horrendous. Farmers who grow crops that have been patented may end up having to pay royalties to the patent holder if they wish to plant them. This subordinates them to the corporations.

Rules relating to intellectual property have no place in a trade agreement. They should be transferred to other organizations like the World Intellectual Property Organization, as Martin Khor suggests. Countries could then be free to decide whether they want to join WIPO treaties.

GATS

The service industry is big business and heavily dominated by the TNCs. These companies want to operate freely within the sector, but much of it is owned and regulated by governments. Freeing up the trade in services will benefit business and this is what the WTO's General Agreement on Trade in Services (GATS) is designed to do.

Corporations have been the driving force behind the GATS agreement, which is a key component in their armoury. Its aim is to remove any restrictions and internal government regulations in the area of service delivery that are considered to be 'barriers to trade'. Services – anything that you cannot drop on your foot – include water supply, libraries, schools, hospitals, banks and rubbish collection: 160 services are traded internationally.

But TNCs do not provide services for nothing; as they are seeking to make a profit out of water, health and education, those without purchasing power are likely to lose out. The GATS therefore threatens the delivery of basic services to the poor. Attempted water privatization in Bolivia shows that a system governed by people's ability to pay will not deliver services to the poor (see Chapter 10.)

Member countries of the WTO can, in theory, decide which services they can open up for privatization. In practice, however, Western country governments have already put pressure on developing countries to open up service sectors for privatization – on pain of losing development aid. The UK government has, for example, put pressure on Ghana to lease its urban water supply to foreign companies, alleges Christian Aid, making £10 million of aid dependent on such a move.[21]

Negotiations are under way to extend the GATS agreement and change its structure so that rules on one sector also apply to related sectors. Governments of developing countries would then come under more pressure to reorganize the ownership and delivery of services, and sacrifice them to the 'free trade' god. Negotiators from Western countries will push for this liberalization process to be speeded up. GATS negotiations are extremely complex and technical, which puts many developing countries at a serious negotiating disadvantage. Moreover, GATS is intended to make privatization irreversible. This means that once governments have opened up particular service sectors to WTO rules, there is no going back. A company could sue a government which tried to bring a service back under public ownership.

If GATS extends, then decisions about how to organize basic services will be removed from the political arena. Citizens would no longer have the democratic right to decide whether or not services should be regulated. There is a strong case for the GATS to be scrapped, or at least for developing countries to be given and guaranteed a total waiver.[22]

Reform – or replace?

WTO agreements favour the transnational corporations at the expense of the poor; on this basis the organization is failing. Any international organization should be judged on its value to the poorest members of our global society. 'Poverty reduction and environmental protections must be made the priority of international trades rules', suggests Christian Aid.[23]

The WTO should be either substantially reformed or replaced. Its role should be limited to areas that are directly linked to trade and where there is a consensus that trade rules will benefit the poor. Instead of reducing the freedom of developing country governments to manage trade for the benefit of their people, it should guarantee their rights to intervene in trade, where necessary. This means turning round the WTO's role.

Ironically while WTO rules dominate world trade, the organization has not played any role in the primary commodities on which millions depend – coffee, cocoa, tea and sugar, for example. Many developing countries earn most of their foreign exchange from the export of such commodities. But the price of almost all of them is touching record low levels. For example, the world price of coffee – grown by around ten million poor farmers – slumped from 125 US cents per pound in December 1999 to under 60 US cents a pound in December 2002. Smallholder coffee growers face destitution. And a coffee-growing country like

Uganda finds that the amount of debt relief it has been granted is more than wiped out by the fall in world coffee prices.

An international trade organization might be expected to put forward ideas for helping people and countries that are affected. Several years ago a Commonwealth Secretariat paper suggested such an idea – a tax on primary products. This is an idea that needs serious discussion, which seems unlikely within the WTO.

Most crucially of all, the WTO can do nothing to regulate the major trading players, the transnational corporations. The organization is based on the assumption that it is countries that trade. But disputes are between companies as well as governments. The dispute between the European Union and the United States over bananas, for example, was largely a dispute between the EU and a leading banana company, Chiquita. It was the company that complained it was losing market share and it was the company that won. Far from having a mandate to regulate TNCs, the WTO is in the corporate pocket.

In theory the WTO is a 'one-member-country, one-vote' democracy; in practice there has never been a vote in its eight years' existence. Developing-country members could vote to change the rules to make the WTO a trade organization that is capable of grappling with the most pressing trade issues that affect the world's poor. Or it might be better to start afresh, possibly to look again at the idea of John Maynard Keynes for an international trade organization that would cover all the major trade issues that affect developing countries.

The MAI

In 1995, a year after the WTO came into being, the twenty-nine member countries of the Paris-based Organization for Economic Cooperation and Development (OECD) began to draw up a Multilateral Agreement on Investment. The agreement, encouraged by and based on WTO principles, would have removed obstacles to companies from abroad that invested in OECD countries and given them greater protection. The OECD claimed that the agreement would give new impetus to growth, employment and higher living standards. The MAI became one of the most controversial agreements on the international agenda. It would have increased the power of TNCs to an enormous extent, giving them unprecedented power but without any corresponding responsibilities. It would have increased the power and freedom of monopoly interests to exploit the poor.

The agreement would not have allowed governments to lay down specific conditions for foreign investors. Governments and local authorities would even have problems passing health legislation that interfered with the activities of foreign investors. Currency controls would have been forbidden. The MAI would have effectively handed over power from elected bodies to unelected business, taking away the democratic rights of ordinary people to insist on reasonable safeguards for any planned investment. National governments could even have been sued by companies whose plans they blocked. A fast-food chain, for example, that wanted to open a restaurant in a country that had signed the MAI could sue the government of that country if it was denied entry or if it introduced environmental or social legislation that might curb the firm's investment. The MAI thus seemed like a severe case of free trade gone mad.

The agreement would have 'eroded the rights of citizens and the role of governments, while extending the rights of transnational corporations', warned WDM director Barry Coates. The treaty could fuel a 'race to the bottom', in which governments 'will abandon their commitments to local communities and sustainable development in their scramble to attract foreign investment.[24] On environmental issues, the MAI could conflict with established treaties. A government may, for example, turn down a proposal from a foreign investor on the grounds that it would increase greenhouse gases and mean it could not meet its obligations under the Kyoto treaty on emissions. It is unclear which treaty would decide the outcome.

After strong protests, the MAI was dropped; it was a victory for the NGOs that had opposed it. But the MAI's ideas live on. They are found in the EU's trade agreement with the African, Caribbean and Pacific group of countries. The British government has continued to negotiate bilateral investment treaties, based on WTO/MAI principles, giving huge rights to the TNCs, including the right to sue governments that stand in their way. 'Foreign investors such as Enron, Vivendi and Mobil are queuing up to use these treaties to sue governments in the developing world, targeting everything from new taxes to regulation of privatised public services', says Luke Eric Peterson.[25]

A bad master

International trade could be a servant of the poor; it is certainly a bad master. The livelihoods of millions in developing countries have been wrecked or severely disputed because of cheap imports which have been permitted since the WTO agreements came into force in 1995.[26] 'We are not against trade', says Haiti's president, Jean-Bertrand Aristide, 'but our fear is that the global market intends to annihilate our markets. We will be pushed to the cities, to eat food grown on factory farms in distant countries, food whose price depends on the daily numbers game of the global marketplace.'[27]

Trade needs to lose its dominance in the world economy. As Chapter 10 shows, there is a strong case for developing countries to put less emphasis on trade and give more to production for domestic consumption. There is a case for them to trade a lower volume of goods. This does not necessity mean lower returns – it depends on the price per unit. If coffee producers were to agree to trade, say, three-quarters of the present volume of coffee, they would be very likely to receive a much higher return. When a severe frost in Brazil's coffee-producing areas, and disruptions in other major producing countries, reduced coffee output by 25 per cent in 1975, world prices shot up eightfold. Producers were selling a lower volume but receiving a great deal more for it. If returns can improve in an unplanned way, they could improve in a planned way.

Cancún 2003

The WTO planned to hold its fifth ministerial conference in Cancún, Mexico, in September 2003. The conference's aim is to 'take stock of progress, provide any necessary political guidance, and take decisions as necessary'.[28] It may launch a round of negotiations for the liberalization of investment, competition policy, government procurement and trade facilitation. This expansion of the 'power and jurisdiction of the WTO – now the most powerful multilateral instrument of the global corporations – is a mortal threat to development, social justice and equity, and the environment'.[29]

Campaigners are therefore likely to make a wide-ranging effort to publicize the implications of an extension of trade liberalization and to confirm the view already held by many developing countries that such an extension is not in their interests.

> For the movement against corporate-driven globalization, derailing the 5th Ministerial or preventing agreement on the launching of a new comprehensive round would mean not only fighting the WTO and free trade to a standstill. It would mean creating momentum for a rollback of free trade and a reduction of the power of the WTO

believes Walden Bello.[30] Changing the rules of the WTO, not least to reduce the power of the organization and to knock free trade off its gilded perch, is seen by campaigners as an essential component of the struggle against corporate-driven globalization. The Cancún meeting could be a landmark in that struggle.

How subsidies distort

The agricultural subsidies that Western covernments pay to
their farmers distort trade and undermine the efforts of
local farmers in developing countries. These subsidies
amount to over US$300 billion a year.* European Union
and United States farm subsidies encourage overproduc-
tion, distort trade and depress prices, making EU and US
farm goods artificially cheap on world markets, resulting
in the dumping of cheap, subsidized produce in poor
countries. A huge double standard operates. While paying
subsidies to their farmers, rich countries have put pressure
on developing countries to reduce or eliminate their
subsidies. It is case of protection for the rich and the free
play of market forces for the poor.

Case studies in an ActionAid report have shown how
Bangladesh, Indonesia, Kenya, Nigeria, Pakistan and
Swaziland are among the countries affected. In 2000 there
was a sudden and dramatic increase in the volume of
cheap, duty-free wheat flour imported by Kenya from
Egypt, undercutting local prices by up to 50 per cent,
threatening the livelihoods of around 500,000 Kenyan
people dependent on wheat for a source of income.

In 2000-01, the USA and EU together supplied Egypt
with almost 4 million tonnes of the grain. Significant
quantities of this were dumped. 'There are strong suspi-
cions', says the report, 'that subsidized US and possibly
EU wheat has been used to manufacture the flour in
Egypt which has been sold to Kenya at cheap prices.'
Cheap wheat imports into Nigeria from the US have
nearly doubled since 2000 and are having a detrimental
impact on the country's production of staple foods.

Subsidized wheat coming into Bangladesh as food aid
is, again, having a negative effect on local farmers. According to the Washington-based International Food Policy
Research Institute the food aid helped to undercut prices

for local wheat producers, acting as a disincentive for them to be more self-reliant and to grow their own crops.

EU subsidies to the sugar sector are also causing problems, eradicating the competitive advantage of sugar-producing developing countries. Swaziland, for example, produces sugar at less than half the cost of EU countries, and yet is unable to compete with the EU imports that increasingly dominate its market. Subsidized EU sugar products into Swaziland have led to the loss of about 16,000 jobs in the Swazi sugar industry and 20,000 jobs indirectly linked to the industry.

* OECD, *Agricultural Policies in OECD Countries, Monitoring and Evaluation 2002.* Paris: OECD, 2002.

Source: *Farmgate: The Developmental Impact of Agricultural Subsidies,* London: ActionAid, 2002.

9

Tackling debt

You talk about structural adjustment as if Africa was some kind of laboratory. But Africa is people!

Chinua Achebe, speech to Western bankers

On the quayside of Salvadore, Brazil, the 'Stone of Weeping' marks what was once the site of the slave auction. But countless 'stones of weeping' are being set up across the poorer countries as a consequence of debt slavery

David Golding, Jubilee 2000 Newcastle Coalition

The debts that developing countries owe to Western countries enslave both people and countries, and can be a serious obstacle to implementing alternative strategies. Indebtedness to foreign governments and their agencies restricts the independent action of developing countries, shackling them in the corporate-driven globalization system.

Debt has forced developing countries to accept austerity programmes that harm their people, especially the poor. They are at the mercy of international financial institutions (IFIs), notably the Washington-based World Bank and International Monetary Fund, that Western governments use to manage debt. If the IFIs say to indebted countries, 'take steps to globalize your economy if you want help with debt relief', then countries are too shackled to do otherwise. Third World debt is now recognized as 'the greatest single cause of poverty and injustice across the earth and potentially one of the greatest threats to peace'.[1] Breaking from this vicious trap could liberate the indebted.

But debt cancellation is something that the World Bank and the IMF deny developing countries except in very limited amounts. Most Third World debt is owed to government departments in Western countries, often to agencies such as the UK's Export Credits Guarantees Department, the IMF, the World Bank and other lending agencies. Much of the debt was run up as a result of irresponsible lending by rich countries in the 1970s and 1980s. Some of the lending enriched elites while condemning many of the poor to continuing poverty. Money which could be spent on health care, education and sustainable development now has to be spent instead on debt repayments.

The origins

The origins of Third World debt burdens date back to the early 1970s.[2] The so-called Bretton Woods system of fixed exchange rate was then abandoned, causing greater uncertainty over export and import prices. Primary commodity prices were also mostly declining or stagnant. In 1973, the US Federal Reserve governor, Andrew Brimmer, noted a sharp rise in lending to less developed countries, and that the main explanation was the 'failure of demand for loans from borrowers in developed countries to keep pace with the expansion of credit availability'.[3] In other words, people in the North were not borrowing enough so far as the banks were concerned. So the banks had to persuade developing countries to borrow money instead. US banks engaged in what Brimmer called 'loan pushing' – encouraging poor countries to borrow money they did not need.

From 1971 to 1976, the debts of developing countries doubled, from US\$62 billion to over US\$125 billion. In the 1950s, 1960s and early 1970s it was also commonplace for Western governments to lend rather than give development aid. Recipients paid interest on the loans. By the mid-1970s, servicing the debt – paying interest and capital when due – was beginning to put a strain on the budgets of a growing number of developing countries. Debt was accordingly one of the main items on the agenda at the Fourth United Nations Conference on Trade and Development (UNCTAD 4) in Nairobi in 1976.

The Group of 77 asked at UNCTAD 4 that the debts of the twenty-nine poorest countries be cancelled. Donor countries were not prepared for the request and hastily threw together a policy of not being willing to consider a general cancellation of debt. They said, rather, that they would respond 'quickly and constructively' to country requests for debt relief.[4]

In March 1978 Western countries agreed to relieve some of the debt of the poorest countries, specifically by cancelling past aid loans. In July that year the UK government announced that it would cancel US$928 million of debt owed to it by seventeen of the poorest countries. Sweden, Canada, Finland, the Netherlands and West Germany also announced schemes.[5]

But the schemes were modest when set against the problems. Rising oil prices – which shot up from US$2 a barrel in 1973 to US$34 a barrel in 1981 – and a doubling of world interest rates, led to a sharp rise in Third World debt in the late 1970s and early 1980s. The debt rose over fourfold between 1976 and 1981, to US$540 billion.

The debt issue sprang to wider prominence in September 1981 when Costa Rica announced a moratorium on its debt. But at least eight other countries – Bolivia, Liberia, Madagascar, Senegal, Zaire, Jamaica, Pakistan and Sudan – were by then seeking to have their debts rescheduled.[6] When Mexico, one of the developing world's largest debtors, announced a moratorium on its debt in the autumn of 1982 there were fears for the global financial system should countries default. But Mexico, like other indebted countries, was persuaded to postpone debts – and to borrow money to pay interest on past debts. The debt postponement industry became huge. Each debt crisis was resolved by loaning more money to the debtor country, to service their foreign debts rather than to meet the needs of their people.

Postponing debt has been a costly option for indebted countries because they pay more interest on the money that is delayed for payment. Interest is added on to interest – it is compounded. John Maynard Keynes described this process as 'a form of magic' whereby 'debts miraculously increase'. In sub-Saharan Africa, 'the process is clearly out of control ... interest and arrears accounted for 65 per cent of new debt since 1988. The creditors seem unable to face reality and stop the process.'[7] Money is even lent by creditors so that debtors can repay existing debts – debtors 'rollover' the money to send it back to creditors, rather than invest it in economically and socially useful outlets.

The business of debt postponement has left untouched the underlying problem: the chronic imbalance in the terms on which developing countries trade. The 1980s, for example, were marked by sharply falling prices for primary commodities, which meant lower revenues. Export earnings were often not enough to meet debt repayments.

The shackle keepers

The debt shackle is firmly administered by the World Bank and the IMF. Since the start of the 1980s, these two IFIs have been allowed to exert enormous pressure on developing countries, insisting that countries implement structural adjustment programmes if they want aid, debt relief and investment.

Introduced in 1980, when many developing countries were in deep recession, structural adjustment programmes (SAPs) typically require governments to liberalize trade, privatize parastatals (government bodies), reduce spending on social programmes, such as health-care and education, eliminate food subsidies and increase the prices they pay to growers of crops for the export market. SAPs are supposed to lead to economic recovery, long-term growth and stability. But their record is dismal. Adjustment programmes have failed even when measured against the Fund's and the Bank's own criteria. Over eighty developing countries have implemented or are implementing SAPs. In most countries, they have not led to the higher economic growth they were supposed to be all about. But poverty levels have risen, rural crises intensified and development has stagnated in many countries. SAPs have made things worse rather than better. 'The evidence accumulated over decades is that those countries which allowed the IMF to dictate the macroeconomic policies they should follow, and who did so blindly, have all suffered major setbacks in poverty eradication.'[8]

Foreign debts, too, have tended to rise rather than decrease under SAPs. Ghana, for example, a country which vigorously implemented IMF/World Bank policies, has become one of Africa's most highly indebted countries.

The SAP prescription was seriously flawed. The programmes concentrated on domestic changes in developing countries, while ignoring the international changes needed if countries were to have a chance of recovery. Encouraging the growth of export crops led only to lower world prices for these crops, and hardship for millions of growers. Furthermore the policy of persuading governments to pay producers higher prices for export crops has led to their expansion at the expense of food crops; food output has often declined as a result. Farmers in Zimbabwe, for example, were encouraged to replace maize with tobacco. Adjustment programmes have also caused governments to reduce their support for small farmers, which again has lowered food output. This has happened in some of the most famine-prone countries, such as Ethiopia.

The indiscriminate promotion of export crops undermined food self-sufficiency while import liberalization led to greater dependence on the global economy. The withdrawal or reduction of support for farmers, under SAPs, hit the poorest farmers the hardest, and led to a huge increase in the number of people who migrated to urban areas.[9]

Developing country debt stock, 1971-2000 (US$ billion)

1971	62
1976	125
1981	540
1986	628
1990	1,457
1996	2,091
2000	2,356

Source: World Bank, *World Development Reports* and debt tables, Washington: World Bank; www.worldbank.org.

HIPC's failure

It was because of their advocacy of SAPs that the IMF and the World Bank became key players in the debt issue. But in the 1980s and early 1990s, the Fund and the Bank did nothing about debt relief, despite the evidence of mounting problems. Not until 1996 did they launch an obviously limited scheme, the Heavily Indebted Poor Countries (HIPC) debt initiative. By this time Third World debt had risen massively – to US$2,091 billion, an almost fourfold increase in the fifteen years since 1981.[10]

The HIPC 'initiative' has been an abject failure. It is not designed to cancel a country's debt, only to write it down. By the end of 2002 it had failed to relieve more than a tiny part of Third World debt. The so-called initiative was from the start lumbered with the strict conditions imposed by the Bank and the Fund. To qualify for relief, indebted countries needed to have had an SAP for at least six continuous years (later reduced to three years). This meant that they needed to prove a history of adopting economic measures such as trade liberalization and cuts in government services.

In the late 1990s, SAPs gave way to Poverty Reduction Strategy Papers (PRSPs), which are basically SAPs by another name. Under their PRSP, countries may be judged by the Fund and the Bank to have reached an interim 'decision point', when officials make a ruling about whether they qualify for debt relief under the HIPC initiative. They may then receive a small amount of relief and are required to jump over further hurdles to what is known as 'completion' point. Qualifying countries may have to wait for several years before they reach this final point.

At completion point, a country's debt is written down to the level where it is judged by the Bank and the Fund to be sustainable – in practice this is to the point where existing debt 'stock' is one and a half times its expected yearly export earnings. This is supposed to give indebted countries a lasting exit from a debt problem. The World Bank and the IMF appear to have decided on this 'one and a half times its yearly export earnings' rule, judging that a country can then repay debt on a sustainable basis. But export earnings are notoriously erratic and the Bank and the Fund tend to take an optimistic view of them. The key point is that the scheme is well short of a 100 per cent debt write-off – it does not offer substantial debt relief.

This also means that indebted countries have to keep on exporting to earn money to pay off debts. So Bank and Fund leverage is maintained. The scheme limits the losses of creditor governments, while increasing their leverage over HIPC countries. 'We are entitled to ask ... whether the debt has become an increasingly sophisticated tool for structuring Third World economies according to the requirements of the developed world.'[11]

World leaders have made the right noises about funds for debt relief, but their actions have lagged far behind. When leaders of the G7 – the seven largest industrial nations – met in Germany in June 1999, they agreed to cancel US$100 billion of Third World debt. In September that year, President Clinton announced that the USA would cancel all the interest and capital owed on development assistance and commercial debt. In December Britain and Italy made similar announcements. France followed in January 2000.

The offers were tied to the HIPC initiative and only become operative when the IMF and the World Bank give the go-ahead. The debt that is written off must be used for poverty alleviation, thus overcoming the criticism that it might be used by governments for other purposes, such as purchasing armaments. By the end of 2000, while the Group of Seven industrialized nations had raised its promise of money for debt cancellation to US$110 billion, only one country, Uganda, had actually had any of its debt cancelled.

Jubilee

On the NGO front there was a great deal more activity than in the Bank and the Fund. In the early 1990s a UK university lecturer Martin Dent and retired civil servant Bill Peters suggested the idea of cancelling Third World debts in the year 2000, as a fitting way to mark the millennium. The idea was inspired by the Old Testament principle of Jubilee, under which slaves were to be freed, property restored to its original owner and debts cancelled every fifty years. Jubilee was a way of ensuring that no matter how poor people became they would have a fresh start.

The idea of a Jubilee-style debt cancellation for the world's poor in 2000 caught the imagination of churches and aid agencies, such as Oxfam and Christian Aid. The Jubilee 2000 coalition of over a hundred NGOs was launched in April 1996, with South African-born Ann Pettifor as director. Jubilee 2000 groups sprang up across the world. While the HIPC scheme was crawling out of the woodwork, the rapidly growing Jubilee 2000 movement was looking at debt from a totally different perspective.

Central to the campaign was the total cancellation of the unpayable debts of heavily indebted countries in 2000 under a fair and transparent process; fifty-two countries were specially identified. Unpayable debt was broadly defined as:

- debt which cannot be serviced without placing a burden on the poor;

- debt which in real terms has effectively already been paid (because of changing terms of trade or rising interest rates);
- debt for improperly designed projects;
- odious debt, apartheid and apartheid-caused debt, and debt incurred by repressive regimes.[12]

The Jubilee 2000 coalition ran a four-year, high-profile campaign to cancel debt and release funds for anti-poverty projects. It pointed out that it costs the fifty-two most heavily indebted countries about US$23 billion a year to service their debt, several times more than they receive in aid from the West. About US$300 billion of debt was estimated by the coalition to be unpayable.

The Jubilee 2000 campaign ended in December 2000 with rhetoric and promises from creditor governments but with only a tiny amount of debt actually cancelled. Despite huge international support, including a petition signed by 24 million people in 166 countries, support from religious leaders and pop stars such as Bono and Bob Geldof, the campaign fell short of its objective but did succeed in putting debt firmly on the international agenda. One of its main achievements was to communicate the complexities of the debt crisis in a way that could be understood, and to persuade world leaders that it was a key issue.

It also put on the agenda the issue of country bankruptcy. Individuals and companies in dire economic straits are allowed to file for bankruptcy, but not countries. In 2002 the IMF accepted the need to look at this issue. At its annual meeting in September 2002, the Fund was asked to draft proposals that would allow sovereign states to go bankrupt and have a fresh start.[13]

While the Jubilee 2000 coalition ended, a follow-up organization Jubilee Plus, later renamed Jubilee Research, came into being.

The human cost

The human cost of the debt burden is enormous. The 1997 UN *Human Development Report* estimated that if severely indebted countries were relieved of their annual debt repayments they could use funds for investments 'that in Africa alone would save the lives of about 21 million children by 2000 (7 million lives a year) and provide 90 million girls and women with access to basic education'.[14]

Education and health care have been severely affected across the developing world. 'Teaching materials are not available in schools, health care facilities have deteriorated' because of Malawi's debt burden, says Francis Ng'ambi of the Malawi Economic Justice Network.

> Around 20 per cent of the adult population are infected with HIV/AIDS, and the money which is going to service our debt is urgently needed to buy drugs to treat these people. Because of the debt, the government has had to remove food subsidies; the prices of basic commodities that people rely on has risen five to ten times. People don't know why.[15]

A short-lived flurry

In late December 2000 there was a flurry of activity from the Bank and the Fund, with an additional seven countries judged to have reached the HIPC initiative decision point, bringing the total to twenty-two: Benin, Bolivia, Burkina Faso, Cameroon, Gambia, Guinea, Guinea-Bissau, Guyana, Honduras, Madagascar, Malawi, Mali, Mauritania, Mozambique, Nicaragua, Niger, Rwanda, São Tomé & Príncipe, Senegal, Tanzania, Uganda and Zambia. But the flurry did not last. In 2001 and 2002 only a further four countries were added to the list: Chad, Ghana, Ethiopia and Sierra Leone.

Most of the twenty-six HIPC qualifying countries are relatively small, with a population between them of around 300 million. The fifty-two most heavily indebted countries have a joint population of over 1,030 million. Countries enjoying a reduction in annual debt servicing therefore account for less than 30 per cent of the population of the fifty-two countries. Even more telling is that the reduction in debt servicing, some US$800 million, amounts to a mere 3.4 per cent of the total annual debt service payment (around US$23 billion) of the fifty-two indebted countries.

Over time the twenty-six qualifying countries may expect debt relief of about US$40 billion. But this amounts to little more than a third of the US$110 billion debt which the G7 promised to cancel. Neither does the initiative recognize that fifty-two countries need debt relief – the HIPC list stops at forty-two. Countries not on the HIPC list include Bangladesh, Haiti and Nigeria. Their debt profiles are not considered serious enough for them to qualify. But all are in desperate need of debt cancellation. Nigeria's debt per head is about US$250, higher than at least six HIPC qualifiers and over twice as high as Burkina Faso.

Included in HIPC's list of forty-two are Kenya, Angola, Vietnam and Yemen, but the Bank and Fund deem that these countries already have sustainable levels of debt. Other countries in the list include some of the poorest and most war-ravaged countries on earth. But they have not yet even been considered for relief. They include Burma, Burundi, the Central African Republic, Democratic Republic of the Congo, Republic of the Congo, Guinea Bissau, Rwanda, Somalia and Sudan.

According to Ann Pettifor, the HIPC initiative 'is not deep enough to provide a lasting exit to the debt burdens faced by indebted countries. It moves far too slowly and is subject to increasingly discredited IMF austerity conditions.'[16]

The case of Malawi

The Malawi case highlights the power of the Bank and the Fund, and their extraordinary interference in an indebted country's affairs. In 2001 the IFIs advised the government of Malawi to reduce the level of its grain reserves to between 30,000 and 60,000 tonnes, on cost-effective grounds. The maize in the reserve – which was almost two years old – should be exported rather than sold locally, they advised, helping the country to repay a £9 million foreign debt. The IMF advised that the maize reserve be replenished in 2002.

In early 2002, it was clear that Malawi's drought meant sharply lower food output. Millions of people had little or no food. Neither did the country have an emergency reserve of grain. In July 2000 the reserve had held 175,000 tonnes of maize. Now the cupboard was bare. The government of Malawi had gone even further than the IMF advised: it had sold off all the grain.

The poor harvest in 2001 meant that food stocks could not be replenished. The IMF also went further. Even though Malawi had taken its advice, and more, and even though hundreds had now died of starvation, the IMF withheld an aid payment of US$47 million to the country in 2002. It seems that the IMF disliked the way the Malawi government helps its farmers. 'The IMF displayed remarkable insensitivity and ideological narrow-mindedness.'[17] 'We cannot underestimate the enormous power wielded by international institutions such as the IMF', says Sakou Jobe, country director of ActionAid in Malawi; 'they have massive influence. The government of Malawi has been guided by their policies and conditions of investment.'[18]

It is possible that pressure from its citizens to ensure food security could have persuaded the government not to sell those maize reserves. But IMF pressure was considerable and it was debt that gave it the leverage. 'Without cutting the noose of debt, Malawi will not be able to challenge the rigged rules and double standards of IMF creditors; and she will not be free to spend money to improve the health of her people', says Ann Pettifor.[19]

Debt takes more

Most of the countries with debt packages under the HIPC scheme will still be spending more each year on debt than on health care and education. Mauritania, for example, will be paying US$63 million on servicing its debt, but only US$51 million on education and US$17 million on health. Haiti is paying US$60 million a year to service its debt, 'while conditions for ordinary people are getting worse every day', says Camille Chalmers, a leading figure in Haiti's Jubilee 2000 campaign; 'this debt payment to the rich is both immoral and profoundly unjust'.[20]

By September 2002, only six countries – Bolivia, Burkina Faso, Mauritania, Mozambique, Tanzania and Uganda – had reached their completion point under the HIPC scheme. The Bank and the Fund released their 'Status of Implementation Report' for the scheme that month, still claiming that the initiative is a success. The facts suggest otherwise. The report shows:

- Nineteen countries were originally expected to reach completion point by the end of 2002. The number of countries expected to face unsustainable debt burdens at completion point is thirteen.
- Thirteen out of the twenty 'interim' period countries have gone off-track with their IMF programmes at some point, thus delaying debt cancellation and denying them interim debt service relief;
- Overall, even according to the narrow definitions of the World Bank and IMF, HIPC only appears to be working for between seven and ten countries out of the forty-two included within the initiative;
- The IMF and World Bank have considered, but rejected, alternative proposals for debt relief on the grounds that they are 'unaffordable' and will create 'moral hazard'.[21] 'The 20 countries that are between decision point and completion point seem to be stuck in a permanent state of limbo', says Jubilee Research.[22]

When they reach completion point, thirteen of these twenty countries are therefore expected to face unsustainable debt burdens. This makes a mockery of World Bank and IMF claims that debt will be reduced to the point where it is sustainable. The 'one and a half times earnings' formula is seen to be a grossly inadequate basis for debt relief.

Although Tanzania has reached completion point in the HIPC process, it will pay out US$168 million in debt servicing compared to US$87 million on health. 'Tanzania has seen its annual debt repayment drop by only 10 per cent. Is this is a lasting exit from debt?'[23]

Mozambique is the poorest country in the world, according to the World Bank, with poverty that results in part from a decade of battering by apartheid South Africa. The World Bank and the IMF agreed that some of the country's debt be cancelled in 1999, subject to the usual strict conditions. They claimed that the deal would free resources and allow Mozambique to broaden the scope of its development effort. This was shown to be false when Jubilee 2000 finally forced the IMF to release the actual figures. For Mozambique, while there has been some reduction from earlier years, there will be no significant reduction in actual debt service paid, after the completion point, from what Mozambique is now paying. Post-HIPC relief, Mozambique will continue to spend US$100 million a year on debt service – 'twice what it spends on running its health service', pointed out Britain's International Development Secretary of the time, Clare Short.[24]

Creditor countries agreed in 2002 that some countries would need additional 'topping up' of debt relief at the HIPC initiative completion point in order to bring their debts down to sustainable levels. At the G8 meeting in June 2002, leaders committed – though have not yet delivered – an additional US$1 billion of debt relief for this purpose.

Even some creditor governments seem unconvinced that the Bank/Fund 'one and a half times earnings' criterion is realistic. 'We will press the Bank and the Fund for more advice for HPIC countries on realistic debt sustainability analysis to ensure that countries exit the initiative with a sustainable debt level', says the UK government.[25] But creditor governments show a disturbing lack of willingness to stand up to the Bank and the Fund and to insist on changes.

In the spring of 2002, the World Bank and IMF released two

reports which confirmed the predictions of NGOs that HIPC countries would never reach the export growth targets they had set out.[26] NGOs, including Jubilee Research, accused the IMF and World Bank of 'cynically using unrealistically high forecasts for export growth in order to limit the costs of debt cancellation for their own pockets'.[27] By late 2002 only 15 per cent of unpayable poor country debts (that is, those of the 'Jubilee 52 countries') have been cancelled. And for every dollar that developing countries received in grants they were paying out $13 in debt servicing.[28]

African countries are especially affected by indebtedness; they owe almost US$300 billion in external debt, about 60 per cent of their gross domestic product, some 12 per cent of total debt owed by all developing countries. Almost half of this – US$149 billion – is owed by the thirty-four African countries included under the HIPC initiative. During the long-drawn-out process of negotiating debt relief under HIPC, Africa has sunk further into poverty. The number of people in extreme poverty in sub-Saharan Africa rose from 242 million to 300 million during the 1990s.[29] African countries now spend US$14.5 billion each year – that is, US$40 million each day – repaying debts, but receive only US$12.7 billion in aid.[30]

The morality of creditor government and World Bank and IMF policy over debt has been called into question by a wide range of people and organizations. 'It is immoral and unethical and a structure of sin for rich countries to continue demanding from poor countries the payment of huge sums of money in debt repayments', say Catholic bishops in eastern Africa, for example;

> The structural adjustments that the IMF and the World Bank have imposed on our countries in various forms, have in many instances resulted in rising poverty, food insecurity, massive job losses, rising cost of living, devaluation of local currencies and accelerated privatization that put the control of the economies in the hands of a small ruling class.[31]

Debt relief works

The tragedy about the slowness of debt relief is that such relief works. A Jubilee Research report says:

- In 1998, education spending was only US$929 million, less than the amount spent on debt service. In 2001 it was US$1306 million more.
- Before debt relief, more than twice as much was being spent on debt service as on health. Since then, spending on health has risen by 70 per cent – and is now one-third higher than spending on debt repayments.
- Debt relief is not being used to fuel military expenditures. In the countries reviewed, we found no increase in military spending as a result of debt relief.[32]

Uganda was the first country to obtain relief under HIPC: US$2 billion of relief, although spread over thirty-five years. Charlotte Mwesigye of Uganda's debt relief network told a meeting in September 2002 what relief has achieved in her country. Since 1998, when debt started to be written down, the money that would have gone into repayments has helped provide an additional ten thousand classrooms, although there are still over a hundred children per classroom. The number of Ugandan children at primary school has risen from 2.5 million to 6.5 million. Public spending on health-care facilities has increased; 93 new health centres have been built. Over 1,700 new boreholes have been dug and over a thousand shallow wells, with the result that around 900,000 more people have access to clean water. Although Uganda has been badly affected by falling world coffee prices, the number of Ugandans living below the poverty line – a dollar a day – has declined from 56 per cent to 35 per cent of the population.[33]

Total cancellation

The HIPC 'initiative' has failed; the need is for the cancellation of 100 per cent of unpayable Third World debts. Only the total write-off of this debt is enough. Cancelling debt is about freedom of manoeuvre, about freedom for countries and people who are enslaved. Debt cancellation helps to open the door to alternatives. With more of their own funds to invest, indebted countries would have more option to invest in the social sector, they would have the freedom to be less dependent on corporate-dominated globalization.

Ann Pettifor says of Malawi:

> Without the debt, it is possible that the people of Malawi could, democratically, set priorities, or affect the priorities of their government; one of these could be to protect Malawian farmers and markets from those who would prey upon their weakness. Malawi might have been able to do what voters in the world's biggest debtor nation – the US – can do: put pressure on their government to subsidize food producers, and protect them from unfair competition from competing producers.[34]

Substantial debt relief, let alone cancellation, is unlikely to happen if the Bank and Fund remain unchanged. NGOs have long campaigned for radical changes in both institutions, with some calling for their replacement with bodies that are more sensitive to the needs of developing countries. Governments too have protested. Austerity programmes championed by the IMF and World Bank offer 'a choice between death and death' in poor countries, according to Haiti's President Aristide; 'Haiti, under intense pressure from the international lending institutions, stopped protecting its domestic agriculture while subsidies to the US rice industry increased.'[35]

The era of corporate-driven globalization has been an era of progressively deeper financial crises and growing debts. The result has been impoverishment and loss of rights for people in indebted countries. Only enormous public pressure will bring change in IMF/World Bank policies and in the pace of debt relief. But as the effects of the policies become more widely known, so the clamour for change will grow. By using indebtedness to keep countries tied to a global trading system which is failing the poor, these institutions have lost any moral authority they might have claimed.

The World Bank's sister

Structural adjustment programmes often oblige developing countries to make bigger cuts in tariffs than is required under World Trade Organization agreements. Pakistan, for example, a country largely self-sufficient in wheat, has come under pressure from a regional development bank, the Asian Development Bank (ADB) – a sister organization to the World Bank – to reduce its support for small-scale farmers.

Up to 70 per cent of Pakistan's wheat production – which totalled 21 million tonnes in 2000 – is consumed locally, leaving a marketable surplus of 5–6 million tonnes. Of this, the government regularly buys in nearly 4 million tonnes for strategic reserves and buffer stocks, leaving very little for disposal on export markets. The government reserves the right to procure more wheat for reasons of food security. In 2000 it exercised this right and bought in over 8.5 million tonnes.

After procurement, the government sells wheat to flour mills at subsidized prices that are then passed to the consumer. The government has thus developed a system to control and stabilize wheat prices that gives farmers a fair return and consumers reasonable prices. But, in early 2001, the government began to implement the conditions of a loan to the agricultural sector from the ADB. These conditions require a move away from government intervention towards a market-based system, with the emphasis on deregulation, liberalization and privatization.

The government slashed its procurement target from 8.5 million tonnes to 4 million tonnes for 2001 and shut

down a large number of procurement centres. These
changes had a dramatic effect on the wheat market.
Farmers had increased wheat output in the belief they
would receive Rs 300 per maund (40 kilos) and in light of
the government's high procurement target for 2000. With
the dramatic reduction in the 2001 target, farmers rushed
to try to sell their harvest as fast as possible, in the hope
that they could obtain the procurement price before prices
began to fall.

In Pakistan, as elsewhere in the developing world,
small-scale, resource-poor farmers are under pressure to
sell their products quickly – they need money to repay
high-interest loans taken from middlemen and dealers, and
to purchase next year's inputs. They are unable to hold
surplus production to see if prices will rise.

Many small-scale farmers in Pakistan (93 per cent of all
farm production is on holdings of between 5 and 12 acres)
found that they could not get the new procurement price
and had to sell at prices as low as Rs 200–240 per maund,
with the market collapsing around them. Selling their
crops at a loss devastated the social fabric of rural communities.

Under the rules of the WTO, Pakistan was not obliged
to reduce its support to wheat farmers, provided the value
of the support did not exceed 10 per cent of wheat
output. It was the influence of the ADB, and of the IMF
and the World Bank, that caused the damage to the
country's small farmers. The ADB is now pushing for the
phasing out of farm subsidies in Pakistan.

Source: *Farmgate*, London: Action Aid, August 2002.

10

Alternative strategies

To be truly radical is to make hope possible, rather than despair inevitable.

Unknown source

In addition to reforms of TNCs and key institutions (as described in the previous three chapters), people throughout the developing world, and also in the North, are taking initiatives at local level which are enabling them to break free from corporate-driven globalization. They are showing that alternatives not only exist but are successful, that communities can organize in such a way that they have less need to trade and submit their future to soulless corporations. They are showing that there is no need to continue as virtual serfs in an international economy that is run for and by the corporations. With an increased determination to build local economies, people are showing that another world is possible.

Too many societies have become overdependent on foreign economies, hence the urgent need for alternative approaches. 'We need to break out of ... our existence as appendages of foreign economies', in the words of a director of a small non-profit food marketing company in the Caribbean.[1]

Strategies for greater self-reliance

The greater the self-reliance, the less people rely on the global economy, the more they break free from corporate-driven globalization. They are able to pursue their own development course. For this to happen, governments of developing countries need to seize back the policy initiative they have lost to the TNCs and the international financial institutions. More priority should go to developing thriving local economies and less to international trade. The rebuilding of 'healthy, stable and sustainable societies can only be done when citizens and nations take back control of their economies'.[2]

Localization is the route to achieving this, believe Caroline Lucas and Colin Hines. They define localization as a 'set of interrelated and self-reinforcing policies that actively discriminate in favour of the more local. It provides a political and economic framework for people, community groups and businesses to re-diversify their own economies'. They believe it 'has the potential to increase community cohesion, reduce poverty and inequity, improve livelihoods, promote social provision and environmental protection and provide the all-important sense of security'.[3]

'Localization' is a concept that industry has not been slow to pick up for its own uses. It has even spawned an industry. The Localization Research Centre, for example, based at the University of Limerick, describes itself as 'the information, educational, and research centre for the localization industry'.[4]

Corporations often try to get themselves accepted as 'local' in the countries where they operate. The US-based Localization Industry Standards Association consists 'of over 200 corporate clients and their globalization solutions partners ... [It] provides best practice, business guidelines and multi-lingual information management standards for making enterprise globalization become a reality!'[5] Localization is therefore seen by some TNCs as a tool, something that can assist their global efforts – complementary to and not replacing globalization.[6]

The *World Development Report 1999/2000* of the World Bank also sees localization as complementary to, rather than opposed to, globalization. It defines localization as 'the growing economic and political power of cities, provinces, and other sub-national entities', and predicts that it will be one of the most important trends in the twenty-first century.[7]

This book's contributors see localization as a definite alternative to globalization, something totally distinct from industry plans. To bring about people-centred localization, the International Forum on Globalization recommends:

- Reintroduction of protective safeguards that have traditionally been used to protect domestic (local) economies, and to aid local economic renewal.
- Changes in subsidy policy to favour vital local enterprises such as small-scale organic agriculture for local markets, small-scale energy and transportation infrastructures.
- New controls on corporate activity, including a 'site here to sell here' policy for manufacturing, banking and other services, whether domestic or regional.
- Grounding capital and investment within the community; profits made locally remain primarily local.
- Major changes in taxation policies such as increases in resource taxes for extraction and depletion of natural capital like forests, water, minerals; and the introduction of pollution taxes.
- Increased direct public participation in policymaking to help ensure equity and diversity of viewpoint.
- Reorientation of international aid and trade rules and the domestic policies that influence those changes so that they contribute to the rebuilding of local rather than global economies.
- New competition policies; global corporations to lose access to local markets unless they conform to local investment rules.[8]

Greater democracy is key to increased decision-making at local level. Local people must feel they can influence their local economy. Governments of developing countries need to democ-

ratize decision-making and enable people to make decisions over
their own livelihoods. Communities are developing the localization idea in many different ways. In around 1,500 villages in India,
for example, the idea has led to a desire for self-rule, with communities declaring themselves village republics.

> In these villages, residents control their natural resources –
> forest, land, minerals and water sources. They have also
> formed effective institutions to manage these resources. They
> plan, execute and resolve all affairs inside the village. Govern-
> ment officials and programmes are accepted only when the
> gram sabha (the only formal institution in the village)
> approves them. In many such villages, the forest department,
> the police and other officials are just restricted to executing
> programmes chalked out in village meetings. Everywhere the
> desire for self-rule comes from the threat to livelihood. Like
> the 125 villages inside the Rajiv Gandhi National Park in
> Karnataka's Nagarhole. When the government declared their
> traditional home as a national park, it meant evacuation.
> What the 40,000-odd residents did was to declare self-rule
> and take control of the area. A taskforce was set up in each
> village to work out the modalities for self-rule. Barriers were
> erected with signboards directing outsiders to seek permission
> of the yajaman (traditional chief) prior to conducting their
> business in the village. Such are the strong linkages of these
> village republics to control over natural resources that they
> can be termed as natural republics.[9]

Some of the villages have formed different committees to look
after different resources. In these villages, natural resources and
their equitable distribution form the core of governance.

Food sovereignty

Most people in developing countries live and work in the rural
areas. The starting point for self-reliant strategies is often the wish
to have greater sovereignty, more say and control over food
supplies. The idea is generally opposed by Western governments.

At the start of the Uruguay Round of trade negotiations in 1986, for example, US Agriculture Secretary John Block said: '[the] idea that developing countries should feed themselves is an anachronism from a bygone era. They could better ensure their food security by relying on US agricultural products, which are available in most cases at much lower cost'.[10]

In 2002, ministers might put that more diplomatically but the sentiment remains. It suits Western countries if developing countries do not produce all their own food, so that their markets are open to food imports, many of which are sold to developing countries below the costs of production – in other words, they are 'dumped'.[11]

Development aid from Western countries for the food and agriculture sectors of developing countries fell by half in the 1990s. With big surpluses to dispose of, Western governments were less than keen to give aid that would help countries to grow more of their own food. Requests for aid for agriculture were declining, they said.

Food sovereignty in developing countries may not suit Western governments or corporations, but there is renewed interest in the idea in the developing world. Food sovereignty means the right of people to decide their own agricultural and food policies, to determine the extent they want to to be self-reliant, and to restrict negative outside factors such as the dumping of food in their areas. It means farmers having control over land and resources such as water and technology.

Efforts by small farmers to increase output can do much to increase family and community self-reliance. Technologies that can produce the necessary food without causing environmental damage are already used in millions of farming communities. Organic agriculture, intercropping, rotation of crops, mulching, and the integration of crops and livestock are among the approaches which yield results. In developing countries, organic agriculture, usually in the form of intercropping, has been the norm for centuries with a long and successful history. Growing and rotating two or more crops in the same land allows the crops to support each other, not least in warding off pests.

Many farmers in developing countries have been persuaded, however, to drop traditional techniques and use chemical fertilizers instead. The persuaders were often the companies selling the fertilizers. An initial rise in yields may have followed the early applications of fertilizers, and the old techniques were scorned and not passed on to succeeding generations. Especially in the last two decades of the twentieth century, however, financial pressures meant that many could no longer afford chemicals. They returned to organic methods, not necessarily with conviction but because they had no option. Interest in recovering and developing traditional techniques, in low external input technologies, for example, is now growing. The essential point about these techniques is that they are more likely to be sustainable than growing crops for export in monocropping fashion. There are many examples of farmers in developing countries increasing their food output with low-cost technologies and in a sustainable manner.[12]

Governments need to question whether they should encourage their farmers to grow crops for export – crops which generally fetch low prices and earn limited foreign exchange. Incentives could usefully be given to their own farmers to grow food for local consumption. Incentives to local firms, such as domestic hotels, to buy food from local rather than from foreign sources would be helpful. Stepping up the amount of food grown locally would not only help greater self-reliance, it would also lower a country's import bill, help to correct balance-of-payments problems, and make it less likely that IMF help is needed.

Local processing of foodstuffs has potential and is often a neglected area of policy. If farmers know there are local markets for their produce they are less likely to want to export. 'Food processing plants could provide more reliable markets for farmers and badly needed jobs for other people. Fruit and other crops that now go to waste could be utilized.'[13]

Agrarian reform

Redistributing land to small-scale farmers can do much to reduce poverty and enhance food sovereignty. Dividing large farms into smaller units often means that more food per hectare is produced. This is happening in a number of countries. In El Salvador, for example, a 10 per cent rise in land ownership has boosted income per person by 4 per cent. In India, the states where poverty has fallen the fastest are those that have implemented land reform. Ethiopia has transformed a feudal land system into family farming. Most strikingly in China, the shift from large farms to smallholding (between 1977 and 1985) witnessed an unprecedented rise in farm output, enabling millions to escape from poverty.[14]

Land reform can give people more power in the community. One of the largest NGOs in Latin America, and one of the most successful grassroots movements in the world, is Brazil's Landless Movement (MST). This movement of the poorest has withstood constant repression to claim and farm the unused land of the wealthy. Less than 3 per cent of the country's population owns two-thirds of Brazil's arable land, and 60 per cent of farmland lies idle. Some 25 million peasants struggle to survive by working in temporary agricultural jobs. The MST is a response to these inequalities.

Under MST, hundreds of thousands of landless peasants have taken upon themselves the task of carrying out long-overdue land reform. In 1985, with the support of the Catholic Church, hundreds of landless rural Brazilians took over an unused plantation in the south of the country and successfully established a cooperative there. They gained title to the land in 1987. Today more than 250,000 families have won land titles to over 15 million acres after MST land takeovers. In 1999 alone, 25,099 families occupied unproductive land. There are currently 71,472 families in encampments throughout Brazil awaiting government recognition; 300,000 families have settled on millions of hectares of land that now produces food.

The success of the MST lies in its ability to organize. Its members have not only managed to secure land, and guarantee food security for their families; they have come up with an alternative socio-economic development model that puts people before profits. This is transforming the face of Brazil's countryside and the country's politics at large.

The gains have not come without a cost. Violent clashes between the MST and police, as well as landowners, have become commonplace, claiming the lives of many peasants and their leaders. In the past ten years, more than a thousand people have been killed as a result of land conflicts in Brazil. Few of the suspected killers have been brought to trial. The MST has resisted this repression and has been able to gather support from a broad international network of human rights groups, religious organizations and labour unions.

In order to maximize production, the MST has created sixty food cooperatives as well as small agricultural industries. Their literacy programme involves 600 educators, who presently work with adults and adolescents, and about 1,000 primary schools in the settlement areas are monitored.[15] In October 2002 the MST supported the successful presidential bid of Luís Inacio Lula da Silva, leader of Brazil's Workers Party (PT).

Local money

Although it seems to have acquired a strange mystique, money is but a means of exchange and a store of 'value'. International exchange in the mainstream trading system is done with the currencies of Western countries – notably the dollar, pound, euro and yen. Even trade between developing countries is often transacted with a Western currency, because governments know that these will be freely accepted worldwide, unlike the currencies of developing countries. Attempts to develop an accepted 'Third World' currency have so far come to nothing. Foreign currencies are difficult to earn and therefore often scarce. But for millions of people in developing countries, their national currency may also be scarce. They are too poor to have money. As a result, money is coercive by nature – people with money exercise power over people without it.

Scarcity of money inhibits the exchange of goods and services, and reinforces poverty. It can therefore make sense for a local community to develop its own currency. This will facilitate the exchange of goods and services in their community, build up community self-reliance, stimulate the local economy and can be an important part of the alternative to economic globalization.

Local currencies have been common throughout history, emerging whenever a community needed to protect its internal economy from outside disturbances. But the economic climate in the early twenty-first century has led to a big increase in their number. In 2001, there were more than 2,000 local currencies in operation, according to David Boyle.[16] But by the end of 2002 there were more than 7,000, he estimates, most of them in Argentina.[17]

The LETSystem – Local Exchange Trading System – is the most advanced form of local currency. LETS schemes are an attempt to help in the building of healthier local economies. The first LETSystem was developed in Canada's Comox Valley in 1983, where some people adapted the 'barter' (straight exchange of goods) network model and turned it into a full-scale community system with greater advantages, yet operating at a fraction of the cost.

This prototype was very successful, despite considerable antipathy and even active resistance from key elements in the local community. About 20 similar systems sprang up across North America. But by 1988 a combination of factors, principally research and development costs and fragile user confidence, caused trading in the Comox Valley system to decline virtually to a standstill. While this created a general loss of confidence in North America, LETSystems began to grow worldwide. Since 1987 some 70 LETSystems have been established in New Zealand and almost

200 in Australia. In Britain the number rocketed from 7 systems in early 1991 to 150 by the end of 1993. All these systems are based on the original prototype in Comox Valley, which has recently resumed trading with improved computer software, administration and more ways of introducing and educating people about LETSystems.

For a local currency to work, it has to stay within the community it serves, be issued by the people who use it, exist in sufficient supply to meet the needs of that community, and have the confidence of local people. The LETSystem meets these criteria. It is friendly, convenient, cost-effective, simple and secure. It works much like a bank or a building society. Everyone has an account, but instead of money transferring from one bank to another, all exchanges are within a single system. A local currency cannot leave the community it serves, so it ensures connections between people exchanging skills, goods and services. With a local currency, the community is less affected by fluctuations in the external money supply.

Each new account starts at zero and thereafter may hold a positive or a negative balance. Those with negative balances have, quite simply, created the money which is in the positive accounts. So this local money is essentially a promise by some members of the community to give service to others. Money like this, which people issue themselves, is personal money; everyone has money to spend. By the same token, nobody needs it, so things only happen when people decide. Nobody can tell anyone else what to do.[18]

There are other alternative currencies – Time Dollars, for example. These differ from the LETSystem in that the aim is not to create an alternative trading system but to build the 'core economy' of families, neighbourhoods and communities. Time Dollar Exchanges are about building social support networks, community, and social capital.

Time Dollars are described as 'a new, tax-exempt kind of money that empowers people to convert their personal time into purchasing power by helping others and by rebuilding family, neighbourhood and community. An hour helping another earns one Time Dollar. For the elderly, Time Dollars look like a new kind of extended family. For teenagers, Time Dollars provide a setting where kids can say to each other: 'Don't do something stupid.' For residents in public housing, they mean doing what neighbours used to do for neighbours. 'The Time Dollars you earn helping others can be used to receive services or help from someone else. When you spend your Time Dollars, someone else earns them. They can be saved up for a rainy day. They can be given to someone else, a family member, friend, or neighbour who needs help. Or they can be donated.'[19]

Nowhere has the rise of local currencies been faster than in Argentina, a country severely affected in 2001 and 2002 by economic upheaval (see Chapter 6). Many people lost confidence in the money issued by government and up to 80 per cent of all financial transactions in Argentina are now carried out in a local currency. The Argentinian capital, Buenos Aires, is 'the epicentre of one of the most extraordinary new kinds of money anywhere in the world', says David Boyle.[20]

Argentina's Global Barter Network in the capital is ten years old, and has grown up independently of any of the local currencies in richer countries. It has 300,000 members in Buenos Aires province alone, many of them increasing their monthly income by the equivalent of US$600 a month, or more than the average wage.

All members are known as 'prosumers' – both producers and consumers. They are given 50 'creditos' – the name of the local currency – when they join, each one printed in different denominations, with serial numbers. Most of the trade goes on at weekly meetings of each local group, which take the form of a large market, attracting anything from home-grown vegetables to remaindered stock from local businesses. There are also bigger monthly markets which attract a range of dentists, doctors and surgeons, performing their skills out in the open among the stalls – all in exchange for creditos.

The Argentine government is encouraging the Barter Network, and visitors from other Latin American governments are looking to see if they can replicate the idea.

> This makes some organisers nervous, but it does mean that current talks to get supermarkets to contribute goods and to let people pay some local taxes in creditos have more chance of success ... Buenos Aires is showing a possible way that ordinary people can survive when there's no cash – not without discomfort or effort but this is survival, after all.[21]

Another initiative is the Exchange Club in Argentina, which is part of a Network of Self-Help. The objective of the network is not profit, but to increase the quality of life. In this system, each member produces goods or services which can be traded with offerings of other members of the club without having to use money. Money is replaced by an instrument of exchange that some clubs call 'Nodine' (No Dinero – No Money), and which is generated for the purchase of labour, goods and services, the initial value being equivalent to conventional money. 'This allows groups of individuals in a region or in different regions in a country to inter-exchange goods and services in a reciprocal and amicable way, with ecological concern and where everyone wins and nobody loses.'[22]

Are local currencies effective? The experience of many communities in both North and South suggests the answer is yes.

> There appears to be solid evidence that complementary currency systems can be effective in stimulating local initiative and cooperation, and in relieving the paralysis that often sets in when communities are hit by sudden economic setbacks such as a national currency collapse or a rise in unemployment. But beyond the practical considerations, there is a fierce idealism among many advocates, a conviction that the local currencies increase cooperation over competition, and increase sustainable development.[23]

Local currencies have a huge and many-sided potential. They help to facilitate exchange where no exchange would take place. They help to bring power back to people and can be a vital part of the alternatives to corporate globalization jigsaw. (See Box for an example of the value of a local currency in a developing country.) They may also bring cultural benefits. According to Susan Witt, executive director of the E.F. Schumacher Society,

> By intentionally narrowing our choices of consumer goods to those locally made, local currencies allow us to know more fully the stories of items purchased – stories that include the human beings who made them and the minerals, rivers, plants, and animals that were used to form them. Such stories, shaped by real life experience, work in the imagination to foster responsible consumer choices and re-establish a commitment to the community. In this sense, local currencies become a tool not only for economic development but for cultural renewal.[24]

New local currencies will not transform globalization 'into a wholly benign force overnight', says David Boyle, 'but they can provide us with some independence, no matter what economic storms shake the world financial system'.[25]

Raising money globally: the Tobin tax

At the other end of the spectrum to local currencies lies an alternative plan for money, in this case for raising money globally. The Tobin tax was proposed in 1978 by Nobel prizewinning economist James Tobin. His idea was that a small tax (less than 0.5 per cent) be levied on foreign exchange transactions to deter short-term currency speculation. While the rate would be low enough not to have a significant effect on longer-term investment, it would cut into the yields of speculators. It would be a check on the movement of massive amounts of currency around the globe as speculators seek to profit from minute differentials in currency fluctuations.

Currency speculation adds volatility and instability to markets, and has been linked to the 1997-98 currency crisis in Southeast Asia, the fall of the Mexican peso in 1994, and the failure of the European exchange-rate mechanism in 1992. About US$1 trillion worth of currency is traded every day in unregulated financial markets. Only 5 per cent of this activity is related to trade and other real economic transactions. The other 95 cent is simply speculative activity as traders bet on exchange-rate fluctuations and international interest-rate differentials. This kind of financial speculation plays havoc with national budgets, economic planning and allocation of resources. Governments and citizens are becoming increasingly frustrated by the whimsical and often irrational activities in global financial markets that have such an influence over national economies and are seeking some means to curb damaging, and unproductive, speculative activity.

As foreign-exchange transactions and financial deregulation have accelerated, so interest in the Tobin tax has grown. The tax would reduce the power that financial markets have over national governments to determine fiscal and monetary policies. It would give more autonomy to governments to set these policies by making possible greater differences between short-term interest rates in different currencies.

This tax would also yield a considerable sum. Assuming a conservative tax rate of 0.2 per cent, and an effective tax base of US$75 trillion annually, the tax would yield US$150 billion annually – almost three times as much as annual development assistance from rich to poor countries. The Tobin tax could therefore generate substantial additional resources to assist development.

There are two political issues involved with putting such a tax in place. First, it would be necessary to forge agreement among the major countries to implement a uniform tax; second, there would have to be agreement on the collection and distribution of the tax revenue. NGOs are putting pressure on national governments and international institutions to support the Tobin tax, as it would help to restore democratic control of national economies.

The Tabu currency in Papua New Guinea

Tabu is the shell currency of the Tolai people of the Duke of York Islands and Gazelle Peninsula in the Province of East New Britain, Papua New Guinea. It is made from the shell of the Nassa Callosa and Nassa Camelus snail, which is harvested from the beaches of New Britain, New Ireland and the Solomon Islands.

The tops of the shells are pinched in a way that reveals a small hole which is then threaded onto cane (rattan) strips. These strips can be bent and broken at lengths appropriate for the purchase of the full range of locally produced goods and services. Tabu is acquired and produced in the home, and is divided into two types functioning as savings, with a third type functioning as a means of exchange.

The first type of savings is of medium-term duration, for the payment of bills as a result of local government court settlements, for 'bride price', paid before marriages, and other medium-scale expenses. The second type of savings, and the method of issuing the currency, involves the long-term storage of Tabu in large rolls which are cut open and freely distributed at the ceremony [after family funerals].

Tabu that is not necessary for either of these types of savings, functions as a medium of exchange until it is of sufficient volume to be added to either the medium- or long-term savings.

Tabu is valued in units of fathoms, which is equal to the Imperial measurement of six feet or 183 centimetres, and divisible down to a unit of 10-12 shells.... The exact length and the number of shells in one fathom, and therefore in its sub- and supra- units, has not yet been standardized....

Tabu is a commodity money, similar to gold or silver coins, which are valued by the Tolai people for its ceremonial and customary uses, as well as a divisible medium of exchange for primarily locally-produced goods and services. To those non-Tolai people who are willing to receive Tabu as payment, it is considered a credit currency good for redemption only from a Tolai person in goods or services, or at the Local Level Government office at which it can be converted into [the national PNG currency, the] Kina.

Source: Stephen DeMeulenaere, 'The Valuation and Production of Tabu Shell Currency', on website: www.ccdev.lets.net/asia/asia.html.

The tax could be an important part of the alternatives jigsaw and help to increase equity and economic sovereignty globally.[26]

Alternative trade: the future lies with the infant

Developing countries want to trade; a country with no oil has no option but to trade if it wants to import oil and have mechanical life. If poor countries did not trade they would deny themselves the possibility of earning money from richer countries and consumers in the North. But they want a fairer deal from trade. The mainstream international trading system is likely to yield only limited benefits, especially for the resource-poor farmers.[27] Such farmers do not trade their produce internationally; the traders are the TNCs. As the mainstream system is synonymous with corporate-driven globalization, the benefits accrue chiefly to the corporations rather than to the poor. The alternative trading system bypasses the corporations and offers the possibility of trade across borders that can enable poor producers to benefit from the global economy.

Under the alternative trading system – also known as ethical trade or fair trade – the actual producers trade with buyers in a more direct way and receive a higher return than under conventional trade. The alternative system enables consumers to buy direct, giving them the satisfaction of knowing that their purchases are helping to improve the livelihoods of producers.

Fairly traded produce is sold through supermarkets, 'One World shops', churches, mail-order catalogues and in other marketing outlets. While still small, in comparison to mainstream trading, the alternative system has huge potential.

The coffee trade provides an example. Coffee is one of the developing world's most important traded commodities, providing employment for more than 25 million people in some eighty countries. Around 70 per cent of coffee growers are small farmers who grow the crop in the hope of a cash income. But their share of the price that coffee fetches on world markets is often well below the cost of production. A sustained period of low prices during the first half of the 1990s left many growers bankrupt and destitute; some lost their land, while others neglected their crop to get casual jobs. Coffee harvests declined in quality as a result. Prices rose in the late 1990s but fell sharply in 2000.

The problem for growers is not just that world coffee prices are low or even that they fluctuate widely. The deeper problem lies in the workings of the world coffee market. Most coffee is traded down a line of dealers before it is exported – it can change hands as much as 150 times – leaving growers with a meagre return even when prices rise.

Fairtrade mark

Some growers, however, are shielded from this system. About half a million coffee growers are members of farmers' organizations which sell directly to coffee-roasting companies that comply with internationally accepted fair-trade criteria and have the Fairtrade mark (see below). The difference between fairly traded and 'conventional' coffee is that all Fairtrade-mark coffee must be bought direct from small grower organizations which are genuinely representative of their members; there must also be advance payments of up to 60 per cent to ensure that the grower organization can finance itself. Fairtrade-marked coffees are independently audited and guaranteed to meet these criteria.

Growth is phenomenal: sales of fairtrade coffee in the UK, for example, grew by over 50 per cent a year in the late 1990s, 2000 and 2001. Fairly traded ground coffees now have 7.5 per cent of the UK coffee market.

Under the Fairtrade system, farmers' organizations receive a guaranteed price which covers the cost of production and allows for investment and a basic living wage. When coffee prices are low, the Fairtrade price can be double the world price. When prices are higher, farmers receive 5 cents per pound more, which goes directly to the farmers' organizations. Fairtrade terms mean higher prices, a direct trading relationship and long-term contracts.

Standards of alternatively traded products are maintained in different ways (see also below). The Netherlands was the first country to launch a Fairtrade consumer guarantee – the Max Havelaar label – in 1989. In 1993, the London-based Fairtrade Foundation was set up by CAFOD, Christian Aid, New Consumer, Oxfam, Traidcraft and the World Development Movement. It works to ensure 'a better deal for marginalized and disadvantaged third world producers'. The Foundation awards the Fairtrade mark to products which meet internationally recognized standards of fair trade. Currently, more than a hundred coffee, tea, banana, chocolate, cocoa, juice, sugar and honey products carry the mark. The Foundation has a partnership agreement and shares a common definition of fair trade with alternative trading organizations in other countries.

There are labelling initiatives throughout Europe and North America, with the product range including coffee, drinking chocolate, chocolate bars, orange juice, tea, honey, sugar and bananas. In Europe, Fairtrade Mark products are available in most supermarket chains, with some products gaining 15 per cent of national market share.

The FairTrade Labelling Organizations International (FLO–International) was set up in 1997 to coordinate the work of the national initiatives and run monitoring programmes more efficiently. FLO–International has seventeen member organizations in Western Europe, North America and Japan, and 186 coffee producer groups on its register, mostly with between 100 and 500 members. One of FLO-International's aims was the introduction of a single international Fairtrade label. This was unveiled in Britain in October 2002 and will be introduced gradually across the FLO member countries, with Belgium and the Netherlands also launching in 2002 and others in 2003.

'Fairtrade is the food of the future', says Harriet Lamb, director of the Fairtrade Foundation. Foods with the Fairtrade mark are now sold in 17 countries through 235 traders and 452 companies, being sourced from 360 producer groups in 36 countries, representing 4.5 million growers and their families. The projected sales of Fairtrade Mark products in the UK for 2002 are between £53 million and £58 million. In 2001, UK sales rose by 40 per cent to a retail value of £46 million, which means consumers spent nearly £1.50 a second on Fairtrade products. Total sales in volume worldwide increased from 39,750 tonnes in 2000 to 48,506 tonnes in 2001, a 22 per cent increase. Recent surveys suggest the majority of people would prefer to buy Fairtrade mark products.[28]

Fairtrade standards

The problems experienced by poor producers and workers in developing countries differ greatly from product to product. The majority of coffee and cocoa, for example, is grown by independent small farmers, working their own land and marketing their produce through a local cooperative. For these producers, receiving a fair price for their beans is more important than any other aspect of a fair trade. Most tea, however, is grown on estates. The concern for workers employed on tea plantations is fair wages and decent working conditions.

Fairtrade criteria address this by using two sets of producer standards, one for small farmers and one for workers on plantations and in factories. The first set applies to smallholders organized in cooperatives or other organizations with a democratic, participative structure. The second set applies to organized workers, whose employers pay decent wages, guarantee the right to join trade unions and provide good housing when relevant. On plantations and in factories, minimum health and safety as well as environmental standards must be complied with, and no child or forced labour can occur.

As Fairtrade is also about development, the generic standards distinguish between minimum requirements which producers must meet to be certified Fairtrade. Requirements also encourage producer organizations continuously to improve working conditions and product quality, to increase their environmental stability of the activities, and to invest in the development of their organizations and the welfare of their producers/workers.

Trading standards stipulate that traders must:

- pay a price to producers that covers the costs of sustainable production and living;
- pay a 'premium' that producers can invest in development;
- make partial advance payments when requested by producers;
- sign contracts that allow for long-term planning and sustainable production practices.

Other products

While food and beverages account for most fairly traded products, other goods are also available. The International Federation for Alternative Trade (IFAT), a global network of over 160 members in more than fifty countries, lists a wide range of products that are sold by its members:

- Household goods: practical and useful household utensils hand made from sustainably managed resources.
- Furniture: original designs made from wood, from metal as well as from natural sources such as water hyacinth, rattan and palm.

- Garments and jewellery: deluxe items created from natural fibres; a wide range of silverware and precious and semi-precious jewellery.
- Food products and beverages.[29]

Carpets are also available through Rugmark. This is a non-profit organization working to end child labour and offering educational opportunities to children in India, Nepal and Pakistan – the carpet-producing countries currently participating in the programme. It does this through loom and factory monitoring, consumer labelling, and running schools for former child workers. Rugmark recruits carpet producers and importers to make and sell carpets without the use of child labour. By agreeing to adhere to Rugmark's strict no-child-labour guidelines, and by permitting random inspections of carpet looms, manufacturers receive the right to put the Rugmark label on their carpets.

The Rugmark label provides the best possible assurance that a carpet is not produced by children. The label also verifies that a portion of the carpet price is contributed to the rehabilitation and education of former child weavers. Labelled carpets are sold in Europe and in North America.[30]

A publicly quoted company that embraces the alternative trade idea, in the form of buying direct from local people, is the Body Shop, which has operated a fair-trading scheme with developing countries since 1987. One project under the scheme involves buying shea butter from a cooperative made up of women from thirteen villages in northern Ghana. 'Trade has changed the status of women in these communities. Because they now have a livelihood, they can pay for books and uniforms for their children ... can call on a health worker when they're ill.'[31]

Alternative trade is ripe for considerable expansion. 'I have seen dozens of fair-trade projects at work in the South, and in every single one of them the benefits were not in question', says David Ransom; 'merely why there wasn't more of it and what could be done to make it bigger. Though fair trade may be an infant among giants, the future lies with the infant, not the giant.'[32] The infant is growing up fast and offers real hope in the task of combating corporate-driven globalization.

The alternative to the flying food scandal

Living in Burkina Faso at a time when West Africa was gripped by drought, a BBC correspondent, Alex Kirby, noticed strawberries sitting on a runway, ready for flying to Paris. Grown in a country where people were starving, the strawberries were flown out several times a week, 'to titilate the jaded palates of the wealthy North.... Developing countries need to be able to sell their goods abroad. But growing nonessential crops to be flown thousands of miles to markets which name their own price is a fragile way of doing it.'[33]

This practice is widespread. Much of the food on European tables has travelled several thousand miles to get there. The trade is part of corporate-driven globalization and is an affront to the hungry. The easy availability of air transport has encouraged the growth of export crops – including fruit and vegetables, and also flowers. Exports such as these distort a developing country's agricultural economy, encouraging small farmers to participate in growing crops for export rather than food crops for local needs. The farmers often realize too late that the prices they receive for these crops are lower than the cost of producing them.

While consumers in the West have become used to unseasonable food on the supermarket shelves, the real cost is hidden. Flying food uses about forty times the amount of fuel used by sea transport. It gives consumers the benefit of 'out of season' fruits but at a heavy cost in terms of fuel and the environment. 'The real cost of food miles madness are seldom reflected in the price of food', says Hugh Raven of the UK-based NGO, SAFE Alliance. Those costs include 'diverting land in food-deficit countries from producing food for local consumption into crops for export as with soya production in Brazil'.[34] The further that food has travelled, the less sustainable and the less environmentally friendly it is.

Under a 'Food Miles' campaign, activists in the North are calculating the distance that food has travelled and opting whenever possible for foods that have travelled a shorter distance. 'Consumers have begun to question the way in which their food is produced', says Sustain, the NGO behind the campaign in the UK.[35] The campaign could help to cut down on food imports which have travelled vast distances, and is doing a great deal more besides. It is challenging the whole notion of food being grown in countries where there is considerable hunger and being traded, usually by the corporations, to feed the already well-fed. This is obnoxious South–North trade. Consumer power is again an important part of ending this scandal.

The search for alternatives has been enormously stimulated by the failures of corporate-led globalization and the insensitivity of powerful institutions such as the World Bank and the WTO. The struggle against TNCs and implementation of alternatives are gathering pace as people across the world find their voice and discover their role.

Local fight-back in Bolivia

People in local communities are fighting back against globalization. The people of Cochabamba in Bolivia, for example, have taken back their water from the hands of a corporation.

In 1999 the World Bank pressurized the Bolivian government into privatizing water companies. The Bank refused credit to the public company which ran the water services, recommended 'no public subsidies' to cushion against price hikes, and insisted on giving a monopoly to Aguas del Tunari, part of the British company International Water Ltd, in turn owned by the US engineering giant Bechtel. The new owners, who had been granted a forty-year concession, announced price hikes before they even began operations; in a region where the minimum wage is under US$100 per month, people faced increases of US$20 per month and more.

People had to buy permits to collect rainwater from their own wells and roof tanks. Many people could only get water for two hours a day. All autonomous water systems had to be handed over without compensation. In response, thousands became involved in a campaign to save their water – old and young, seasoned activists, the employed, the unemployed, and those usually too busy surviving to get politically involved.

Many of them came from comfortable backgrounds. At the barricades they met people from all walks of life. Resisting offers from political parties, which arrived bearing gifts of money, they formed the Coordinadora – Coordination for the Defence of Water and Life. This is a unique coalition of labour activists, rural organizations, coca growers, politicians, non-governmental organizations, local professionals and young people.

The Coodinadora organized the first protest in December 1999, when 20,000 people occupied the central plaza. The government then used teargas against people for the first time in eighteen years. For two months no one paid their water bills. Then in February, when negotiations broke down, the Coordinadora called for a symbolic seizure of the central square, the plaza. This time, 30,000 turned up. Police fired on the crowd: 175 people were injured and two youths were blinded. In April, 30,000 people were again in the plaza when martial law was declared. A state of siege was imposed; crack military units were sent in.

Television cameras focused on a man on bent knee, rifle pointed, eye in the sights, in civilian clothes. He was an army captain shooting into the demonstrators. One of them said: 'I became aware of sharpshooters pointing at my face, and then I felt the shots near me; there are three bullet holes in the flag I was carrying. More than one person fell.' A 17-year-old boy was killed; many more were injured. People were incensed. There were now more than 80,000 in the streets. The official line was that the protesters were drug traffickers. Indignant old ladies blockading the streets said: 'What, us, drug dealers?'

The company made a rapid exit from the country. La Coordinadora talked with a government delegation and they agreed that the water contract should be broken. The water is now controlled by the people. The company, meanwhile, is suing the Bolivian government for loss of the profits that it would have made.

If the WTO's GATS is tightened in a way that makes privatization irreversible (see Chapter 9) it would not be possible for a government to go back on its decision. The power of people to make their views known would be curtailed.

Source: Based on Marcela López Levy, 'The damn water is ours', *New Internationalist*, September 2001.

I I

Conclusion:
the urgency of alternatives

> There is a time for everything ... a time to tear down, a
> time to build.
>
> *Ecclesiastes* 3

In 1999, 51 of the world's 100 largest economies were corporations, 49 were governments, according to the UK's Institute for
Policy Studies. To put this in perspective, General Motors is bigger than Denmark and over three times the size of New Zealand;
the top 200 corporations' combined sales are bigger than the
combined economies of all countries except the largest ten. Size
matters. It is size, with the protection afforded by company law
and governments, that gives corporations power to make the rules
and that encourages their arrogance. It is size that makes them
believe that they have a divine right to rule through globalization.

When ministers and officials attended the WTO ministerial
meeting in Seattle in 1999 they were each given a complimentary
bag which contained, among other things, an umbrella. The
umbrella might have kept off the rain, although it could not
shield ministers from the tear gas that police fired in the air in a
futile attempt in keep protesters in order. But the umbrella is
unusual. Inside is a map of the world with the words 'Seattle
Round' printed on the northwest coast of the United States.

The words were premature and symptomatic. There is no Seattle

Round. No round was launched. But corporate America – Seattle-based Microsoft and Boeing helped to organize corporate lobbying of ministers – fully expected that a new round of talks to liberalize international trade would be kick-started in the city. It was wrong: the free-trade juggernaut was derailed and the 'Seattle Round' was stillborn. The assumption that a round would be launched illustrates the way that TNCs think they rule the world.

The corporate world expects economic globalization to continue. 'The system presents itself as eternal', Eduardo Galeano, one of Latin American's foremost writers, told the first World Social Forum; 'the power system tells us that tomorrow is another word for today'. People around the world are saying in this book: you are wrong. For the sake of the world's most vulnerable people you have to be wrong; there are alternatives that work.

The need for alternatives is more urgent than policymakers seem to imagine. In the early twenty-first century, the world economic system is tottering, hanging on to a precarious existence. At best the present system might muddle through; at worst it will collapse. Whatever happens, alternatives are needed.

Alternatives can come in gradually or they can be needed quickly as a result of something going catastrophically wrong. When a system is unstable it cannot take shocks. A series of economic shocks, corruption scandals, 9/11, served to shake confidence in the system in 2001. But it wasn't just big shocks. Investor confidence was already ebbing. In early 2000 a leading *Financial Times* share index stood at just under 7,000. In January 2003 it was around 3,700. Nor was it only companies like Enron and WorldCom whose shares collapsed. Shares in companies once considered rock-solid, 'blue chip', have taken a hammering.[1]

'Our present economic system is inherently unstable and is heading not just for recession, but for very serious breakdown', believes Harry Shutt. Signs of these imbalances and market failures are all around. Economic and financial globalization have exacerbated the plight of Third World and former Communist countries. There is growing popular disgust in Western countries about the destructive impact of World Bank/International Monetary Fund structural adjustment policies on poor countries, and at the influence of the big corporations over official policy – 'their ability to buy the political process', says Shutt. The world's leadership is in thrall to corporate America and 'appears to resemble the doomed Soviet Union in its final phase', and the United States in particular persists in trying to impose 'unworkable solutions' such as free trade on developing countries.[2]

Argentina is a country in shock, a country cruelly failed by the international system. Argentina has taken IMF advice, liberalized fast – much faster than most other Latin American countries – and borrowed heavily. By 2001, it could not repay its US$140 billion of foreign debt and the economy virtually collapsed, causing millions to lose their jobs and bringing financial chaos to millions more. The currency lost most of its value, and people could only watch as the value of their savings sank. The ability of the international financial system to cope was tested and failed. Mismanagement of the Argentinian economy by successive governments was a factor, but so also was the IMF. By September 2002, the country was threatening not to repay its foreign debt from hard currency reserves, a move that could have serious implications for the global financial markets.[3] Crisis was averted when Argentina was allocated about $6.8 billion in credit from the IMF, in January 2003, so that it could repay the Fund for past loans. It smacked of a short-term fix that did not address the underlying problems.

Today Argentina. The global economy tomorrow? Unless alternatives to corporate-driven globalization are accepted and phased in, the global economy is heading for a crash and it will be the poor who suffer most.

Democracy

If there is one overriding theme that comes out of the alternatives in this book it is the need for greater democracy – genuine democracy. Especially since 1990, democracy has become the norm in developing countries, notably in sub-Saharan Africa. Political democracy has not, however, brought the anticipated boost to economic and social development. But then the democracy has been limited. While millions more people now have a say in the polling booths, they have no say over the economic systems and institutions which affect their lives.

The international trading system, on which corporate-driven globalization depends, is profoundly undemocratic. It is corporations and the international finance institutions that rule, not governments. Western governments seem trapped by the very IFIs they set up. These pages contain many examples of the changes that are needed for greater democracy.

In many developing countries there is a high level of corruption. In Western countries, corruption takes a different form – the political democratic process has been corrupted by market forces. The mainstream political parties in Western countries are seen as being in the pockets of big business. People are not fooled: they are deserting the mainstream political parties in droves.

Since the mid-1980s membership of political parties in European Union countries has almost halved. Party members have become aware of how little influence they can exert on the policies of their parties, and of how little influence their parties have, of the limited difference they make when in government.

Even governments supposed to be reformist have disappointed. 'All over the world, citizens have worked to elect social democratic and workers parties, only to watch them plead impotence in the face of market forces and IMF dictates. In these conditions, modern activists are not so naive as to believe change will come from the ballot box', says Naomi Klein.[4] Such a dangerous position has arisen because of the failure of politicians to understand the true nature of corporate-driven globalization.

In Western Europe, electors are abandoning their support for political parties in both membership and at the polling booths.

Voter turnout in national elections in the UK has dropped steadily over the past forty years. In the 2001 general election, only 59 per cent of the electorate voted, compared with 71 per cent in 1997 and 77 per cent in 1964. People may write to and lobby their Members of Parliament on corporate-driven globalization but there's little or no evidence that it has any effect.

Losing faith in the conventional political process, millions have switched to non-violent direct action NGOs such as Greenpeace and Friends of the Earth. In this way they believe their voices can be heard more effectively, and that they can help change to come more quickly. And it will be change that people have worked for themselves, not tossed to them by governments like crumbs from a rich man's table. The Gandhian principle of non-violent direct action is often evoked. This is based on *Ahimsa.* While this means non-violence 'it is also an active engagement in compassion … Ahimsa implies that our systems of production, trade and consumption should be small and controllable, not dominant and destructive – of societies, the environments and other life forms'.[5]

Related Gandhian concepts of *Swadeshi Satyagra* and *Swaraj* are also valid today in the struggle again the economic colonization of corporate-driven globalization. Swadeshi is a spirit of regeneration and economic freedom. 'According to Swadeshi philosophy, everybody possesses both materially and morally what they need to design their own society and free themselves of oppressive structures.' Satyagra means 'the struggle for truth' and is the 'key to self-rule, or Swaraj'.[6]

In Western Europe, many have switched to Green parties that are not afraid to tackle corporate power or the IFIs. The rise of these parties gives cause for hope; they can be expected to win more support as people see that the mainstream parties are not tackling one of the major issues of our time. A yawning gap is being left that mainstream parties ignore at their peril. Any democratic party needs to believe in economic democracy, part of which means effective control over the corporations and the IFIs.

As TNCs have huge power over people's lives, citizens deserve a say in the way these corporations are run. There is a strong case for changing company law so that limited liability companies are responsible not just to their shareholders, but to the public as a whole. If the directors of TNCs believe in democracy they should support, not block, such a move.

IFIs such as the World Bank and the IMF may, in theory, be run by Western governments, but in practice they seem to do much as they please – again a thwarting of democracy. One of the biggest public lobbies in recent years was for debt cancellation (see Chapter 9). In the UK, Chancellor of the Exchequer Gordon Brown made all the right noises and seemed personally committed to the cause. 'The UK government continues to be at the forefront of the international debate on debt relief issues, and has repeatedly pushed for the process to be speeded up.'[7]

Yet the pushing has been to no avail. There has been no quickening of the pace on debt cancellation at the World Bank and the IMF. The influence even of a committed, high-level government minister was minimal. It was Bank and Fund officials who were in the driving seat. Western governments seem incapable of standing up to, not just to the TNCs, but even the IMF and the World Bank, which they are supposed to own – a veritable corruption of the democratic process.

To curtail the power of the corporate sector, it seems advisable to limit corporate size, to allow corporations to be active in only one economic sector, or, in the case of foodstuffs, only one part of the food chain. No patents on life forms, including plants, should be allowed. This would make TNCs less dominant, removing a key part of agribusiness corporate power. 'Monopoly' power needs to be considered from a much wider perspective than it is at present. No TNC should be permitted to have monopoly power over small farmers. TNCs should not be permitted to run basic services, such as health care and education. The US-based Program on Corporations, Law and Democracy

(POCLAD) recommends that corporations 'should be prohibited from owning stock in other corporations'.[8]

Huge public pressure – in the form of non-violent direct action, or through the party process – is needed to persuade governments, especially of Western countries, to wake up to how corporate-driven globalization is failing; to persuade them to tackle the injustice that lies at the heart of the system and to urge them to encourage and not to thwart alternatives. Governments need to remove the factors that stand in the way of people in developing countries implementing their own alternatives.

Sustainable development

Sustainable development has become the buzz term of our age. Yet TNCs fail the sustainable development tests. Their interest lies in maximizing profits in the short term, not necessarily sustaining them over the long term. Shareholders want their dividends, this year. Companies have to deliver, in the short term.

Corporate-driven globalization is also inherently unsustainable as it relies on ever-increasing amounts of goods being flown around the world. The energy requirements seem too great for long-distance transport to be compatible with sustainable development. As Peter Fleming points out, energy shortages can be expected to lead to destabilized and interrupted oil supplies.

The destabilizing nature of globalization is belatedly being recognized in the United States. Globalization 'is a profoundly disruptive force for governments to manage ... many of the politically and economically rigid Arab countries are feeling many of globalization's stresses, especially on the cultural front, without reaping the economic benefits', said the director of the US Central Intelligence Agency, George Tenet, in February 2003.[9] That would be true of the great majority of developing countries, rigid or flexible.

Corporate-driven globalization also looks unsustainable because it resembles economic totalitarianism that centralizes power – a mirror image of Communism. Like Communism, it seems more and more like a phase through which the world is being forced to pass. Devinder Sharma suggests that globalization will not survive because it is built on the exploitation of the poor. And the forces behind globalization are not as solid as they might seem. 'The mighty forces driving globalization are surely impervious to the petty aggravation of street protests.... Certainly one would have hoped so, but it is proving otherwise.'[10]

It is proving otherwise because protesters have the stronger arguments, because the alternatives are growing in credibility, range and scope. At the Johannesburg summit on sustainable development, in 2002, world leaders ended with a statement that said: 'Fundamental change in the way societies produce and consume are indispensable.'

The changes run deeper than leaders appear to expect. Both the concept and the word 'globalization' should be dropped. The word is ambiguous, tainted and discredited, a dirty word among those who are globalized. It is little use the globalizers talking about making it work for the poor. The mindset that created corporate-driven globalization is in no position to offer a solution. Corporate-led globalization, with its uniform 'one-size-fits-all' philosophy is proving, in J.K. Galbraith's words, to be 'not a serious concept'. Rather it is being shown up as an impostor. In the words of Shakespeare's Macbeth, it may turn out to be a 'brief candle ... a poor player, that struts and frets his hour upon the stage, and then is heard no more ... a tale told by an idiot, full of sound and fury...'

A key question is how to make the global economy work for the poor. It is the global economy which can and must be radically changed to remove corporate domination, to allow the poor to breathe and have a chance. It is the international economy which is a fact, not corporate-driven globalization. If Western governments are willing to break free from corporate control and stop parroting the corporate line, they just might find that making the international economy work for the poor is also what non-governmental organizations want. This is a bridge between the two. It would need, however, to be an international economy with very different rules and practices, allowing for many alternatives, a diverse and not a single system. Only then can the poor share in the benefits.

Instead of a monolithic system governed by the free-trade ideology, an alternative system might be seen as a large jigsaw, containing many different pieces. All the pieces are needed to enable the full picture to emerge. It is little use poor farmers organizing locally, for example, if WTO/World Bank/IMF rules act against them. Action needs to be taken in a number of mutually reinforcing ways if the power of the corporations is to be tackled. The alternatives jigsaw will have room for flexibility; it will not be rigid and dogmatic as is the existing system, but have multiple checks and balances, based on people's values, rhythms, and strategies of their choosing.

The kind of world that millions want to see would devolve the greater part of production, trade and economic decision-making to the national and local levels; it would put development policy above trade policy, giving the poor priority – developing an economic system that would give the poor entitlements to food, for example. International trade is part of the jigsaw, but only a part, a piece marked 'fair' and pro-poor rather than 'free'. Corporations just may be a piece of that jigsaw but they would look very different from the TNCs of today – small, accountable, non-threatening and genuinely democratic.

Hope

Running through this book are messages of hope, that alternatives can work. Many are of course radical. But, in the words of British prime minister Tony Blair: 'the radical decision is usually the right one. The right decision is usually the hardest one. The starting point is not policy. It's hope.'[11] The hope is that changes to the global economic order are coming.

Change may appear to happen only slowly. But when people come to an understanding of their true values, when human well-being is considered more important than corporate profit, then change could be dramatically quick. 'The flash point of change will be that moment when we come to a new understanding of what we truly are.... When change comes, it comes like lightning.'[12]

Understanding is growing, values are shifting, changes are coming and could be sudden and dramatic. The alternatives are turning upside down the world of corporate-dominated globalization. If we are prepared for it, we shall be better able to handle it.

ANNEX

Sources on alternative ideas and campaigning social movements

Action Group on Erosion, Technology and Concentration (ETC)

Formerly Rural Advancement Foundation International (Canada). Supports socially responsible development of technologies useful to the poor.
www.etcgroup.org

AgBioIndia, the Forum for Biotechnology and Food Security (India)

Information on food and related issues.
www.agbioindia.org

ATTAC (France)

International network of citizens campaigning for democratic control of financial markets.
www.attac.org

Campaign Strategy (UK)

Has 'modest suggestions for anyone trying to save the world'.
www.campaignstrategy.org

Centre for Development Alternatives (India)

Tamil Nadu-based NGO working on alternatives.
www.cfdachennai.org

Centre for Environment and Society, University of Essex (UK)

Database with case studies on sustainable agriculture.
www.essex.ac.uk/centres.ces

Coalition against Bayer-dangers (Germany)

Focuses on Bayer.
www.CBGnetwork.org

Corpwatch (USA)

Keeps watch on transnational corporations.
www.corpwatch.org

Corporate Watch (UK)

Provides information on corporate issues.
www.corporatewatch.org.uk

Development Alternatives Information Network (India)

Information system for sustainable development in the Indian
subcontinent.
www.dainet.org

Development Alternatives with Women for a New Era
(DAWN) (Fiji)

Deals with the priorities of women's and civil society organizations;
helps strengthen capacity to deal with issues arising from the
impacts of globalization.
www.dawn.org.fj

Earth Policy Institute (USA)

Provides 'a vision of what an environmentally sustainable economy
will look like'.
www.earth-policy.org

Fairtrade Foundation (UK)

Alternative trade initiatives, including the Fairtrade Mark.
www.fairtrade.org.uk

Focus on Trade, website of **Focus on the Global South**
(Thailand)

Autonomous programme of policy research and action of the
Chulalongkorn University Social Research Institute, Bangkok.
Particular focus on the impact of trade and the WTO on
developing countries.
www.focusweb.org

Food First (US)

Alternative ideas for achieving food security.
www.foodfirst.org

Food Miles (UK)

Encourages people to think about how many miles their food has travelled.
www.sustainweb.org/chain_fm_index.asp

Friends of the Earth (FoE)

Campaigns for improvements to 'the conditions for life on Earth'.
www.foe.org

Global Exchange (USA)

Aims to help build an 'international grassroots movement that puts people before profits'.
www.globalexchange.org

Greenpeace International

An international organization 'that uses peaceful activity to protect the global environment'.
www.greenpeace.org

Independent Media Center (Indymedia) (USA)

A collective of independent media organizations and journalists offering grassroots, non-corporate coverage 'for the creation of radical, accurate and passionate tellings of truth'.
www.indymedia.org

Institute for Agriculture and Trade Policy (IATP) (USA)

Keeps track of the latest developments.
www.iatp.org

Intermediate Technology Development Group (ITDG) (UK)

Promotes small-scale, alternative technologies.
www.itdg.org

International Baby Food Action Network (IBFAN).

Researches abuses of the WHO code on the marketing of breast-milk substitutes.
www.babymilkaction.org

International Federation for Alternative Trade (IFAT)

Global federation promoting fair trade, social justice, and the sustainable livelihoods of Third World farmers, artisans and crafts producers.
www.ifat.org/dwr

International Forum on Globalization (IFG)

An alliance of activists, scholars, economists, researchers and writers, representing 60 organizations in 25 countries.
www.ifg.org

International Institute for Environment and Development (IIED) (UK)

Promotes sustainable patterns of development through research, policy studies, networking and knowledge dissemination.
www.iied.org

Jubilee Research (UK)

Successor organization to the Jubilee 2000 Coalition.
www.jubileeresearch.org

KMP Peasant Movement of the Philippines

Movement of peasant farmers.
www.geocities.com/kmp_ph

LETSystem (USA)

Local money system.
www.gmlets.u-net.com

McSpotlight

Puts McDonald's under the spotlight.
web: www.mcspotlight.org

Movement of the Landless (MST) (Brazil)

Leading grassroots movement for agrarian reform.
www.mstbrazil.org

New Economics Foundation (UK)

Alternative ideas for new economies.
www.neweconomics.org

One World.net

Several hundred organizations, many concerned with alternatives, are listed.
www.oneworld.net

Permaculture.net (USA)

Permaculture is a design system that reconciles human communities with ecological imperatives. For farmers it is an alternative system of agriculture.
www. permaculture.net

People for Fair Trade (USA)

Works against 'corporate globalization and for trade laws which protect people's right to safety, health, a sustainable environment and democratically enacted laws'.
www.peopleforfairtrade.org

Peoples' Global Action

Network of radical grassroots groups.
www.agp.org

StopEsso (UK)

Information on the campaign to stop buying Esso petrol.
www.stopesso.com

Third World Network (Malaysia)

Wide-ranging information on globalization issues.
www.twnside.org.sg

Time Dollars (USA)

Local money system.
www.timedollar.org

Tobin Tax

Campaign for an international tax on currency movements.
www.waronwant.org

Trade Justice Movement (UK)

Network of NGOs campaigning to change the rules of international trade to benefit the poor.
www.tradejusticemovement.org.uk

Transnational Institute (Netherlands)

Worldwide fellowship of scholar-activists, seeking 'to create and promote international cooperation in analysing and finding possible solutions to such global problems as militarism and conflict, poverty and marginalization, social injustice and environmental degradation'.
www.worldcom.nl

Via Campesina

International movement which coordinates peasant organizations of small and middle-scale producers, agricultural workers, rural women and indigenous communities.
www.viacampesina.org

World Bank Bonds Boycott (USA)

A campaign to cut off World Bank funds at source.
www.worldbankboycott.org

World Development Movement (WDM) (UK)

Campaigns on development and poverty issues.
www.wdm.org.uk

World Social Forum

Groundbreaking international forum for alternatives.
www.forumsocialmundial.org.br

WTO Watch (USA)

Operated by IATP as above. Includes the former 'Trade
Observatory'.
www.wtowatch.org

Notes

Chapter 1

1. Madeline Bunting, 'Dam buster', *Guardian*, 28 July 2001.
2. William Pfaff, 'The West's globalisation drive is proving a massive failure', *International Herald Tribune*, 29 September 2000.
3. Percy Barnervik, Asean Brown Boveri, quoted in Percy Makombe, 'Transnational companies must be made accountable', *Financial Gazette* (Harare), 16 January, 2003.
4. Charles Reed, ed., *Development Matters: Christian Perspectives on Globalisation*, London: Board for Social Responsibility/Church House Publishing, 2001, p. 6.
5. Most people were asked by email. Some I interviewed personally at the World Trade Organisation ministerial meeting in Doha, November 2001, and at the 'World Food Summit – Five Years Later' meeting in Rome in June 2002. Some contributors did not offer a definition. A strict North–South divide was not possible. Some contributors are from the South but work for organizations in the North, and vice versa. Nico Verhagen is based in Europe but is included as a Southern voice, as he is giving the view of Via Campesina, a movement of peasant farmers largely, although not only, from the South. Views expressed are the views of the contributors and not of the organization they work for.
6. *Eliminating World Poverty: Making Globalisation Work for the Poor*, UK Government White Paper Cm 5006, London: HMSO, December 2000.
7. 'Making globalization work for the poor', *Finance & Development*, March 2002, Washington DC: IMF.
8. George Soros, quoted in Faisal Islam, 'Soros: "May day protesters

do have a point"', *Observer*, 6 May 2001.

9. I am indebted to Malcolm Rodgers of Christian Aid for the notion that we should break down globalization into the 'globalizers' and the 'globalized'.

10. *World Investment Report 2002*, New York/Geneva: United Nations, 2002, p. xv.

11. See *Crops and Robbers*, London: Action Aid, 2001.

12. Eric Schlosser, *Fast Food Nation*, London: Allen Lane, 2001, p. 261.

13. United Nations Development Programme, *Human Development Report 1999*, New York: Oxford University Press, p. 30.

14. UNICEF staff working papers, No. EPP-00-00, January 2000. See Walden Bello, John Cavanagh, Michael Chossudovsky, Victoria Tauli-Corpus, Martin Khor, Bruce Rich and Vandana Shiva, *Does Globalization Help the Poor? A Special Report*, San Francisco: International Forum on Globalization, 2000.

15. United Nations, *The Least Developed Countries Report 2002*, New York/Geneva: UNCTAD, 2002, p. iii.

16. Speeches to the World Trade Organization ministerial meeting, Geneva, May 1998.

17. International Forum on Globalization, *Alternatives to Economic Globalization: A Better World is Possible*, San Francisco: Berrett–Koehler, 2002.

18. See John Madeley, 'Poor rail at free trade', *Independent on Sunday*, 1 March 1998.

19. Speech to a meeting in London, April 1998.

20. Joseph Stiglitz, 'The disastrous consequences of a world without balance', *Financial Times*, 23 September 2002.

Chapter 2

1, Caroline Lucas and Colin Hines, *Time to Replace Globalisation*, The Greens/European Free Alliance, European Parliament, 2001.

Chapter 3

1, Mike Davis, *Late Victorian Holocausts: El Niño Famines and the Making of the Third World*, London: Verso, 2001.

2. Ibid.

Chapter 7

1. UNCTC leaflet, DESI E. 130, New York: UNCTC, 1986.

2. E. von Bern, *The Infiltration of the UN System by Multinational*

Corporations, Zurich: Association pour un Développement Solidaire, 1978.

3. See website: globalcompact.un.org.
4. 'Global Compact: official engagement of UN and big business', *People, Planet and Prosperity*, A Seed Europe magazine (Amsterdam), August 2002,
5. Tony Juniper, 'Smoke screen', *Guardian*, 31 July 2002.
6. 'Corporations Behaving Badly', *Multinational Monitor*, Washington, December 2001. The other companies listed were Abbott (pharmaceuticals), Argenbright (security), Coca-Cola, Enron, ExxonMobil, Philip Morris, Sara Lee, Wal-Mart and Southern (utilities).
7. Website: www.ibfan.org/english/news/press/press30oct02.html.
8. See Judith Richter, *Dialogue or Engineering of Consent*, Geneva: IBFAN-GIFA, 2002.
9. Martin Khor, *Corporate Accountability*, Penang: Third World Network, September 2002.
10. WSSD Declaration, September 2002, paragraph 45.
11. The UN-related agency, the International Labour Organization, has set up a World Commission on the Social Dimension of Globalization 'to respond to the needs of people coping with the unprecedented changes that globalization has brought to their lives and their communities'. The Commission – co-chaired by President Tara Halonen of Finland and President Benjamin Mkapa of Tanzania – is expected to report in 2003.
12. International Forum on Globalization, *Alternatives to Economic Globalization: A Better World is Possible*, San Francisco: Berrett–Koehler, 2002, pp. 131–40.
13. Richter, *Dialogue or Engineering of Consent*.
14. See website: www.foe.co.uk.
15. Gabrielle Palmer, *The Politics of Breastfeeding*, London: Pandora Press, 1988, p. 237.
16. Update, *Baby Milk Action Newsletter*, July 2002.
17. Ibid.
18. *Human Development Report 1999*, New York: UNDP, 1999, p. 100.
19. Ibid.
20. *Britain: The Preferred Location – An Introduction for Investors*, Invest in Britain Bureau, London: Department of Trade and Industry, 1993, p. 7.
21. Richter, *Dialogue or Engineering of Consent*.
22. *Master or Servant?*, London: Christian Aid, 2001, pp. 37, 45.
23. Ibid, pp. 42–3.
24. *Alternatives to Economic Globalization*.
25. See David Bollier, 'Common sense: community ownership and the

displacement of corporate control', and Patrick Bond, 'An answer to marketization: decommodification and the assertion of rights to essential services', *Multinational Monitor*, July/August 2002, Washington DC: Essential Information.

26. Richard Holme, 'Giants tread carefully', *Guardian*, 7 August 2002.
27. Quoted in Anita Roddick, *Take it Personally*, London: Thorsons, 2001, p. 30.
28. Naomi Klein, 'Welcome to the net generation' in ibid., p. 35.
29. 'Genetically modified crops – thinking global, acting local', *The Ecologist*, May/June 1999, p. 205.
30. Patrick Tooher, 'Iceland boss reaps GM ban rewards', *Daily Telegraph*, 22 April 1999.
31. HRH Prince of Wales, 'Seeds of disaster', *Daily Telegraph*, 8 June 1998.
32. John Ingham, 'U-turn by genetic food firm', *Daily Express*, 8 July 1998.
33. 'Supermarket goes GM-free', *Financial Times*, 20 July 1999.
34. 'Modified products banned by three fast food chains', *Financial Times*, 8 March 1999.
35. Terry Slavin, 'Testing times for firms that say no to gene foods', *Observer*, 7 March 1999.
36. McSpotlight website: www.mcspotlight.org.
37. Eric Schlosser, *Fast Food Nation*, London: Allen Lane, 2001.
38. McSpotlight website.
39. Lawrence Donegal and Paul Webster, 'McTrouble', *Observer*, 20 October 2002.
40. 'Burgers off', *Guardian*, 9 November 2002.
41. StopEsso website: www.stopesso.com.
42. Ibid.
43. See Terry Macalister, 'Greenpeace hails Deutsche warning', *Guardian*, 11 October 2002.
44. Website: www.babymilkaction.org.
45. Coalition against Bayer-dangers, website: www.CBGnetwork.org.
46. Ibid.
47. See *Crops and Robbers*, London: ActionAid, 2001.
48. *Human Development Report 1999*.
49. *Crops and Robbers*.
50. Website: www.eccr.org.
51. John Madeley, 'Unsuitable for use – profile of paraquat', *Pesticide News* 56, June 2002.

Chapter 8

1. See Debi Barker and Jerry Mander, *Invisible Government – The World Trade Organization: Global Government for the New Millennium?*, San

Francisco: International Forum on Globalization, 2001.

2. Speech to a meeting at the Royal Institute of International Affairs, London, January 1998.

3. Statement to the second WTO ministerial meeting, May 1998.

4. Communication to author.

5. Tony Clarke, *By What Authority!* Polaris Institute and the International Forum on Globalization, n.d.

6. See *The World Investment Report 2002*, New York and Geneva: UNCTAD, 2002.

7. Myriam Vander Stichele, speech to NGO meeting in Geneva, May 1998.

8. Kevin Watkins, 'Global market myths', *Red Pepper*, June 1996, p. 14.

9. *Human Rights and Economic Globalization: Directions for the World Trade Organisation*, New York: PDHRE, November 1999.

10. The Zanzibar Declaration of least-developed countries, July 2001.

11. Naomi Klein, speech in London, November 2001.

12. Thomas Chafunya, 'WTO throws out Africa's request', *Daily Times* (Malawi), 14 November 2001.

13. Five leading UK-based NGOs urged industrialized countries to sign 'a code of conduct' pledging that would not use economic and diplomatic threats and bribes during the trade talks. (Press release 9 November 2001). Industrialized countries declined to make such pledges.

14. Comments at press conference in Doha, November 2001.

15. Conversation with the author, November 2001.

16. Conversation with the author, November 2001.

17. Mark Curtis, Christian Aid, conversation with the author, November 2001.

18. Conversation with the author, November 2001.

19. Conversation with the author, November 1999.

20. Amy L. Kazmin, 'WTO chief urges India to back new trade talks', *Financial Times*, 11 January 2000,

21. *Master or Servant? How Global Trade Rule Can Work to the Benefit of Poor People*, London: Christian Aid, 2001, p. 2.

22. The World Development Movement is running a vigorous campaign in opposition to the GATS. See website: www.wdm.org.uk.

23. *Trade Justice*, London: Christian Aid, 2002, p. 27.

24. WDM website.

25. Luke Eric Peterson, 'Dusted-off trade treaties ensure there is no such thing as a free riot', *Guardian*, 6 May 2002.

26. *Farmgate: The Developmental Impact of Agricultural Subsidies*, London: ActionAid, 2002.

27. Jean-Bertrand Aristide, *Eyes of the Heart: Seeking a Path for the Poor*

in the Age of Globalization, Monroe, ME: Common Courage Press, 2000.

28. See John Madeley, *Hungry for Trade*, London: Zed Books. 2000, ch. 5.
29. WTO website: www:wto.org.
30. Walden Bello, 'The Oxfam debate: from controversy to common strategy', Focus on the Global South, Bangkok, May 2002, website: www.focusweb.org.

Chapter 9

1. Britain's Chancellor of the Exchequer, Gordon Brown, speech to a Jubilee 2000 meeting in London, 7 March 1999.
2. Many NGOs and writers on debt take 1982 as the start of the Third World debt crisis: the year that Mexico announced a moratorium on its foreign debt. By the mid-1970s, however, the debt problem had become a significant factor.
3. Quoted in Joseph Hanlon and John Garrett, *Crumbs of Comfort*, London: Jubilee 2000 Coalition, 1999.
4. See John Madeley, 'Third World pressures at Nairobi', *Round Table*, London, October 1976.
5. See John Madeley and Geoff Tansey, *Your Money or Your Lifestyle*, London: Christian Aid, 1978.
6. See John Madeley, 'Owing to forces beyond our control', *Development Forum*, March 1982, Geneva: United Nations, 1982; and Harold Lever and Christopher Huhne, *Debt and Danger: The World Financial Crisis*, Harmondsworth: Penguin, 1985.
7. John Garrett and Angela Travis, *Unfinished Business*, London: Jubilee 2000 Coalition, 1999.
8. Ghanaian MP Ben Turok, quoted in Linda Ensor, 'The real truth behind IMF–World Bank SAPs', *Business Day*, Johannesburg, 8 October 2002.
9. See John Madeley, *Hungry for Trade*, London: Zed Books, 2001.
10. See *World Development Report 1998/9*, Washington DC: World Bank, 1999.
11. Jacques B. Gélinas, *Freedom from Debt*, London: Zed Books, 1998, p. 43.
12. Hanlon and Garrett, *Crumbs of Comfort*; also Patricia Adams, *Odious Debts*, London: Earthscan, 1991.
13. David Tether and Larry Elliot, 'IMF shores up debt defences', *Guardian*, 30 September 2002.
14. *Human Development Report 1997*, New York: United Nations

Development Programme, 1997.

15. Speech to a meeting in London, September 2002.
16. Quoted in John Madeley. 'No end to shackles', *Observer*, 21 January 2001.
17. Stephen Devereux, *State of Disaster*, London: Action Aid, June 2002.
18. Press release, ActionAid, 14 June 2002.
19. www.jubileeresearch.org.
20. Madeley, 'No end to shackles'.
21. *HIPC Initiative: Status of Implementation*, Washington DC: World Bank/IMF, 16 August 2002. Analysis by Jubilee Research based on a draft of the report. See www.jubileeresearch.org/hipc/hipc_ news/ hipc290402.htm.
22. Ibid.
23. 'Still waiting for the Jubilee', Jubilee Debt Campaign, 2002.
24. Quoted in Hanlon and Garrett, *Crumbs of Comfort*.
25. Letter to MPs from Gordon Brown and Clare Short, 17 September 2002.
26. See 'Heavily Indebted Poor Countries Initiative – status of implementation', March 2002; and 'The Enhanced HIPC Initiative and the achievement of long term external debt sustainability', Washington DC: World Bank, 27 March 2002.
27. See 'HIPC – flogging a dead process', Jubilee Plus report, at www. jubileeresearch.org/analysis/reports/deadHIPCpdf
28. *Global Development Finance 2002*, Washington DC: World Bank, 2002.
29. Romilly Greenhill and Sasha Blackmore, *Relief Works: African Proposals for Debt Cancellation – and Why Debt Relief Works*, London: Jubilee Research, 2002.
30. NEPAD Capital Flows, May 2002, NEPAD Secretariat, website: www.nepad.org.
31. See website: http://allafrica.com/stories/200208050363.html.
32. Greenhill and Blackmore, *Relief Works*.
33. Speech to a meeting in London, September 2002.
34. Website: www.jubileeresearch.org.
35. Aristide, *Eyes of the Heart*.

Chapter 10

1. Kathy McAfee, 'Strategies for greater self-reliance', in *Storm Signals*, London: Zed Books, 1991, p. 159.
2. Colin Hines, *Localization: A Global Manifesto*, London: Earthscan, 2000, p. 239.
3. Caroline Lucas and Colin Hines, *Time to Replace Globalisation*, The Greens/European Free Alliance, European Parliament, 2001.

4. Website: www.localisation.ie.
5. Website: www.lisa.org.
6. 'Localization' is also a computing term. Sometimes shortened to '110n', it is the process of adapting a product or service to a particular language, culture, and desired local 'look-and-feel'. A product or service is developed 'so that localization is relatively easy to achieve – for example, by creating technical illustrations for manuals in which the text can easily be changed to another language and allowing some expansion room for this purpose'. See www.whatis.techtarget.com.
7. *World Development Report 1999/2000*, Washington DC: World Bank, 1999.
8. International Forum on Globalization, *Alternatives to Economic Globalization: A Better World is Possible*, San Francisco: Berrett–Koehler, 2002.
9. Richard Mahapatra, Prabhanjan Verma, Nidhi Jamwal and Kazimuddin Ahmed, 'The second independence', *Down to Earth*, New Delhi, 31 August 2002.
10. Cited in 'Cakes and caviar; the Dunkel Draft and Third World agriculture', *The Ecologist*, vol. 23, no. 6, November 1993, p. 220; and in Kevan Bundell, *Forgotten Farmers*, London: Christian Aid, June 2002.
11. See *Farmgate: The Developmental Impact of Agricultural Subsidies*, London: ActionAid, 2002; and *Dumping on the Poor*, London: CAFOD, 2002.
12. See Jules Pretty and Rachel Hine, *Feeding the World with Sustainable Agriculture: A Summary of New Evidence*; and *Safe-World Research Project, The Potential for Sustainable Agriculture to Feed the World*, University of Essex, 2000. www2.essex.ac.uk/ces/; Helena Norberg-Hodge, *Bringing the Food Economy Home: Local Alternatives to Global Agribusiness*, London: Zed Books, 2002; John Madeley, *Food for All: The Need for a New Agriculture*, London: Zed Books, 2002.
13. McAfee, *Storm Signals*, p. 163.
14. See *Rural Poverty Report 2001*, Rome: IFAD, 2001.
15. MST website: www.mstbrazil.org.
16. David Boyle, 'Time as currency' in Anita Roddick, *Take it Personally*, London: Thorsons, 2001, p. 216.
17. Communication to author. September 2002.
18. Website: www.gmlets.u-net.com.
19. Website: www.timedollar.org.
20. David Boyle, 'Learning from the supermarkets of Buenos Aires', London: *Town & Country Planning*, July/August 2001.
21. Ibid.
22. Website: www. trueque@eirelink.com.

23. Walter Truett Anderson, *Green Money: Local Currencies Filling a Niche in the Global Economy*, San Francisco: Pacific News Service, November 1999.
24. Website: www.schumachersociety.org.
25. Roddick, *Take it Personally*, p. 218.
26. See War on Want website (www.waronwant.org) for more details of the Tobin tax.
27. See UN Conference on Trade and Development, *Globalization and Liberalization*, New York/Geneva: UNCTAD, 1996, ch. 3.
28. See website: www.fairtrade.org.uk.
29. Website: www.ifat.org.
30. Website: www.rugmark.org.
31. Anita Roddick, foreword to *The No-nonsense guide to Fair Trade*, Oxford: New Internationalist, 2001.
32. Ibid., p. 124.
33. Alex Kirby, 'UNEP – turning aspirations into agreements', *The Courier*, Brussels: EU/ACP, July–August 2002.
34. *The Food Miles Report*, London: SAFE Alliance, 1994.
35. Sustain website: www. sustainweb.org.

Chapter 11

1. Between March 2000 and October 2002, for example, shares in the once-venerated media giant Reuters fell from 1600 pence to 160 pence – losing 90 per cent of their market value.
2. Harry Shutt, *A New Democracy: Alternatives to a Bankrupt World Order*. London, Zed Books, 2001.
3. Thomas Catan, 'Buenos Aires hits back at IMF attack on politicians', *Financial Times*, 25 September 2002.
4. Naomi Klein, *Fences and Windows*, London: Flamingo, 2002, p. 21.
5. Vandana Shiva, 'Reversing globalisation: what Gandhi can teach us', *The Ecologist*, May/June 1999, p. 225.
6. Ibid. p. 224.
7. Letter to author from UK Treasury official, 2 July 2002.
8. See website: www.poclad.org.
9. George J. Tenet. 'The worldwide threat in 2003: evolving dangers in a complex world', CIA briefing paper, 11 February 2003. Website: www.cia.gov
10. 'The case for globalization', *The Economist*, 23 September 2000.
11. Speech to Labour Party conference, September 2002.
12. Stephen Verney, *Into the New Age*, London: Fontana/Collins, 1976, pp. 29, 49.

Index

Abuja Declaration, 143
accountability, 116–17
Achebe, Chinua, 158
ActionAid, 12, 24, 42, 50, 156
Africa: debt in, 172; shrinking
    economy of, 41
Africa Gender and Trade Network,
    22, 36
agrarian reform, 183–4
AgrEvo company, 126
Agri-Health Initiative, 52
agriculture, 69, 71, 75, 86;
    campaigning required, 105;
    organic *see* organic agriculture;
    prices of, 74; to be taken out of
    WTO, 63, 68, 70, 74
agrochemicals, use of, 34
Aguas del Tunari, 199
alternative strategies, 177–201;
    urgency of, 202–11
Amnesty International, 132, 133
Andersen company, 101
Angola, 60
Annan, Kofi, 39, 114
anti-globalization, 3, 6, 11, 16, 93, 99,
    102
Anti-Globalization Network, 23,
    44
Antrobus, Peggy, 21, 43–4, 62
apartheid, 166

Argentina: economic crisis in, 48,
    204; local currencies in, 187–8
Aristide, Jean-Bertrand, 154, 174
arms trade, 58, 59
Asian Development Bank, 175
Asian financial crisis, 29, 48, 190
Association pour un Développement
    Solidaire, 113
AstraZeneca company, 133
Australia, 40; LETSystem in, 186
Aventis CropScience, 131

Baby Milk Action, 130
bananas, trade in, 138–9
Bangladesh, 91
Bangladesh People's Solidarity Centre
    (Belgium), 24, 58
bankruptcy of countries, 166
Barnet, Richard J., 6
basic needs, right to, 80
Baycol drug, 131
Bayer company, 114–15, 130–31
Bechtel company, 200
Bello, Walden, 12, 17, 37–8, 63, 155
Berger, John, 32
Berne Declaration, 133
biopiracy, 73
biotechnology, 31
Blair, Tony, 9, 145
Block, John, 181

Body Shop, 197
Boeing, 203
Bolivia, water privatization in, 150;
     campaign against, 199–201
Bono, 166
Bose, Manabe, 48, 63
Bové, José, 127
boycotting of corporations, 124, 130
Boyle, David, 185, 189
brands, global, 49
Brazil, 183; coffee production in,
     154–5; economic crisis in, 48–9
breastfeeding, stengthening of, 119–20
Bretton Woods system, 18, 159
Brimmer, Andrew, 159
Bristol Myers, 149
British South African Company, 6
Brown, Gordon, 207
Brown, Kathy-Ann, 52, 63
BSE crisis in Britain, 125
Bunzl, John, 26, 55–7, 77–9
Bush, George W., 128, 129

CAFOD, 22, 48, 194
capital flows, regulation of, 67
Cargill company, 134–5
Caribbean Association for Feminist
     Research and Action, 50
Caritas, 94
Catholic Church, 183
Central Sandinista de Trabajadores
     (Nicaragua), 10
centralism, economic, 38
Chalmers, Camille, 170
Chang, Ha-Joon, 18, 40, 66–7
child labour, 196, 197
China, 140; growth in, 41
Chiquita company, 139, 152
Christian Aid, 121, 122, 150, 151,
     165, 194
CIDSE, 94
Cipro drug, 130–31
citizenship, global, 95
civil society, 64
climate change, 102
Clinton, Bill, 9, 164
Coalition Against Bayer-dangers, 114,
     130

Coates, Barry, 21, 42, 79–81, 146,
     153
Coca-Cola company, 49
Cochabamba, fighting water
     privatization in, 199
coffee: fair trade, 193, 194; price of,
     51, 151–2, 173; volume of
     production of, 154
Cold War, 19
colonialism, 8, 39; globalization as,
     20–26
Common Agricultural Policy, 148
Communism, fall of, 41
community, longing for, 98
Comox Valley, LETSystem in, 185–6
comparative advantage, theory of, 46,
     47
competition, destructive, 55–7
concentration of political and
     economic power, 45
conditionalities, 98
Confederation of Education Workers
     (Argentina), 10
Congo, war in, 60
consumers, power of, 199
Consumers International, 17, 54,
     146
'contraction and convergence' model,
     104
cooperatives, 196, 197
Coordination for the Defence of
     Water and Life (Bolivia), 200–201
corporate charters, revocation of,
     117–18
corporate dismantling, 118
corporate domination, 42–7, 112–35,
     122; within WTO, 139–41
corporate mobility, limiting of, 123
corporate removal, 117
corporate responsibility, 116
Corporate Watch, 22, 36
corporations: control of, 179; liability
     of officers of, 123; personhood of,
     116, 118; power of, 121
     (excessive, 8)
corruption, 123, 203
cosmetics, tested on animals, 37
currencies: local, 185 (in Argentina,

187–8); Third World, 184 *see also* tabu currency

currency: controls on, 153; system of, and arms trade, 58; speculation in, 189–90; transaction tax, 101

Custers, Peter, 24, 58

customer. revolt, efficacy of, 124–31

cynicism, as form of violence, 32

Dabhol power plant, India, 121

Dan Church Aid, 25, 48

Davis, Mike, 27

debt, 12, 28, 168–9; cancellation of, 19, 35, 96, 101, 159, 160, 164, 165–6, 171, 173–6, 207; human cost of, 166–7; morality of, 172; odious, 166; relief of, 152, 158–76; servicing, 171 (costs of, 168)

decentralization, 84, 87–8, 109

decolonization, 32

deglobalization, 12

Demichelis, Alejandro, 10

democracy, 19, 28, 32, 56, 63, 65–6, 67, 70–71, 76, 77, 79, 80, 81, 95–6, 97, 103, 109, 116, 179–80, 196, 204–8, 207; economic, 206; global, 23; participatory, 11

Dent, Martin, 165

deregulation, 17, 43, 53–5, 120, 121

despair, prevalence of, 32

Development Box, in WTO, 146, 148

Development Alternatives with Women for a New Era (DAWN), 21, 43

Development Fund of Norway, 15, 45

diamond trade, 60

disparate exchange, 24–5, 58–61

diversity, 69, 96, 100; cultural, 105; disappearance of, 37–40; economic, 87; of culture, 29

Doha development agenda, 146

Doha meeting of WTO, 142–7

Dole company, 139

Dove, Fiona, 16–17, 43, 81

drought, 198

Du Pont company, 132, 149

dumping, 86, 156; prevention of, 73, 75

Durai, Jayanti, 17, 54–5, 63–4, 146

ecological accounts, 101

ecological debt, 104

e-commerce, 18

economies, separation between, 63

Ecumenical Council for Corporate Responsibility, 133

education, 34, 54, 65, 80, 95, 167, 169–70, 173, 197

Egypt, grain dumping in, 156

E.F. Schumacher Society, 189

11 September attacks, 94, 143, 203

El Niño, 27

El Salvador, agrarian reform in, 183

Emmett, Susie, 17, 57–8, 82

energy, generation and conservation of, 83

Enron, 86, 101, 116, 121, 154, 203

environmental issues, 19, 28, 29, 33, 44, 53, 72, 77, 100, 105, 117, 132, 151, 181

Equina, Pedro, 25, 48, 64–5

Esteva, Gustavo, 14, 18, 31, 65–6, 110

ethical issues of globalization, 93–5

Ethiopia, 162; agrarian reform in, 183

European Exchange Rate Mechanism, 190

European Union, 37, 49, 138, 143, 145, 148, 152, 156; policy on development cooperation, 94

Exchange Club (Argentina), 188

exchange, traditions of, 65

exchange controls, 86, 93

Export Credits Guarantees Department, 159

export crops, growing of, 198

extinction of species, 45

ExxonMobil (Esso) company, boycott of, 128–30

fair trade, 91; 104–5, 192–3; coffee, 193, 194; model of, 62

Fairtrade Foundation, 194, 195

FairTrade Labelling Organization (FLO–International), 194–5

Fairtrade standards, 195–6
Fairtrade-mark, 193–5
farmers, alliances of, 76; small farmers, 175, 176, 196 *see also* subsistence farmers
Farmers' Initiatives for Ecological Livelihoods and Democracy (Indonesia), 48
Fernando, Sarath, 10
fertilizers, chemical, 182
firewalls, 93
First Conference of People's Global Action against Free Trade and the World Trade Organization, 10
Fleming, Peter, 55, 82, 208
Focus on the Global South, 17
food: imports of, 9; long-distance transportation of, 104, 198; measures of productivity, 82; self-sufficiency, 162
'Food Miles' campaign, 199
food security, 132, 135, 172; local systems, 71
food sovereignty, 73–6, 180–82; enhancement of, 70
footprints of products, 82
foreign direct investment, 86, 89–90
Foro Emaus, 133
France, 164
free spaces, creation of, 71
free trade, 58, 88, 91; dishonesty of, 44
Friends of the Earth, 46, 47, 117, 126, 133, 206

G7, 103, 164, 168
G8, 28, 171
Galbraith, John Kenneth, 3, 209
Galeano, Eduardo, 203
Gallop, Pippa, 22, 36, 84–5
Gandhi, Mahatma, 102
Gelber, George, 22, 48–9, 85–7
Geldof, Bob, 166
General Agreement on Tariffs and Trade (GATT), 53, 137
General Agreement on Trade in Services (GATS), 7, 54, 90, 137, 149–51, 201; alternatives to,

79–81; negotiations to be halted, 75
General Motors company, 202
genetically modified organisms (GMO), 45; ban on, 74; foods, 31, 37, 45 (customer revolt against, 125–6)
Ghana, 150, 197; debt of, 162
Global Barter Network (Argentina), 187–8
Global Climate Coalition (GCC), 129
global economy, reshaping of, 88–9
Global Regulatory Authority (GRA), proposed, 122
global warming, 129
globalization: aggressive nature of, 5; alternatives to, 9–12, 62–76, 77–105, 109–10; and wealth gap, 30; as imperialist domination, 26; control of, 66–7; criticism of, 13; cultural, 49; definition of, 3–5, 15–26; demerits of, 27–61; dependent on cheap gas and oil, 55; destabilizing nature of, 208; economic, 16, 17–18; ethical, 93–5; failure of, 40–41; financial, 48, 86; from below, 93; relation to militarism, 61; tainted word, 209; triggers a race to the bottom, 33 *see also* deglobalization *and* anti-globalization
globalized people, 8–9
globalizers, 6–8
gobal warming, 101
Golding, David, 158
governance, 78; reform of, 67
Green parties, 16, 206
Green Revolution, 45
greenhouse gases, 99, 101, 104
Greenpeace, 206
Group of 77, 160
growth, slowdown of, 41

Haiti, 170
Hall, Ronnie, 23, 46–7, 87–8
handmade goods, 51
health and safety, 196
health care, 53, 65, 167, 169–70, 171,

173; access to, 80, 123
van Hees, Ted, 23, 48, 88
Hehir, Byran, 38
Heilbroner, Robert, 101
Henderson, Hazel, 18, 35, 88–9
herbicides, 133–4
Hewitt, Patricia, 145
Highly Indebted Poor Countries
    (HIPC) initiative, 167–8, 169, 170,
    171, 173; failure of, 163–5
Hilary, John, 17, 53, 89–92
Hines, Colin, 178
HIV/AIDS, 131, 167
hope, 210–11
Houtart, François, 21, 46, 92
human rights, 19, 32, 72, 73, 94, 95,
    96, 100, 105; challenge to WTO,
    141–2

Iceland supermarket, 125
India, 71, 72, 90, 119, 144–5, 180,
    197; agrarian reform in, 183;
    growth in, 41
indigenous peoples, rights of, 72
Indigenous Women's Network (Asia),
    10
Indonesia, economic crisis in, 49
industrialization, 39
inequality, 58, 85, 93; increase of, 47
Institute for Policy Studies, 202
intellectual property rights, 25, 68,
    71, 74
intercropping, 181
International Baby Food Action
    Network (IBFAN), 130
International Court of Justice, 75
International Federation for
    Alternative Trade (IFAT), 51, 196
International Food Policy Research
    Institute, 156
International Forum on Globalization
    (IFG), 4, 15, 116, 118, 122, 179
International Gender and Trade
    Network, 21, 50
International Labour Organization
    (ILO), 117
International Monetary Fund (IMF),
    14, 21, 23, 28, 30, 39, 46, 49, 56,

70, 72, 79, 81, 86, 94, 97, 103,
    109, 111, 141, 158, 159, 161–3,
    164–5, 168–72, 174, 204, 207,
    210; quota system in, 68
International Society for Ecology and
    Culture (ISEC), 16, 99–100;
    Global to Local Programme, 100
International Simultaneous Policy
    Organization, 26, 55–7
International Water Ltd, 199–200
Internet, 18, 89
Invest in Britain Bureau, 120
investment, localization of, 179
Iran, 59
Iran–Iraq war, 60
Ireland, agriculture in, 94
Italy, 164

James, Edison, 139
Jobe, Sakou, 169
Jubilee movement, 35, 158, 159–61,
    165–6
Jubilee Research, 166, 172, 173

Kamal, Mr, 146
Karnataka State Farmers' Association
    (India), 10
Kaukab, Rashid, 139
Keene, Chris, 23, 44, 92–3
Keynes, John Maynard, 102, 152, 161
Khor, Martin, 7, 13, 25, 67–8, 115
Kirby, Alex, 198
Kissinger, Henry, 3, 59
Klein, Naomi, 205
Korea, economic crisis in, 49
Korten, David, 25, 43, 93
Kyoto protocol, 128–9, 153

labour laws, 51
labour regulation, in UK, 120
labour standards, 105
Ladakh: effects of globalization on,
    34; social campaigns in, 100
Lamb, Harriet, 195
Le Pen, Jean-Marie, 56
least developed countries (LDCs), 9,
    91
Leen, Maura, 17, 38–9, 93–5

liberalization, 7, 9, 25, 47, 53, 74, 80, 105, 143, 161, 204; progressive, 63
limited liability of corporations, elimination of, 118
Lincoln, Abraham, 70–71
Lipobay drug, 131
literacy programmes, 184
local economies, 10; developing of, 82
Local Exchange Trading System (LETSystem), 185
localization, 65, 98, 110, 178, 179; of finance, 93; of food production, 83, 84; of money, 184–9; of production, 92–3, 95; of trade and investment, 65
Localization Industry Standards Association, 178
Localization Reseach Center, 178
Lomé Convention, 138
Lucas, Caroline, 16, 37, 95–6, 178

Mahato, Bir Singh, 25, 68
maize, production in Malawi, 168–9
Malawi, 91; debt in, 168–9, 174; drought in, 169
Malawi Economic Justice Network, 167
Malaysia, 140
malnutrition, of children, 8
Maran, Murasoli, 144–5, 148
Marks & Spencer company, 126
Marshall-Robinson, Nelcia, 50, 69
Mauritania, 169
Max Havelaar, 194
Mazhar, Farhad, 136
McDonald's, 7, 49, 126–8; criticisms of, 127; day of action for workers of, 127
Mchumo, Ali, 142–3
McSpotlight, 128
Mexico, 140; financial crisis in, 190; moratorium of debt of, 160
Microsoft, 203
migration: control of, 67; international, 18; urban, 162
military spending, 173
Mitsui, 132

Mobil company, 154
mobility, of people, 17
Monbiot, George, 3
money, local, 184–9
monocropping, 182
monopoly power, 207
Monsanto company, 126, 132, 149
Moore, Mike, 138
Morris, Dave, 127
Mourin, Jennifer, 8, 21, 38, 69
Movement for National Land and Agricultural Reform (Sri Lanka), 10
Movement for the Survival of the Ogoni People (MOSOP) (Nigeria), 10, 132
Movimento Sem Terra (Brazil), 10, 13, 183–4
Mozambique, 171
Mueller, Ronald E., 6
Multilateral Agreement on Investment (MAI), 138, 152–4
multilateralism, 93
Mwesigye, Charlotte, 173

Nader, Ralph, 147
Naerstad, Aksel, 15–16, 45–6, 96–8
National Indigenous and Peasant Coordination (Guatemala), 48
nations, role of, 70–71
neoliberalism, 5, 12, 42, 46, 47, 87, 96
Nepal, 197
Nestlé, 115, 119–20; boycott of, 130
New Consumer organization, 194
New Economics Foundation, 24, 27
New Zealand, 40, 91; LETSystem in, 185
Ng'ambi, Francis, 167
Nissan factory, Sunderland, 89–90
Nixon, Richard, 59
non-discrimination, principle of, 140
non-governmental organizations, 12–13, 93, 94, 105, 172, 174, 190
non-violent direct action, 206
Norberg-Hodge, Helena, 5, 16, 33–5, 98–100
North, viewpoints of, 77–105

North American Free Trade Agreement (NAFTA), 44
Novartis company, 133

Ocaya-Irama, Jane, 24, 50, 68
oil: price of, 59, 160; supplies, disruption of, 84, 208
One World shops, 193
organic agriculture, 82, 83, 84, 179, 181, 182
Organization for Economic Cooperation and Development (OECD), 152, 152
Organization of Petroleum Exporting Countries (OPEC), founding of, 59
Oxfam, 12, 105, 165, 194

Pakistan, 175–6, 197
Papua New Guinea, 191–2
paraquat, 133–4
participation, 11, 67, 179
patenting: limitation of, 75; of food crops, 132, 147; of life forms, 73, 97, 207 (ban on, 74)
Peasant Movement (Philippines), 10, 35
peasants, rights of, 75
People for the Ethical Treatment of Animals (PETA), 127
People's Decade for Human Rights Education (PDHRE), 141
People's Global Alliance, 11
people's rights, protection of, 62
Pesticide Action network (PAN), 21, 38, 133, 134
pesticides, 131
Peters, Bill, 165
Pettifor, Ann, 19, 35–6, 100–101, 165, 168, 169, 174
Pfizer, 149
Pheko, Mohau, 22, 36, 69–70
Philip Morris, 45
Philippines, 45, 117; breastmilk substitutes in, 130
Play Fair Europe, 10
Poland, 57–8
political parties, falling membership of, 205
politicians, confrontation of, 105
pollution, 28, 99
Popper, Karl, 103
Porto Alegre, 11, 92
poverty, 5, 45, 85, 91–2, 102, 109, 158, 159, 171, 172, 183; directing economy for poor people, 209; elimination of, 80, 95, 101, 151; empowerment of poor people, 88; in Africa, 172; suffering of poor people, 48–50; worsening of, 8–9
Poverty Reduction Strategy Papers (PRSPs), 48, 163–4
Prince of Wales, 125
privatization, 43, 46, 80, 102, 161, 172; of water, in Bolivia, 150, 199–201
productivity, measurement of, 82
profit motive, 52
Program on Corporate Law and Democracy (POCLAD), 207–8
prosumers, 187
protectionism, 110
proximity principle, 102

quantitative restrictions (QRs), 31

Rajiv Gandhi National Park, 180
Ramos, Danilo, 26, 35, 70
Ransom, David, 197
Raven, Hugh, 198
regional cooperation, 69–70
regulation, 92; at the national level, 28; multilateral, need for, 73–6; of transnational corporations, 120–24, 136; self-regulation of industry, 121; Sunday as, 101
renewable energy, 129
resistance, 69
Rhodes, Cecil, 6
rice, varieties of, 45; high-yielding, 51
rich people, getting richer, 30
Richter, Judith, 116, 121
Right Livelihood Award, 132
Robinson, Mary, 95
Roy, Arundhati, 3

Ruggiero, Renato, 137
Rugmark carpets, 197
rules-based system, 77

SAFE Alliance, 198
Sainsbury's, 126
sanitary and phytosanitary measures
  (SPS), 31
Saro-Wiwa, Ken, 132–5
satyagra, 206
Saudi Arabia, 59
Save the Children (UK), 17, 53
Schlosser, Eric, *Fast Food Nation*, 127
Seattle meeting of WTO, 144, 202;
  protests at, 11
self-determination, 39
self-reliance, strategies for, 178–80
shareholder pressure on companies,
  132–5
Sharma, Devinder, 20, 30, 70–71, 209
shea butter, 197
Shell, 124; boycott of, 132–3;
  shareholder action in, 116
Shiva, Vandana, 20, 32–3, 71
Short, Clare, 171
Shutt, Harry, 203
da Silva, Luis Inacio, 184
Simba, Iddi Mohamed, 145
Simms, Andrew, 24, 27, 101
simultaneous policy, 77–9
slave trade, 50
smoking, campaigning against, 53–4
social forms of ownership, 81
solidarity, 64–5, 81, 96
South: transfer of resources to, 85–7;
  viewpoints on globalization,
  62–76
South Africa, 171; government taken
  to court, 131
South Asian Peasant Coalition, 48
sovereignty: of people, 140; respect
  for, 96 *see also* food sovereignty
Steel, Helen, 127
Stiglitz, Joseph, 30
strategic options for tackling
  corporate power, 116–18
structural adjustment, 35, 56, 158,
  161–3, 172

subsidiarity, principle of, 87, 102
subsidies, 179; agricultural, 33 (in
  Pakistan, 176); distortion caused
  by, 156–7; of food, 34, 167, 174;
  reduction of, 148
subsistence farmers, 146, 148;
  destruction of, 31, 39
sugar, production of in Swaziland,
  157
Sunday, regulatory role of, 101
supermarkets: as food retailers, 57; as
  vacuum cleaners of wealth, 103
Sustain organization, 199
sustainability, 19, 46, 47, 71–2, 73, 80,
  82, 87, 96, 101; ground rules for,
  47
sustainable development, 208–10
swadeshi, 206
swaraj, 206
Swaziland, sugar production in, 157
Swedish Society for Nature, 133
Syngenta company, 132, 133–4

tabu currency (Papua New Guinea),
  191–2
Tamil Nadu, Du Pont blocked in,
  117
Tanzania, 91, 171
Tauli-Corpuz, Victoria, 15, 39, 71–2
taxation, 179; of primary products,
  152 *see also* Tobin tax
technology, transfer of, 90
Tenet, George, 208
Thailand, 119; ban on tobacco
  imports, 53–4
Thatcher, Margaret, 96
Third World Network, 25
Time Dollars, 186–7
tobacco, smoking, control of, 64
tobacco companies, tactics of, 129
Tobin, James, 189
Tobin Tax, 78, 92, 189–92
tourism, 34
trade, alternative, 192–3
trade and development, links
  between, 62
trade and investment rules,
  reorientation of, 89–92

trade domination, dealing with, 136–57
trade unions, recognition of, 120
Trade-Related Intellectual Property Rights (TRIPs), 7, 31, 40, 70, 137, 145, 147, 149
Trade-Related Investment Measures (TRIMs), 90, 137, 138, 149
Traidcraft, 194
transnational corporations (TNCs), 6–7, 11, 16, 33, 45, 50, 63–4, 72, 74, 86, 110, 111, 192, 208; code of conduct for, 113, 119–20; dismantling of, 118; domination of, 112–35 (in service industry, 149); interest in localization, 178; power of, 111, 140–41, 153, 207 (reduction of, 99); reform of, 177; regulation of, 39, 120–24, 136; US-based, 117
Transnational Institute, 16, 43
transparency, 96
transportation, 208; minimization of, 99; of food, 104, 198–9
trickle down, theory of, 40, 46
Tripathi, Ruchi, 24, 42, 72–3
Trocaire organization, 17

Uganda, 152; debt relief of, 173
unemployment, 31, 40
unequal exchange, 60
Union Carbide Corporation, Bhopal disaster, 118
Union Oil Corporation, 117
UNITA movement, 60
United Kingdom (UK), 164, 171; labour regulation in, 120; LETSystem in, 186; pressure on Ghana over privatization, 150; voter turn-out in, 206
United Nations (UN), 9, 23, 64, 68, 72, 75, 103, 112; corporate colonization of, 112, 113–15; framework convention on tobacco control, 64; Global Compact, 114–15; reform of, 75; strengthening of, 93
UN Centre on Transnational Corporations (UNCTC), 39, 113; downgraded, 114
UN Children's Fund (UNICEF), 8
UN Conference on Environment and Development (UNCED), 115
UN Conference on Trade and Development (UNCTAD), 8, 160
UN Development Programme (UNDP), *Human Development Report*, 8, 120, 132, 166
UN Financing for Development Conference, 85–6
UN Millennium Development Goals, 29, 87
UN Millennium Summit, 9
UN Security Council, veto in, 94
UN World Summit for Social Development, 115
UN World Summit on Sustainable Development (WSSD), 115
United States of America (USA), 49, 59, 102, 129, 143, 148, 152, 156, 174, 208; tobacco exports of, 54
Universal Declaration of Human Rights, 141–2
universal economic well-being, 102
urbanization, 98
Uruguay Round, 49, 137, 147, 181

Vajpayee, Behari, 145
Verhagen, Nico, 49–50, 73–6
la Via Campesina, 98
village republics in India, 180
Vivendi company, 101, 154

wages of workers, 117; low levels of, 44, 51
Waithima, Simeon, 52, 76
Wallach, Lori, 11
water: access to, 54, 80, 123, 173; privatization of, 150, 199
Watkins, Kevin, 5
wealth gap, 30, 104
Wegrzyn, Marian, 57–8
West Bengal, 45
wheat: production of, in Pakistan, 175–6; subsidised, 156–7

White, Harry Dexter, 103
Wienarto, Nugroho, 21, 48, 76
Williams, Mariama, 21, 50, 76
Wills, Carol, 19–20, 51, 104–5
With, Peter, 25, 48, 105
Witt, Susan, 189
women: rights of, 72; work of, 50
Women's Alliance of Ladakh (WAL), 100
Workers' Party (PT) (Brazil), 111, 184
World Bank, 14, 21, 23, 39, 46, 49, 70, 72, 79, 81, 86, 94, 97, 103, 109, 111, 141, 158, 159, 161–3, 164–5, 167, 174, 204, 207, 210; quota system in, 68; *World Development Report*, 179
World Commission on Sustainable Agriculture and Food Sovereignty, 75
World Development Movement (WDM), 42, 146, 159–61, 194
World Environment Organization (WEO), proposed, 99
World Health Organization (WHO), 53–4, 64, 131; International Code of Marketing of Breastmilk Substitutes, 115, 119, 130
World Intellectual Property Organization (WIPO), 68, 149

World Social Forum, 11, 12, 92, 95, 203
World Trade Organization (WTO), 7, 14, 20, 21, 23, 28, 33, 37, 39, 46, 49, 53, 60, 70, 72, 78, 79, 81, 88, 89, 90, 91, 94, 97, 99, 109, 111, 112, 137–9, 175, 210; Agreement on Agriculture (AoA), 31, 70, 74, 75, 137, 139; agriculture to be taken out of, 63, 68, 70, 74; as mortal threat, 155; Cancún ministerial meeting, 155–7; corporate influence on, 139–41; decision-making in, 68; Doha meeting, 142–7; human rights challenge to, 141–2; need for change in, 147–9; protests against, 11; 'Seattle Round', 202–3; Singapore Ministerial Decision, 142; voting in, 152
World Wide Fund for Nature, 133
WorldCom, 86, 101, 116, 203

Xerox, 101

Zimbabwe: Cargill's activity in, 134–5; tobacco production in, 162
Zimbabwean Agricultural Commodity Exchange (ZIMACE), 135

Zed Titles on Globalization and International Financial Institutions

Yilmaz Akyuz (ed.), *Reforming the Global Financial Architecture: Issues and Proposals*

Samir Amin, *Capitalism in the Age of Globalization: The Management of Contemporary Society*

Samir Amin, *Obsolescent Capitalism: Contemporary Politics and Global Disorder*

Walden Bello, *Deglobalization: New Ideas for Running the World Economy*

Walden Bello, Nicola Bullard and Kamal Malhotra (eds), *Global Finance: New Thinking on Regulating Speculative Capital Markets*

Robert Biel, *The New Imperialism: Crisis and Contradictions in North–South Relations*

Patrick Bond, *Against Global Apartheid: South Africa Meets the World Bank, IMF and International Finance*

Greg Buckman, *Globalization: Tame it or Scrap it? Mapping the Alternatives of the Anti-Globalization Movement* (forthcoming)

Ha-Joon Chang, *Globalization, Economic Development and the Role of the State*

Carlos M. Correa, *Intellectual Property Rights, the WTO and Developing Countries: The TRIPS Agreement and Policy Options*

Carlos M. Correa and Nagesh Kumar, *Protecting Foreign Investment: The WTO and the New Global Investment Regime*

Bhagirath Lal Das, *Trade and Development Issues and the World Trade Organisation*, Vol. 1, *An Introduction to the WTO Agreements*; Vol. 2, *The WTO Agreements: Deficiencies, Imbalances and Required Changes*

Bhagirath Lal Das, *The World Trade Organization: A Guide to the New Framework for International Trade*

Bhagirath Lal Das, *WTO: The Doha Agenda: The New Negotiations on World Trade*

Wim Dierckxsens, *The Limits of Capitalism: An Approach to Globalization without Neoliberalism*

Graham Dunkley, *The Free Trade Adventure: The WTO, the Uruguay Round and Globalism – A Critique*

Graham Dunkley, *Free Trade: Myth, Reality and Alternatives* (forthcoming)

William F. Fisher and Thomas Ponniah (eds), *Another World Is Possible: Popular Alternatives to Globalization at the World Social Forum*

Jacques B. Gélinas, *Juggernaut Politics: Understanding Predatory Globalization*

Peter Griffiths, *The Economist's Tale: A Consultant Encounters Hunger and the World Bank*

François Houtart and François Polet (eds), *The Other Davos: The Globalization of Resistance to the World Economic System*

Fatoumata Jawara and Aileen Kwa, *Behind the Scenes at the WTO: The Real World of International Trade Negotiations*

Martin Khor et al., Third World Network, *WTO and the Global Trading System: Development Impacts and Reform Proposals*

Arthur MacEwan, *Neoliberalism or Democracy? Economic Strategy, Markets and the Alternatives for the 21st Century*

John Madeley, *A People's World: Alternatives to Economic Globalization*

John Mihevc, *The Market Tells Them So: The World Bank and Economic Fundamentalism in Africa*

Heikki Patomaki, *Democratising Globalisation: The Leverage of the Tobin Tax*

Richard Peet, *Unholy Trinity: The IMF, World Bank and WTO*

James Petras and Henry Veltmeyer, *Globalization Unmasked: Imperialism in the 21st Century*

Jan Nederveen Pieterse (ed.), *Global Futures: Shaping Globalization*

Vijay Prashad, *Fat Cats and Running Dogs: The Enron Stage of Capitalism*

Robbie Robertson, *The Three Waves of Globalization: A History of a Developing Global Consciousness*

SAPRIN, *Structural Adjustment: The SAPRIN Report. The Policy Roots of Economic Crisis, Poverty and Inequality* (forthcoming)

Harry Shutt, *The Trouble with Capitalism: An Enquiry into the Causes of Global Economic Failure*

Harry Shutt, *A New Democracy: Alternatives to a Bankrupt World Order*

Kavaljit Singh, *The Globalisation of Finance: A Citizen's Guide*

Kavaljit Singh, *Taming Global Financial Flows: Challenges and Alternatives in the Era of Financial Globalization*

Joost Smiers, *Arts under Pressure: Promoting Cultural Diversity in the Age of Globalisation*

Susanne Soederberg, *The Politics of the New International Financial Architecture: Reimposing Neoliberal Domination in the Global South* (forthcoming)

David Sogge, *Give and Take: What's the Matter with Foreign Aid?*

Bob Sutcliffe, *100 Ways of Seeing an Unequal World*

Teivo Teivainen, *Enter Economism, Exit Politics: Experts, Economic Policy and the Damage to Democracy*

Oscar Ugarteche, *The False Dilemma: Globalization – Opportunity or Threat?*

Paulo Vizentini and Marianne Wiesebron (eds), *Free Trade for the Americas? The United States' Push for the FTAA Agreement*

David Woodward, *The Next Crisis? Direct and Equity Investment in Developing Countries*

For full details of this list and Zed's general catalogue, please write to: The Marketing Department, Zed Books, 7 Cynthia Street, London NI 9JF UK or email Sales@zedbooks.demon.co.uk.

Visit our website at www.zedbooks.co.uk.